Becoming a Whole Person

In appreciation and the love of Christ

Ed Dawson

Becoming a Whole Person

◆

A Year of Devotions full of Humor,
Truth, and Love

by Cid Davidson

To Becky, who is in the process of becoming a whole person... From Judy, who is still working on becoming a whole person!

iUniverse, Inc.
New York Lincoln Shanghai

Becoming a Whole Person
A Year of Devotions full of Humor, Truth, and Love

All Rights Reserved © 2004 by Cid Davidson

No part of this book may be reproduced or transmitted in any form or by any means, graphic, electronic, or mechanical, including photocopying, recording, taping, or by any information storage retrieval system, without the written permission of the publisher.

iUniverse, Inc.

For information address:
iUniverse, Inc.
2021 Pine Lake Road, Suite 100
Lincoln, NE 68512
www.iuniverse.com

ISBN: 0-595-32002-3

Printed in the United States of America

Bible translations used in *Becoming a Whole Person*:

(CEV) Contemporary English Version copyright 1995, Used by permission of the American Bible Society. All rights reserved.

(KJV) The King James version

(NIV) HOLY BIBLE, NEW INTERNATIONAL VERSION®. NIV®. Copyright©1973, 1978, 1984 by International Bible Society. Used by permission of Zondervan. All rights reserved.

(NLT) Scripture quotations marked (NLT) are taken from the *Holy Bible*, New Living Translation, copyright 1996. Used by permission of Tyndale House Publishers, Inc., Wheaton, Illinois 60189. All rights reserved.

DEDICATED TO

Lissa, Will, Allen, Virginia, Margaret

Children: Bone of our bone, flesh of our flesh—
brothers and sisters: born of His spirit, washed in His blood.

The dear love of family touches the heart
squeezed dry by the demands of others—
with the springs of living water from the indwelling Spirit.
They go beyond sympathy, and even compassion,
and dig deep into their own resources
to do what is both generous and inconvenient
in order that those who have known the discouragement of darkness
may have the relief of light.

Stumbling words of thanks cannot express the depth of gratitude,
for tears and tongues are but poor vessels to carry repayment
for what has been given without instruction or recrimination.

But may they know the joy of His heart;
and may they reap as generously as they have sown.

Contents

Introduction

January

1 Discovered
2 Dogged by Fear
3 For Butter or Worse
4 My Father's House
5 Green Eggs and Sham
6 Step by Step
7 Discouragement
8 The Limp
9 Oysters
10 The Seat Next to Mine
11 Morning Manna
12 Knit One and Purl, Too
13 Golf Equation
14 The Feline is Mutual
15 Right Motive, Peculiar Result
16 Cover-up
17 Musk Oxen
18 Alarming News
19 A Hearing Ear
20 Strawberry Fields Forever
21 Warm Silence
22 What is it about January?
23 Weather or Not
24 Bulbs
25 As Time Goes By
26 Macro Thinking
27 Disasterville
28 Leaning
29 Ants
30 Choices
31 Life With Father

February

1 Malfunction Junction
2 The Diner's Club
3 Insulated
4 Goodbye, Mrs. Zips
5 The Woman in White I
6 The Woman in White II
7 On Cows
8 Wool Coats
9 Cat and Mouse
10 Word of Mouth
11 The Sky is Falling!
12 A Dillar A Dollar
13 Little Red Schoolhouse
14 My True Love
15 Worry Warts
16 Changed Your (S)oil Lately?
17 Picnic Time
18 I.B.M. Compatible
19 On Termites
20 It's a Shoe-in!
21 Service, Please!
22 Death Valley Days
23 Memory Lapse
24 Traveler's Aid
25 What's in Your Hand?
26 A Walk in the Dark
27 Undone
28 Orange Blossom Christianity

March

1 Days Like a Shadow
2 The Pit of Sin
3 Road Rage
4 Through Glasses Darkly
5 Trees and Temples
6 The Jumping-off Place
7 Blessed Assurance
8 Small Comforts
9 The Bruiser
10 Present and Accounted For
11 Wash Day
12 Elephants and Flies
13 Toupee Tape
14 Workshops
15 Night Train To London
16 Close Encounters
17 Knowing Christ
18 Shoulder Your Boulder
19 A Little About the Ephod
20 The Fallen Woman
21 Alien-Nation
22 Fire Drill (Almost)
23 Cue from Fescue
24 A Fungus Among Us
25 Looking Ahead
26 Hiding
27 Rain
28 Buttons (and no Bows)
29 Caution: God at Work
30 Lesson from the Laundromat
31 Ship to Shore

April

1 April Fool
2 Are You Lumpy?
3 Signs and Wonders
4 Advance Preparation
5 A Rainy Lesson
6 Alligators and Crocodiles
7 A Happy Medium
8 Little House on the Freeway
9 Presence, Not Presents
10 Accent-u-ate the Positive
11 Scarlett and God
12 Word Stuck
13 Castles in the Air
14 Time on Your Hands
15 Mexican Sunday
16 Leaf it to Beaver
17 Provision
18 Perspective
19 I'll Take Vanilla
20 Ground Work
21 The Man in the White Suit
22 A Message in Flowers
23 Foxes
24 Golden Oldies
25 Mountain Sights
26 Body Language
27 White/White
28 The Scientific American
29 Coming Home
30 Stop, Look and Listen

May

1 Slip—Not
2 Driven by Distraction
3 Ants in the Plants
4 A Listening Heart
5 Hard to Look Impressive
6 Fireside Chat
7 In Nonessentials, Charity
8 The Greatest of All....
9 Family Business
10 A Mother of Love
11 Listen Up
12 I See What I See
13 Standing Firm
14 Hope Chest
15 Special Delivery
16 Night Flight
17 Open Doors
18 One-Way Signs
19 A Near Glimpse of Eternity
20 Packin' It In
21 Open Window
22 An Old Injury
23 Flying High
24 Sight and Insight
25 The Only Proper Dress
26 S.O.S.
27 Jaws
28 Be prepared
29 Balloons
30 Salads to Desserts
31 Lesson from a Boat

June

1 The Maine Thing
2 The Road Not Taken
3 A Gifted People
4 The Love of God
5 Buckle Up
6 Golf Tips
7 Field Hand
8 Built to Specification
9 My Father's Whistle
10 Ravens

11 Reigning Cats and Dogs
12 Charge Account
13 Fat of the Land
14 A Rabbit Tale
15 Tick Talk
16 Put Hair on Your Chest
17 Dressed to Kill
18 Addiction
19 A Light in South America
20 Linkage

21 Hanging On
22 Fire Man
23 Building Blocks
24 Turtles
25 The Heart of the Matter
26 Japanese Lesson
27 On Closets
28 Overlooking Facts
29 Yokefellows
30 Family Reunion

July

1 Clap Your Hands
2 Beavers
3 Rejected
4 True Freedom
5 Nitpicking
6 Armor in Place
7 The Devil and Idle Hands
8 What's Your Rag Content?
9 Parcels and People
10 God's Wisdom from Bill

11 And the Answer is…
12 Two Worlds
13 God's Messenger
14 Golf Advice
15 Weight a Minute!
16 Out of Sequence
17 Elastic Editing
18 Help Wanted
19 Island Invasion
20 Name Tags

21 Peacocks
22 Tidal Thoughts
23 Mirror, Mirror on the Wall
24 Who's in Charge Here?
25 The Greatest Gift
26 Harley Davidson
27 Desert Traveler
28 Singing in the Rain
29 A Counter Encounter
30 What Goes Up…
31 On Fireflies

August

1 Plan B
2 Western Lesson
3 A Taste of Honey
4 Bed and Breakfast
5 Not Miss America
6 Rip Tide
7 Animal Life on the Windshield
8 Watch Where You're Going
9 The Ice Cream Machine
10 Toy Test

11 Children 101
12 On the Road
13 The French Fool
14 Original Creations
15 Flatlander
16 Television
17 Communion Service
18 Viewpoint
19 Golf Games and Golf Clubs
20 Bridging the Gap

21 Impression at the Dentist's
22 Our Creator God
23 Smoke Gets in Your Eyes
24 The Helper
25 Disappointments
26 Jiminy! It's a Cricket!
27 Lettuce Pray
28 Wedding Plans
29 Anniversary Gratitude
30 Hearing Loss
31 A Change in the Weather

September

1 As I Stood Dyeing
2 Airport Vignette
3 PMA
4 Let's Play Concentration
5 Captain Hornblower's Wife
6 Weasels
7 Reflections on Reflections
8 Satisfied
9 Eat What's on Your Plate
10 Modern Desert Meeting
11 Remember
12 Incredible Edibles
13 Our Checkbook
14 Radio Daze
15 Plastic Encounter
16 Golden Triangle
17 My Way
18 The Eyes Have It
19 Selective Memory Syndrome
20 On the Bench
21 Reverse Psychology
22 Lost in (Cyber) Space
23 Glove Boxes
24 Locked In
25 Becoming a Child
26 The Carry All
27 Bravery
28 The Portrait
29 Centipedes and Millipedes
30 A Grateful Heart

October

1 Canned Spaghetti
2 Free Advice
3 Caught by a Prayer
4 Needed: A Life
5 In Good Time
6 On Course
7 Learning About Prayer
8 Let Down
9 Putting it Together
10 Laundry 101
11 It Was the Best of Times
12 Speaking of Limpets…
13 Traffic Signals
14 Aunt Fanny's Money
15 The Real Dirt
16 The Old Man and the She
17 Heaven Scent
18 The Everlasting Fur Coat
19 Façade
20 The Mattress Firm
21 Home Sweet Home
22 Dilly Crystal
23 The Teacher
24 Chair Person
25 A View from the Top
26 Do It Yourself
27 Restaurant Life
28 A Closer (& Depressing) Look
29 A Good Patient
30 An Interesting Discovery
31 Unmasked

November

1 Authorization
2 Haarlem Globe Trotters
3 Clock Talk
4 No Favorites
5 Scrambled
6 Washing Behind Your Ears
7 Correction
8 Art Lesson
9 Good Business Techniques
10 Adventure *En Francais*
11 Jeep Thrills
12 Blackout
13 When in Rome…
14 Non-Sightseeing
15 Rainy Day In Munich Town
16 Trouble
17 Back to London
18 The Nose Knows
19 Home Sweet Home
20 Hope
21 Llamas
22 Tunnel Vision
23 Breezy Rider
24 Encouragement
25 Malice in Wonderland
26 Counting Blessings
27 Giving Thanks
28 Check Mate
29 Ship to Shore
30 The Writing on the Wall
31 Car Talk

December

1 The Bear Essentials
2 The Anchovy Paste Saga
3 Hot Spot
4 Humble and Proud of It...
5 A Winter's Tale
6 A Comforting Voice
7 Horses
8 Pats and Hugs
9 Jumbled Jungle Gym
10 Dear Mother

11 The FPW Syndrome
12 Big Britches
13 Coach Shoes
14 Mockingbirds
15 A Fall From a Tree
16 A Heart That Sings
17 The Instructor
18 Charlotte and Wilbur
19 Movers and Shakers
20 ABC

21 The Christmas Caroler
22 An Unexpected Gift
23 Joys-R-Us
24 Christmas Future
25 Christmas Present
26 Christmas Passed
27 Cache of Clay
28 The Giver and the Gifts
29 A Bell and a Trumpet
30 The Lion and the Lamb
31 An Open Door

Introduction

This book contains a years worth of daily readings: musings and vignettes from a life that was not particularly (well actually, never) spectacular. I started out life as a flibberty gibbet who flitted from one enthusiasm to another. My parents, in stark contrast, were very dignified and never did anything out of line. They led, I felt, very boring and predictable lives. This held no interest for me, so, using what little brain I had, I bent every effort to circumvent being boring and predictable, and instead did everything I could to get everything I wanted.

Much to my surprise, I became very predictable (I always did what I wanted), and became, to be honest, very selfish.

Everyday I am very thankful that, while I was in graduate school at Yale University, I met a darling Southern gentleman. We married, and three children later, there was an enormous change in my life (and it had nothing to do with diapers). My focus changed from thinking about what I want, to thinking about what God wants.

Believe it or not, when my life's focus changed, things suddenly became very unpredictable. My life now contained great joys and great difficulties—certainly not what I was expecting! Even now, my story is not finished. I am still, as the title of this book suggests, *Becoming a Whole Person*.

Sometime after our fifth child was born, I met Helen Baugh and Mary Clark, the founders of Stonecroft Ministries. They, along with a team of women, were establishing Christian Women's Clubs around the country. Not long after that, I began speaking at these clubs across the U.S., telling audiences about how God had changed—and is changing—my life. I have spoken in almost every state in the Union, in Canada and in Europe. I also speak at seminars, church retreats and conferences, and any other venue foolish enough to book me.

In case you're wondering, this book is not a thesis on relativity, an inner look at medieval architecture, or an in-depth study of ethical theology. In fact, when you read these daily devotions, you will immediately discover that I am neither a theologian nor a philosopher. I am merely a woman who is a little weird around the edges—but who loves to laugh, and does her best to help others laugh with her.

As a final note, these daily thoughts are not meant to be gulped down in one indigestible lump. If you take the time to read one a day, you will find all kinds of things that will make you laugh, cry or possibly want to come to Florida to strangle the author (too bad, we're moving!). The thing is, everyone, whether they know it or not, is on a journey. This book held in your hands is the story of my journey. Some of these stories you may relate to, some of them you may not; they are meant to challenge you to set your life goals differently than I did, for like Winnie the Pooh, I was a "bear of little brain." But I found out that God loves everyone, people with little brains, big brains and no brains. I am a walking example—so read this, and believe in God's love for you.

January 1: Discovered

I was engaged in one of my favorite afternoon activities (naptime) when I heard the doorbell ring. Jerking upright, I reached for my glasses and ran for the door. I usually wear glasses only for reading, but since I sometimes have to sign for something, I thought I should be prepared.

I noticed that the deliveryman looked at me a little strangely. I panicked momentarily, thinking I had perhaps dashed to the door in my nightgown. Much to my relief, a quick glance downward reassured me that I was fully (and appropriately) clothed. Perhaps he was looking at me strangely because he couldn't figure out why I lived so far from civilization. Unfortunately, the truth was a little wilder than I had imagined. After he departed, I glanced in the mirror. Not only was I wearing glasses; the glasses had a long dangling string of green dental floss firmly entangled in the earpiece. The real me had been exposed.

Some people think the real me is the one who speaks at seminars. Others think it is the one who fixes meals and takes classes entitled "Aerobics for the Habitually Clumsy." The real me includes all those things. I also make mistakes, do things I know I shouldn't, cry, laugh, and look scary when I wake up. The truth is, I'm a conglomerate—a mixture of everything, just as you are. God knows all these different facets of our lives, and they are in no way hidden. He knows who we really are, and He is not surprised even when we show up wearing green dental floss. We have a God who perfectly loves the imperfect.

"For the word of God is full of living power. It is sharper than the sharpest knife, cutting deep into our innermost thoughts and desires. It exposes us for what we really are. Nothing in all creation can hide from him. Everything is naked and exposed before his eyes." (Hebrews 4:12-13b NLT)

January 2: Dogged by Fear

In the fourth grade, I passed from being driven to riding to school on my bicycle. It was a big step up, I thought, and I reveled in this early taste of independence. The thrill of that bike ride was marred each day, however, when I pedaled past the Colonel's house on the corner. His house was set way back from the road and had no fence—so there was nothing to stop the daily mad dash of the Colonel's roaring Doberman Pinschers. These ferocious dogs evidently had a fixation not only on bikes but also on those who rode them. Unfortunately, it didn't take many trips to school before I was fixated on <u>them</u>. No matter how early or late I left the house, or however quickly or quietly I pedaled, those dogs would come out at full growl. I tried throwing dog biscuits in their direction, but the treats were scorned as bloodless and uninteresting.

The dogs never actually grasped their target, of course, or I wouldn't be here to tell the tale. At the time, I attributed this solely to good luck. I was many years from beginning my spiritual journey, and I didn't know of God's promise in Isaiah 41:10 that says, "Don't be afraid, for I am with you. Do not be dismayed, for I am your God. I will strengthen you. I will help you. I will uphold you…" (NLT).

Even though I didn't know to pray for God's protection, He was there. One statement by psychologist Carl Jung remains clearly in my mind: "Bidden or unbidden, God is present."

"The Lord is my light and my salvation—so why should I be afraid? The Lord protects me from danger—so why should I tremble?" (Psalm 27:1 NLT)

January 3: For Butter or Worse

Restaurants that have those individually wrapped pieces of butter always make me uncomfortable. The painful fact is that I am a butterholic. This is well known to my family, and was graphically pointed out to me one time by the welcoming statement of a grandson when I went to visit.

"Hi, Mom Dee," he said cheerily. "We went to the store and bought real butter just for you!"

When butter is served in a "lump sum," so to speak, and then passed around the table, no one really knows who took the lion's share (unless someone's peeking, of course.) But with wrapped pats, there is an unattractive pile of crunched-up paper right next to my plate. This leads everyone to one of two conclusions: either I have no self-control, or I am trying for an entry in the Guinness book of records.

I also leave a trail of "wrappings" as I journey through life. Some are kind deeds and helping hands, and others are piggy, selfish acts that I would rather sweep off the table. Jesus warned the teachers of religious law by saying, "You clean the outside of the cup and dish, but inside they are full of greed and self-indulgence" (Matthew 23:25b NIV).

May the wrappers beside my plate be wrappers of kindness and love, not of selfishness.

January 4: My Father's House

When my father would say, "Come into the den, I want to talk to you," my heart rate would accelerate, knowing I was being called on the carpet for one of my little capers. I'm sorry to say that my father's little talks about my little capers went in one ear and out the other, for I don't remember a single one of them. It wasn't that I didn't <u>hear</u> the words; I just didn't <u>absorb</u> the words (so much for parental advice…).

I must have been about eighteen or so the last time I heard those dreaded words inviting me to a private conversation. Even at that advanced age (at least <u>I</u> thought it was advanced), I found myself trembling on the chair next to the desk wondering what mischief had finally come to light. But instead of a lecture, Daddy pulled his Bible from a shelf, and read the words of Jesus found in the Gospel of John, chapter 14, verse 2, "There are many rooms in my Father's house. I wouldn't tell you this, unless it was true. I am going there to prepare a place for each of you" (NLT).

My father stopped reading and looked at me. "Ciddy, you could use the phrase 'If it were not so I would have told you' after all of Christ's statements, for they're all true. Did you know that?"

"Yes," I replied.

My father smiled and said, "Good."

I thanked him and quickly made my way out the door and to the stairs. <u>As I traipsed down, I could not have been more delighted, for I had escaped unscathed from the "*sanctum sanctorum*" (my father's name for his private domain), with nary a hint of reproof or correction.</u>

It wasn't until several years after my father's death that I, too, became a follower of Jesus. I don't remember any of the other conversations with my father, but how thankful I am that I remember this one!

January 5: Green Eggs and Sham (with apologies to Dr. Seuss)

The president of Chrysler's De Soto division had agreed to come to Florida to participate in Bradenton's annual De Soto celebration (which celebrated the explorer, not the car). He was coming with several top executives and a small army of press, and, so, we wanted Florida to be at its tropical best. My husband was president of the De Soto Historical Society, the organization that sponsored the weeklong event, and as we were to be the hosts for the first party, we made preparations for an evening that would delight winter-weary visitors. Unfortunately, the weather was not cooperative in the slightest: there had just been a severe freeze, so our lawn looked like ratty, brown industrial carpet.

Suddenly, an idea popped greenly into focus. We called a friend of ours who was in the nursery and landscape business, and he obligingly sent out a crew of men armed with pressure hoses and cans of green paint. Within four hours, our lawn never looked better. It didn't quite have enough time to dry, however, before a light drizzle greeted the first guests, who were unanimous in their amazement at our "verdant sward" (as they say in English novels). I did notice, however, that several of the guests had undeniable touches of green on their shoes; and I could only hope that they couldn't imagine where they got it.

We had tried to cover up deadness with the appearance of life, but it was fairly obvious that it was merely an outward show, not the real substance of life.

"…He has given us eternal life, and this life is in his Son. So whoever has God's Son has life; whoever does not have his Son does not have life." (I John 5:11-12 NLT)

January 6: Step by Step

When it comes to athletics, I am a wimpette. My wrists tire at golf, my ankles at ice skating, and abdomen at aerobics. In grade school I was the one left unchosen, staring with simulated interest at a brick in the wall. At prep school, I knew there was no use trying out for the field hockey team, as I was terrified someone would bean me with a stick. I had a brief career as a cheerleader, but the school colors were pink and white, and I just couldn't work up much enthusiasm for yelling "Pink and white, fight, fight!"

So, since I failed at everything else athletic, I tried walking. I didn't walk very far or very fast, but I did manage to stumble around. I discovered that there are lots of ways to walk... "Let me count the ways" (forgive me, Elizabeth Barrett Browning): steadily, strolling, slogging, plodding, traipsing, trudging, sauntering, staggering, and the above-mentioned stumbling. I was especially encouraged to find that walking is mentioned a lot in the Bible, and I discovered that <u>everyone</u> can walk on God's paths—no matter how unathletic they may be.

"He will teach us his ways, so that we may walk in his paths." (Micah 4:2 NIV)

January 7: Discouragement

Even with all the years I spent in many, many schools, I was a poor, unmotivated scholar. My parents were sure that if I just found the right school, I would be a wonderful student. They were incorrect…and I was usually asked to move on to a different school. The school administrators would convince my parents that I would be "happier somewhere else." I know now that the school was happier when I was somewhere else!

At any rate, my lollygagging began in second or third grade—whichever it was that tried valiantly to instill arithmetic into me. My brain was already stuffed with stories, jokes, and the best ways to tell them. Unfortunately, for some strange reason, my teachers did not encourage jokes or story-telling in the classroom. Not only that, but those silly teachers progressed on to things like science, history, and, (Horrors!), ALGEBRA (I took this twice and I still don't get it).

As I mentioned, my long downfall began with arithmetic. When I had to add anything with more than five numbers, I folded my tent. At least I tried to. But my father (an engineer who couldn't understand how he had produced a child who was a dunce at numbers) wouldn't let me fade into the background, and he forced me to stick with it. I tried hard to convince him I was "a bad arithmeticker" but he didn't buy it, and he would make me add and subtract over and over again until I got it right.

And then (evil child that I was), I discovered my father had an adding machine. I would wait until he was out of the house, sneak up to his office, and make the machine work its magic. Unfortunately, when my father noticed my amazing newfound (and unerring) mathematical prowess, he put two and two together (I told you he was good at math), and he made sure the machine was under lock and key. To make matters worse, it wasn't long before he moved me on to math that even the adding machine couldn't do: multiplication, division, and even fractions. It was a very black time in my life, indeed.

There are many of things in my life that I face with fear and trembling—and they can't be solved with an adding machine, either. So, I tell God that I am just no good at it. But God doesn't buy that any more than my earthly father did. He keeps me at it with gentle insistence. When I run out of answers, I turn to Him in confidence, for he is always there with help and comfort; and He is willing to help me be a good student.

"I am the Lord All-Powerful. So don't depend on your own power or strength, but on my Spirit." (Zechariah 4:6b CEV)

January 8: The Limp

"Jacob got up in the middle of the night and took his wives, his eleven children, and everything he owned across to the other side of the Jabbok River for safety. Afterwards, Jacob went back and spent the rest of the night alone. A man came and fought with Jacob until just before daybreak. When the man saw that he could not win, he struck Jacob on the hip and threw it out of joint. They kept on wrestling until the man said, 'Let go of me! It's almost daylight.' 'You can't go until you bless me,' Jacob replied. Then the man asked, 'What is your name?' 'Jacob,' he answered. The man said, 'Your name will no longer be Jacob. You have wrestled with God and with men, and you have won. That's why your name will be Israel.' Jacob said, 'Now tell me your name.' 'Don't you know who I am?' he asked. And he blessed Jacob. Jacob said, 'I have seen God face to face, and I am still alive.' So he named the place Peniel. The sun was coming up as Jacob was leaving Peniel. He was limping because he had been struck on the hip, and the muscle on his hip joint had been injured."(Genesis 32:22-32a CEV)

The story in Genesis of God wrestling with Jacob has always fascinated me, even though I have never done any wrestling. To be perfectly honest, I've never done any sort of fighting. If someone even gives a menacing look in my direction, my immediate impulse is to hightail it away as fast as my two little feet can carry me (of course, there was the time when my brothers armed me with an iron golf club so I could bonk a neighborhood bully on the head, but that's another story). When someone starts wrestling with you, though, you don't have any choice but to wrestle. And, so, when God started to wrestle with Jacob, Jacob had to wrestle.

After the fight was over, God asked Jacob his name. God was not asking for information but for confession, because Jacob means "he grasps." Jacob was called that because, when he was born, he was holding on to his brother's heel. Later, that name came to mean even more, for Jacob stole his older brother's birthright as well as his blessing. I think that when Jacob "spent the rest of the night alone" (see verse 24 above), he finally had the chance to face who he really was. Even though he was a supplanter (and a trickster!), God knew him and loved him anyway. God loved Jacob, but God still touched his thigh and injured him.

My legs are healthy, but I have something like Jacob's limp. In 1984, I developed a neuro-musuclar disorder called blepharospasms that caused my eyes to clamp shut so tightly that I was functionally blind. There was actually nothing wrong with my eyes *per se*; I just couldn't open my lids to see. This meant no driving (it makes the person in the next lane really nervous if they see you driving with your eyes closed), no reading, no writing, and no housework (that last part wasn't so bad!). But I got to the point where I would have even been glad to do oven cleaning, if I could only see. One day I came across a Bible verse (blurrily, to be sure) that said, "In fact, we expected to die. But as a result, we learned not to rely on ourselves, but on God who can raise the dead." (II Corinthians 1:9 NLT)

I pray that my "limp" will always remind me to depend on my heavenly father. If you also have a physical or emotional problem, count yourself blessed: God can use it not only for your good, but also for the good of many others.

January 9: Oysters

Lots of people like to eat oysters, but they are a little too slippery for me. The only way I can get one down is to douse it with lemon juice, horseradish, and ketchup…and if I'm going to all that trouble, why not put the lemon juice, horseradish, and ketchup on something I like?

Oysters on the half shell are not the subjects of my discussion here, however; I'm thinking of oysters in the whole shell. They will never qualify as one of the stars in the sports world, or be noticed on the best-dressed list, because they are simply not newsworthy. They major in lying quietly on the sea bottom, content to let the more flashy members of their world cruise past. But in their solitary and rather somber existence, they not only provide food for the body, but food for thought.

Everyone knows that pearls are made from bits of sand or grit that enter or are placed inside the hard shell. The irritant is then covered over with shell-building cells that attach themselves to the particle and build up in layers, layers that eventually become pearls. I need to apply this principle to my own life. I have plenty of irritations, some small and some quite irritatingly large. I may not choose the "sand" that enters my life, but I'm able to choose my response—either wasting energy trying to get rid of it, or accepting it and covering it over with layers of love. It then becomes "a pearl of wisdom and understanding." May I never forget that God gives "a crown of beauty instead of ashes" (Isaiah 61:3 NIV) and that layers of love don't add a thing to my weight!

"Not only so, but we also rejoice in our sufferings, because we know that suffering produces perseverance; perseverance, character; and character, hope. And hope does not disappoint us, because God has poured out his love into our hearts by the Holy Spirit, whom he has given us." (Romans 5:3-5 NIV)

January 10: The Seat Next to Mine

Coming home from a speaking itinerary in Wyoming necessitated three connections each way. This gave me the opportunity to worry about losing my bags six different times. In Denver, on my way home, I was told that since my flight was already an hour late, they would put me on a different airline and send me to Orlando. From there I would have to fly from Orlando home to Tampa (I visualized one more lost bag opportunity). But while I was thinking about my bags, God was thinking about something else.

On the plane departing from Orlando, I found myself seated next to an ex-Vietnam soldier who was wearing leather, a lot of medals, a beard, and several tattoos. His glasses had "Harley Davidson" on the earpiece.

He said, "You know I used to be nervous about flying, but I read a book that helped me get over it."

"It wasn't *it* the Bible, was it?" I asked.

He nodded and smiled.

He told me he had run amok in Vietnam, and I told him I had run amok right here in the States. (Probably not the same "mok" of course) and we exchanged the stories of how we came to begin our spiritual journeys. He also told me he was on his way to the Veteran's hospital in St. Petersburg, and had been feeling anxious. It was wonderful to talk with him. When our plane landed I rejoiced with him because, on the day of his worrisome trip, God had arranged for him to meet a little old lady to reassure him that the maker of the universe is still in charge of lives, meetings, and even baggage (yes, all my bags were present and accounted for).

"He will rescue the poor when they cry to him; he will help the oppressed, who have no one to defend them. He feels pity for the weak and the needy, and he will rescue them." (Psalm 72:12-13 NLT)

January 11: Morning Manna

"And the Lord said to Moses, 'I have heard the people's complaints. Now tell them, "In the evening you will have meat to eat, and in the morning you will be filled with bread. Then you will know that I am the Lord your God." That evening vast numbers of quail arrived and covered the camp. The next morning the desert all around the camp was wet with dew. When the dew disappeared later in the morning, thin flakes, white like frost, covered the ground." (Exodus 16:11-14 NLT)

"In time, the food became known as manna." (Exodus 16:31a NLT)

There are a lot of strange breakfast products out there guaranteed to make you thinner as well as filled to the brim with wonderful nutrition. Instead, I'd rather think about manna.

I remember reading somewhere (I can't remember where!) about manna. First, the dew was formed in the quietness of the night, and when the manna came, there was dew on the manna. In a spiritual sense, the dew will only come when there is quietness, so the meaning behind this picture is clear. First we must be quiet, and then eat of the heavenly food; and then we must be quiet again while we think about what God has given us. In that way, God's dew will be absorbed, and we will be nourished with heavenly manna.

Bishop Handley Moule said, "Even if you have not a long time to spend in the morning with your God, hem it with quietness."

January 12: Knit One and Purl, Too

The girl's college that I attended my fist two years was awash with knitters. Since I was trying very hard to fit in and not look like the nerd I was, I took up this indoor sport with gusto (but not much talent). The most impressive girls were those who did argyle socks, and I watched enviously as they dangled various colored bobbins from every surface. I was afraid to start on anything so complicated, though, and so I contented myself with buying some yellow wool to make a pair of socks for my favorite brother, Bill.

If I had been smart, I would have stuck to squares and made an afghan, because I had no idea what I was doing. I had to be nursed through cuffs, heels, and toes and it took me over a year to finish. I dragged those socks through trains, planes, and in cars. Because the yarn was constantly being dropped and rolling around in dusty places, the color turned more and more from yellow to gray. Moreover, I had only enough yarn to make them short, and they ended up looking like ladies golf socks. My brother was a compassionate man, however, and he not only accepted them with enthusiasm, he valiantly wore them on many family occasions for years. He really went the second mile!

It's a funny thing, but there never seems to be much traffic on that second mile. There are a lot of people who show love, but there are not many who keep it up when it is inconvenient. It is when we are busy, tired, or hurting, however, that Jesus is most clearly seen. He was never too busy or tired or hurting to show love, even on the cross.

"And if someone wants to sue you and take your tunic, let him have your cloak as well. If someone forces you to go one mile, go with him two miles." (Matthew 5:40-41 NIV)

January 13: Golf Equation

As a part-time golfer (more part than time), I sometimes look through golf magazines just to see if they have come up with any new techniques that will take 20 points off my score. And, indeed, they always do. It's usually a club, a different stance, a new grip, different gloves, or some gadget that will "revolutionize" my game. There is also a lot of hoop-la over balls that go so far you can't even see where they land (I don't see mine either, but it's not because they go that far…). All of these are pictured as absolute necessities if you want to stun the onlookers—which I can do without all that equipment.

At the risk of seeming cynical, I'm afraid the only thing that will take strokes off my game—or anyone else's—is practice. People who hit and miss (and I am an authority on this) are going to have a hit and miss golf game. To put it in a formula: P + MP = ASYWHTH. Translation: Practice plus more practice equals a score you won't have to hide.

As goes the golf game, so goes my spiritual journey. If I limp along on my journey with only a blessing before meals or only a sermon once a week, I will not only hit and miss, I will mostly miss. I will miss strength, joy, insight, guidance, perspective, and the knowledge that my circumstances are not too great for God to handle. I need to "enlarge my muscles" by practicing prayer, love for others, showing others patience and kindness, and by spending time meditating on God's word.

"I have not yet reached my goal, and I am not perfect. But Christ has taken hold of me. So I keep on running and struggling to take hold of the prize." (Philippians 3:12 CEV)

January 14: The Feline is Mutual

Sometimes our Resident Cat and I have a midnight meeting. If I get up and he is awake, he waits until I am back in bed and then jumps up on me for a snuggle. I have learned to be on my side for this attention, because if I lie on my back, he typically aims for my chest…and twelve pounds of dead weight on the lungs makes breathing, not to mention sleeping, difficult. However, I am always pleased that he has chosen to spend this time with me.

When I wake up at night, I can also have a midnight meeting with God. He is always there waiting, for He never leaves me. It is a great comfort to talk things over with Him. Sometimes He brings someone to mind that is in special need of prayer. When He reminds me of someone, and I pray in response, my prayer goes back to Him in a way that brings a blessing both to me and the one for whom I pray.

Prayer: Father, how glad I am that dark and light are both alike to you, and that you know all my thoughts even before I do. Thank you for your listening ear and a heart that is always open to your children.

"A song for the ascent to Jerusalem. I look up to the mountains—does my help come from there? My help comes from the Lord, who made the heavens and the earth! He will not let you stumble and fall; the one who watches over you will not sleep. Indeed, he who watches over Israel never tires and never sleeps." (Psalm 121:1-4 NLT)

January 15: Right Motive, Peculiar Result

When we lived in Jacksonville, our oldest daughter, Lissa (then about ten), owned an EZ bake oven. It was truly an amazing little cooking appliance. Much to our amazement, it made cupcakes from the heat of a light bulb. I still find it hard to believe that it actually worked. I only know I ate many completed projects. Many.

On my birthday, Lissa decided to go all out and bake a cake for me. She applied herself diligently to the project and ended up with a beautiful, small, round birthday cake. She frosted it, and prepared to squeeze out a message to me with a tube of frosting. Unfortunately, she discovered that we did not have any tubes on hand. She was not deterred. She came up with the idea of breaking up spaghetti into tiny pieces, and placed them carefully on the cake.

Lissa planned for the cake to say "Happy Birthday, Mom," but unfortunately the word "Happy" took up most of the small cake's surface area. So she had to settle for abbreviating the rest. When she presented it after dinner with shining eyes and an expectant heart, the cake read "Happy B.M."

Those of you with experience in potty-training will understand that it nearly killed us not to laugh. But one look at Lissa's precious, earnest face squelched all of our chuckles. So we managed to get through in one piece (we saved our laughter for later!). I was appreciative and I know that God was pleased that one of His children put forth the time and effort to wish her mother a happy birthday.

We should follow David's instructions to Solomon, "Solomon, my son, get to know the God of your ancestors. Worship and serve him with your whole heart and with a willing mind. For the Lord sees every heart and understands and knows every plan and thought. If you seek him, you will find him" (I Chronicles 28:9a-c NLT).

January 16: Cover-up

There was a big, old, ugly tree at the back of our yard that, I think, was struck by lightning. Since it was opposite the window where I sit at my desk, I had the opportunity to see it often. I noticed later that some vines had sprung up around its base and were slowly creeping upward (in Florida, we seem to have a lot of things creeping around…).

At any rate, it has taken three years, but now that ugly, old tree is completely covered with beautiful flowering vines. The birds have discovered it too, and it is now home to several different kinds of birds, accompanied, of course, by many baby birds. We thought at first that the vines would pull down the tree, but they just seem to have made it stronger. Evidently, all those little tendrils are holding everything together in spite of wind, rain, woodpeckers, and squirrels.

There are times in life when lightning hits all of us. There's very little you can do when you feel as if your heart has been ripped out. But God still uses ugly, old trees, as well as people who have been badly shaken. When we are willing to give God time to heal our scars, he will send little vines of love and encouragement that will hold us together, make us stronger, and someday, we can pass on that love and encouragement to others. We will find we have become a nesting place, a resting place for others who are weary.

"Though he brings grief, he also shows compassion according to the greatness of his unfailing love." (Lamentations 3:32 NLT)

January 17: Musk Oxen

Musk oxen would never be included in the category of "beautiful people." They are big and chunky (which makes them sound a bit like a candy bar), and they have so much hair you would think they had stumbled into an Arctic version of Rogaine. If attacked, musk oxen will stand to face its enemy, because its horns are its only means of defense. These animals live in herds, and if there are mothers and calves, the males stand outward in a circle to offer protection to the weaker ones inside.

Musk oxen band together to keep the young from being preyed upon. As older believers, we are called to do this too, standing shoulder to shoulder so that the enemy cannot get in to attack a new believer. God's word tells us, that, "Three are even better, for a triple-braided cord is not easily broken" (Ecclesiastes 4:12b NLT). Since this is so, how much more a cord made of up many Christians who band together to pray and minister to those who are weak and unable to fight? Even if we're not "big and chunky", if we stand shoulder to shoulder in the strength of the Lord Jesus Christ, God will be glorified.

January 18: Alarming News

The morning sun was just peeking over the trees as I opened the door of the lovely home where I was a guest for the night. I was dressed in walking shoes and suitable shirt and pants, prepared for a little exercise.

One moment later, however, I was extremely exercised: for when I opened the door, the loudest burglar alarm in the state went off. The scream that came from my throat nearly matched the scream coming from the alarm, and I jumped back inside, hoping irrationally that the noise would stop if I stepped back inside and closed the door. It did not. The owners of the house did not show up to turn it off. I desperately hoped that they had not slipped away to Europe during the night.

I tip-toed upstairs (I don't know why) and timidly knocked on their bedroom door. There was no answer. Maybe they had both died in there, I thought—for I could still hear that incredibly loud alarm. It sounded even louder upstairs. I banged on the door. Twice. Finally, I heard a sleepy voice saying, "Yes?"

"The alarm is ringing!" I shrieked through the closed door. (I had to scream to be heard over the blaring alarm.) "Do you have a way to turn it off?"

Unfortunately, it took a while for the owners to locate the alarm off switch. It took even longer for me to recuperate from the jangled nerves received while waiting. The ensuing silence was blissful.

I had unknowingly opened a door without entering the proper code; in my life, I sometimes purposefully cross lines that I shouldn't. And sometimes, even with a shrieking alarm, I am so intent on my own way that I ignore the sound and proceed merrily on my way. May I always stay alert for what God wants me to do, and take the time to listen to Him (not to mention alarm bells!).

"Although the Lord gives you the bread of adversity and the water of affliction, your teachers will be hidden no more; with your own eyes you will see them. Whether you turn to the right or to the left, your ears will hear a voice behind you, saying, 'This is the way; walk in it.'" (Isaiah 30:20-21 NIV)

January 19: A Hearing Ear

"Then Moses said, 'I pray that you will let me see you in all of your glory.' The Lord answered: 'All right. I am the Lord, and I show mercy and kindness to anyone I choose. I will let you see my glory and hear my holy name, but I won't let you see my face, because anyone who sees my face will die. There is a rock not far from me. Stand beside it, and before I pass by in all of my shining glory, I will put you in a large crack in the rock. I will cover your eyes with my hand until I have passed by. Then I will take my hand away, and you will see my back. You will not see my face.'" (Exodus 33:18-23 CEV)

"About eight days later Jesus took Peter, John, and James with him and went up on a mountain to pray. While he was praying, his face changed, and his clothes became shining white. Suddenly Moses and Elijah were there speaking with him." (Luke 9:28-30 CEV)

When our son-in-law, Gary, was in high school, he had a prayer answered in an unexpected way. Gary had begun to feel guilty about the kind of music he listened to. He had quite a large music collection, and he especially liked to listen while riding in the car. He hesitated to ask God for guidance, because he was afraid he wouldn't like the answer (this is often true of me, too!).

Gary was "willing to be made willing," however, so he prayed like this: "Lord, if you really want me to give up those tapes, please show me in a definite way." He drove to school as usual that morning, but when he got through that afternoon, he found that someone had broken in to his car and stolen all his tapes.

Moses also had his request answered differently than he was expecting. When Moses was alive he was able to see only God's back from a cleft in the rock, but, 1500 years later, when he saw Jesus, he finally saw the face of God.

Sometimes, I have a prayer that I have to wait to see answered, but I don't know anyone else who had to wait 1500 years! We may be discouraged about the silence that seems to surround our requests, but take heart. God may indeed have the answer waiting for us in the future…and He always has a listening ear.

"You willingly forgive, and your love is always there for those who pray to you. Please listen, Lord! Answer my prayer for help. When I am in trouble, I pray, knowing you will listen." (Psalm 86:5-7 CEV)

January 20: Strawberry Fields Forever

When I was a child, my family would travel to Florida to spend the winter. I can remember the excitement as we went further and further south and began to see palm trees and, then, orange trees. The sun felt so delicious after all the snow and ice we had traveled through. I just couldn't wait to jump into my bathing suit and sit in our little sulfur water pool, even though it smelled like rotten eggs and had icky strands of some kind of white material that floated out from the well (I never inquired too closely into this).

The biggest thrill, though, was on Christmas day when we always had fresh strawberries and ambrosia, which is made of sliced oranges mixed with fresh coconut. We would absolutely pig out on this, exclaiming and raving all the while (in those far-off days fruit didn't travel around the way it does now).

Today, of course, it's a different story, and strawberries and oranges are common and humdrum. No one's face lights up with excitement over a bowl of red strawberries nestled next to a pile of confectioner's sugar, because you can buy them any time and anywhere.

Sometimes I treat God like this. I allow him to become common and humdrum in my life.

Prayer: Dear God, I ask forgiveness for being so lukewarm. Make my heart an altar for your fire.

"Since we are receiving a kingdom that cannot be destroyed, let us be thankful and please God by worshiping him with holy fear and awe. For our God is a consuming fire." (Hebrews 12:28-29 NLT)

January 21: Warm Silence

A soldier in the trenches during World War I is said to have turned to the commanding officer and said, "Emergency call from Sergeant Smith. He said, 'The bullets is whizzing all around!' What should he do, sir?"

The officer's crisp reply was, "Tell him he needs to work on his grammar."

Sometimes, I shoot out irrelevant answers when confronted by someone in need. It is good to have suggestions, of course, but more often than not, people need to be listened to rather than talked to. They need the silent encouragement of your presence. In *Hamlet*, Polonius says, "Give every man thine ear, but few thy voice" (*Hamlet* I.iii). And in *Lorna Doone*, the hero John Ridd sums up his lifestyle by saying, "I have come to love silence…so little harm came come of it."

These are what I call "Ouch" statements. I am often shooting off my mouth at the wrong time. For me to be quietly encouraging is easier said than done (or rather, easier not said than done). Silence can be warm and comforting, especially when someone is going through a personally bleak time.

I have felt love from silence several times, but one time stands out in my memory. It was not a bleak time, but it was certainly a time of struggle and distress. It was the night I decided to give my life to God. The woman sitting next to me was the mother of our Associate Pastor, and when I heard the Gospel, as if for the first time, I wept (under the blanket which I had wrapped around my head). She said not a single word. She was praying for me, I'm sure, but she kept her words to herself. I knew she was there, and she knew I was there, and she loved me in silence.

"A truly wise person uses few words…." (Proverbs 17:27a NLT)

January 22: What is it about January?

It's really too bad about January. After all, a new start to a brand new year ought to make one burst with zeal and fresh ideas. And perhaps it does for some…but not for me.

January has a lot of bluster, but none of the tentative palette of April, the lush green of June, the blazing colors of September, or the bubbling excitement of December. Somehow, it just lies there grumpily, putting in time until I can face the fact that the date I put in my checkbook is going to be different from the year I had just gotten used to.

January, with its mounds of swirling snow, can be quite exciting, of course, but this is not a likely occurrence in Florida. Let's face it: Christmas is only a memory, family and friends have all disappeared, there are decorations all over the house (several of which will not be discovered until February), and I am always left with a solid bulk of fruitcake that remains untouched by human hands. To put it bluntly, I find January dull and drab—sort of like the mildewed washcloth I just unearthed from behind the hamper in the guest bathroom.

There are lots of days when I would even be glad for a small earth tremor. God, however, wants me to remember that He is with me as much in the drab days as He is in the bright ones. The temple of my life can be a place of worship in the low places just as much as on the high. In fact, I believe that He is more pleased when I praise Him with a heart that wants to be listless and just lie down until spring, than He is with one that is jumping up and down with energy.

"…and I praise and honor you all day long." (Psalm 71:8 CEV)

January 23: Weather or Not

When we lived in Michigan, we decided to go skiing for the weekend. On Monday, following three days of unmitigated adult humiliation due our lack of skill and our general ineptitude, we arose at 5:00 a.m. to get the children back in school. At that hour, however, the world was shrouded in fog so thick we couldn't see the road except in brief open and shut patches. We inched along at five miles an hour, having little or no idea where we were going.

Suddenly, we noticed two taillights in front of us. Since we could see them better than the road, we crawled behind them. The unnerving thing was that we didn't know if those lights were going to the drugstore or all the way to California. We had little choice at this point, however, so our little caravan of two crawled on in what we devoutly hoped was a southerly direction.

Eventually, the fog cleared, and we made it home in one piece, but I couldn't help thinking how different it is for those who follow Jesus. He can be trusted to lead us; he won't disappear in bad weather; he will lead us. He truly is the Good Shepherd!

"After he has gathered his own flock, he walks ahead of them, and they follow him because they recognize his voice." (John 10:4 NLT)

January 24: Bulbs

In the process of drifting off to sleep one night, I began thinking about the difference between plant bulbs and light bulbs. If you were to ask someone which one represented spiritual life more, the answer would probably be the plant bulb. And although it is certainly true that we are living only because our heavenly Gardener planted us, waters us, and expects us to grow, I wanted to offer a few thoughts in favor of light bulbs.

A light bulb does not shine until it is connected to the source of power. Furthermore, plant bulbs call attention to themselves, while light bulbs just sit quietly lighting the darkness. Neither bulb will nag, pester, or harangue, but light bulbs show others the way.

When we are firmly attached to the Almighty One who is our source of power, we can't take any credit for shining light, for it all comes from Him. So, we may thank Him for the privilege of shining in a dark world, keeping in mind always that we are "distributors," not "manufacturers."

Whether you prefer to be a plant bulb or a light bulb, grow or glow, and give the credit to God!

"Neither do people light a lamp and put it under a bowl. Instead they put it on its stand, and it gives light to everyone in the house. In the same way, let your light shine before men, that they may see your good deeds and praise your Father in heaven." (Matthew 5:15-16)

January 25: As Time Goes By

When I lean over the tub to scrub it and my tummy is hanging over the edge, I know time has passed. When my twenty-minute walk takes a half hour to finish, I know time has passed. When I no longer fly down the stairs unless I am in free-fall, I know time has passed. When the glasses I wear tend to make the blur on the directions a bigger blur, I know time has passed.

It can be very frustrating to find that joints and limbs no longer have a spring, and that hair has lost its appetite for living. But I think God has two lessons for me in this department. The first is found in Ecclesiastes 3:1, which says, "Everything on earth has its own time and its own season" (CEV). When time has passed, our season is not the same season it was when we were younger. So, life would seem to become "seasoned," so to speak.

The second lesson for me can be read in II Corinthians 4:17-18, "These little troubles are getting us ready for an eternal glory that will make all our troubles seem like nothing. Things that are seen don't last forever, but things that are not seen are eternal. That's why we keep our minds on the things that cannot be seen" (CEV).

While it is not really marvelous news to be told that I will not last forever, it is part of His plan. It is imperative that I work on renewing my inner person instead of bemoaning the decaying of the outer. In other words, may I focus on what I can change, instead of what I can't!

January 26: Macro Thinking

Three words familiar to most Americans in the 1960's and 70's were: mini, midi and maxi. Although I originally had the feeling that they were Latin for "I came, I saw, I shopped," I soon found out they referred to skirt lengths.

Two buzzwords from the late 1980's were "macro" and "micro". I was amazed to hear that they had nothing to do with any sort of pasta dish (my brain kept circling back to macaroni). When our daughter Virginia took the course "Micro- & Macro-Economics" for her master's degree, I couldn't imagine how macro and micro could make up one course (I mean, after all, it's either macaroni or it's not.). The dictionary was not all that much help; it confirmed that "micro" meant small and "macro" meant large. Virginia finally spent some time explaining what the course entailed, unfortunately I can't share that with you, because her explanation is lost somewhere in the murky recesses of my brain.

I do wonder, though, if these terms could be applied to my worldview. Most of my vision is pretty microscopic and is limited to family and friends, but God's desire for my view is <u>macro</u>! In my prayer life, in my giving, in my ministry, I can be a macro woman (all without gaining weight!).

My vision should continually be stretched and extended, so that, in looking at needs, I will see not only those close at hand, but those across the world. I should be praying for brothers and sisters in France, Germany, Spain, Niger, Nigeria, Ethiopia, South Africa, Senegal, China, Russia, Bolivia, Brazil, the Middle East, Israel, Palestine, Pakistan, and India. I should be giving money for projects marked for literature, medicine or buildings. I can also enlarge the scope of my ministry by reaching out to people I don't really know well and bringing them to places where they can hear the Gospel. That's Macro thinking with a capital "M."

"...you will receive power and will tell people about me everywhere—in Jerusalem, throughout Judea, in Samaria, and to the ends of the earth." (Acts 1:8b NLT)

January 27: Disasterville

When I was a guide for Pioneer Clubs, which is a church program somewhat similar to Boy and Girl Scouts, we had to pick a bird name by which to be called. Mine was not exactly a bird, but I chose "Mother Waddles"—which should tell you something. I continued to flesh out the role as Mother Waddles long after I stopped working with Pioneer Clubs, and I eventually reached new heights of duckiness on my way to a conference at Cape Cod. After four hours of waiting for an evening flight, the small airline scheduled to take me to my destination decided that it was getting late and that the weather was uncertain. My flight was canceled. A man with a cell phone standing beside me managed to find a room for me at a nearby hotel. The desk clerk was absolutely the smarmiest individual I have ever seen, and he greedily informed me it would be $150.00 for one night. I was more or less stuck with this, even though there wasn't that much of the night left. I set my alarm so I could get back to the airport to catch a 5:00 a.m. flight.

When I went to check in the next morning, the airline personnel told me that I would have to change airlines if I wanted to get there by 10:00 a.m. I needed to get there by 10 because that was when I was scheduled to give my first talk (I wondered if they were routing me via Acapulco). This change required that I walk, in pitch darkness, to another terminal, dragging my too-many bags. While I was buying the second ticket, someone managed to steal one of my suitcases. I then had to go back to the other terminal to get my original ticket, which they had taken. I limped back to the other terminal. My first ticket had vanished. I trudged wearily back to the original starting place, and as I did so, the elastic on my panty hose broke. It is very hard not to walk like a duck when you are lugging suitcases while hampered by falling stockings (even though I did have one less suitcase than when I started). Mother Waddles didn't make it to the conference in time to speak, but we had a wonderful time when I finally showed up…feeling much older and very much tireder.

Sometimes people can't help the way that they look, and appear very "waddly" with problems and sore feet. If you are looking at any ducks today—be kind!

"But those who hope in the Lord will renew their strength. They will soar on wings like eagles; they will run and not grow weary, they will walk and not be faint." (Isaiah 40:31 NIV)

January 28: Leaning

The person who stole my bag at the airport (see January 27!) didn't really get much in the way of material goods, as it was mostly underwear. However, it did have all my devotional books in it, as well as my notes from an entire year of Bible study.

I'm ashamed to say I was quite un-spiritually furious, and I stomped around for quite a while before I began to try James advice in chapter 1, verses 2-4: "My friends, be glad, even if you have a lot of trouble. You know that you learn to endure by having your faith tested. But you must learn to endure everything, so that you will be completely mature and not lacking in anything." (CEV)

I really didn't know if I wanted endurance or not…but gradually I began to see two things. Maybe the person who took the case looked at some of the Bible verses (one never knows!). Secondly, maybe I had been leaning a little too hard on spiritual materials instead of on the Lord. I put great store on God's Word (the Bible), but it must be the Lord himself who has my full devotion.

January 29: Ants

Ants are interesting to watch at work mainly because they are ALWAYS at work. You never see an ant sitting under a leaf with his feet up having a coffee break, or being a "twig potato" after the sun has set. The Bible commends them for their constant industry. It's not that God expects us to be busy without rest, but he does urge us to lay in a supply of stores for the winters of our lives. These will come whether we are ready for them or not.

When the frost of tragedy or disaster is upon me, and the cold winds of bleak adversity are plucking at my heartstrings, it is too late for me to be thinking about gathering food for the soul. All this must be done in advance of the crisis. A day-by-day storing up of the warmth and sustenance of God's word is the only thing that will see me through the barrenness of winter. While it is a real and precious truth that God will never leave me, he is more REAL to me if I have spent time in close fellowship with him during the sunny, cloudless days. I have to plan ahead for my winter of adversity!

"Take a lesson from the ants, you lazybones. Learn from their ways and be wise! Even though they have no prince, governor, or ruler to make them work, they labor hard all summer, gathering food for the winter." (Proverbs 6:6-8 NLT)

January 30: Choices

"But people who aren't Christians can't understand these truths from God's Spirit. It all sounds foolish to them because only those who have the Spirit can understand what the Spirit means. We who have the Spirit understand these things, but others can't understand us at all. How could they? For, 'Who can know what the Lord is thinking? Who can give him counsel?' But we can understand these things, for we have the mind of Christ." (I Corinthians 2:14-16 NLT)

I was talking with a woman who was new to our town, and, for some reason, the conversation turned to banking. She asked me where I banked, and then I asked her where she banked. She told me.

"Why did you choose that bank?" I asked her.

"Why, it's the tallest bank in town!" she said, a little defensively.

Well, I'm certainly no expert on banking (just ask my husband!), but I am sure that height should not be the criterion for choosing a financial institution. It reminds me that some people choose books simply because they like the title or the cover, or (horrors!) simply because it's on the bestseller list. Some people choose churches the same way, more or less. They like the way it looks (imposing—with Gothic overtones) or because they know it has a lot of members and want to see what all the fuss is about. Or, perhaps, they know some prominent people who go there.

Churches need to be chosen carefully; be wary of ministers who are immature in the faith. If the words that they speak go against God's truths, it's difficult to deepen your faith.

When Jesus ascended into heaven, God sent the Holy Spirit to Jesus' followers. To those who are willing, the Spirit will grant wisdom; which includes the ability to correctly judge false teaching from true. May I be open to receive this gift from the Holy Spirit, and may I use it to determine what is right and true.

January 31: Life With Father

My life with a father who was a civil engineer consisted of many things, not the least of which was "planning trips." He would spend hours studying maps for the best routes to and from Florida, and consulting with AAA as though he were going to Outer Mongolia. Hotels were considered and discarded depending on where he wanted to be, in order to get the best room, the best dinner, and, last but not least, the best oatmeal. This last was imperative, because he ate oatmeal every day of his life, and it had to be just right. He considered the best kind to be oatmeal that had cooked all night in a double boiler, because that's the way it was done at home…and he would surely turn over in his grave if he could see people sticking a bowl in a microwave and using the instant stuff.

The most important preparation for a trip was putting all the information down in a little black book with two columns: one headed "approximate," and the other, "actual." Then he would note down times for gas, breakfast, lunch, and dinner, as well as the mileage (using of course the most efficient speed which was, at that time, 45 miles per hour). This was torture for me, because I am the kind of person who likes to just zoom and get things over with…. Sometimes, I wondered if we really were related.

During the actual trip, the person in the front seat had to fill in the exact times and mileage for each day. If the numbers were off more than a squeak, Daddy would spend hours re-adjusting the schedule so it would be better next time.

If my earthly father spent so much time preparing for a journey, do you not think our heavenly Father has done this for our life's journey? Psalm 40:5 reminds us, "You, Lord God, have done many wonderful things, and you have planned marvelous things for us. No one is like you! I would never be able to tell all you have done" (CEV). Not everyone had a father who planned, but we can all look to our heavenly Father and know that his plans stand firm forever.

"The Lord is truthful; he can be trusted. He loves justice and fairness, and he is kind to everyone everywhere on earth." (Psalm 33:4-5 CEV)

February 1: Malfunction Junction

A few years ago, our town opened a brand new YMCA with excellent facilities for all ages. I joined not long after they opened.

My first aerobics class was a shock. The class was euphemistically called "Slo and E-Z." The participants were certainly Slo, but the instructor was the only one who thought it was E-Z. We huffed and puffed our way around the room for an entire hour, bending, stretching, and trying to hold in what was supposed to be in.

The next morning was a truly painful experience as I undid my wounded body from its crabbed contour. I had allowed my muscles (if you could call them that) to become so rigid that when I stretched them it was, indeed, a painful experience.

I seem to allow myself to become rigid in my spiritual life, as well. Often, when I hear a new idea, my first reaction is to turn away and say, "I've never done it that way." A while ago, I even discovered (to my amazement!) that I had labeled certain tasks as "necessary spiritual chores." When these chores were completed, I would cross them off with great satisfaction. Somehow, I had come to think that God would be terribly pleased with my efforts; the truth was that I had drifted into legalism.

I find I must continually examine my Christian walk. I must always remember I am not under law but grace, and I need to allow my mind to be stretched by a few fresh new ideas!

"I want to know only one thing. How were you given God's Spirit? Was it by obeying the Law of Moses or by hearing about Christ and having faith in him? How can you be so stupid? Do you think that by yourself you can complete what God's Spirit started in you?" (Galatians 3:2-3 CEV)

February 2: The Diner's Club

One of the most exciting and rewarding experiences of my life came at a time when I was "just too busy." We had been in Tampa less than a month, and our children were still trying to adjust to their fifth school in five years. I realize this happens more and more as Americans move around the country, but it never gets any easier, and the groans never get any less.

Our oldest daughter was a junior in high school, and one of the reasons we had left the Detroit area was so that she (and those following immediately after!) could have a few years in one place. The kids all liked their new schools, but Lissa was having a hard time finding friends who were also followers of Christ. She had found one (a darling girl by the name of Leah), and the two of them finally located two boys who were new believers. The girls set about the job of turning them into well-grounded believers with a great deal of enthusiasm and a lot of tapes on living the Christian life. This paled rather quickly, though, and soon the girls came to me and asked if I would teach a class of kids at night. "Oh, I just couldn't," I said and I enumerated all the things I had my fingers in. However, I ended up agreeing to teach one month, and we would see how things went.

Ten more brand new believers were unearthed, and we started in with some Friendship Bible Coffee material from Stonecroft Ministries. Instead of doing the workbooks ("too much like school," I was assured), I asked the study questions as we went along. Because all of the kids except Lissa and Leah were new to Bible study, nobody minded expressing ignorance and/or opinions. At the end of the lesson, we divided up into two groups of six and started learning to pray out loud (a scary project for most of them, but not so bad in a group of contemporaries.)

It was marvelous! The kids were like sponges that hadn't ever seen water…and we decided on the name "Diner's Club—a little meat for all to eat." There was much growth, much hilarity, and much love for each other…. Before we knew it, the group mushroomed into about seventy who squashed into living rooms every Tuesday night without fail (some may have come just for the refreshments!). I had to change the format, of course, as people came and went, and there wasn't much opportunity for continuity in a regular Bible study. So, I did subjects instead, with each lesson standing on its own: we studied subjects such as peace, true success, disappointments, grief, etc.

These studies lasted seven years and, then, just shut off like a faucet. I still meet these "kids" once in a while as I go across the country, and most of them are going on with the Lord. What a privilege to be involved in changed lives, and all because there were two girls who longed to show others the love and light of Jesus.

"The lion has roared—tremble in fear! The Sovereign Lord has spoken—I dare not refuse to proclaim his message! (Amos 4:8 NLT)

February 3: Insulated

Several years ago, there was an article in a Christian publication that was very thought provoking. The question asked was something like this: If you had the opportunity to live in a town where everyone was a Christian, would you do it? The article went on to say that not only would everyone be a Christian, but they would also be super-spiritual, well taught, and overflowing with love and good deeds. In other words, there would be no crabbiness, greed, pride, or selfishness. I thought that sounded pretty sensational, and I would have been among the first to put in my bid (although the more I thought about it, the less I was sure I would qualify!).

The author then went on to say (sneaky thing) that this little set-up was not what Jesus had in mind, because if we live in a community that didn't have any one but believers, how could we be lights to the world? Who would be watching to see what difference Christ made in a life as we work, suffer, face death? The problems and heartaches we face are the same as those who do not yet know the Lord, and it is to be our duty and privilege to show them God's love working in and through our lives.

"You are the light of the world. A city on a hill cannot be hidden. Neither do people light a lamp and put it under a bowl. Instead they put it on its stand, and it gives light to everyone in the house." (Matthew 5:14-15 NIV)

February 4: Goodbye, Mrs. Zips

I stood on the doorstep of a friend and rang her bell. When she opened it and saw my face, she gasped, "Oh my goodness! What's the matter?" "It's my birthday," I said, bursting into tears. "Your birthday?" she echoed. I nodded miserably, and waited for the sympathy I felt I deserved. Feeling impatient with her lack of understanding, I wailed dramatically, "I'm 30!" (after all, I had been an actress!). I remember that day with clarity (and laughter). I thought I had come to the end of everything because I was "over the hill" and well on my way to senility. Little did I know.

A year later, I met Jesus Christ. Have you heard the saying, "Life begins at forty?" For me, it began at thirty-one. Now, of course, I really am over the hill, but strangely enough, gray hair, wrinkles, and the inability to stay up much past 8:00 p.m. are no longer major considerations. I have come to realize that youth and vigor are not prerequisites for joy and peace. I have found, with relief, that the Lord loves me just as much with gray hair as He did with black hair. He will continue to love me with His everlasting love even when I am no longer a contributing member of society because He is God. All I'm responsible for is not to let the wrinkles in my face turn into wrinkles of the heart.

"You survivors in Israel, listen to me, the Lord. Since the day you were born, I have carried you along. I will still be the same when you are old and gray, and I will take care of you. I created you. I will carry you and always keep you safe." (Isaiah 46:3-4 CEV)

February 5: The Woman in White

I realize this is the title of a novel by 19th century author Wilkie Collins, so I hope no one is offended that I am temporarily purloining it. When we lived in Pittsburgh, I used to talk to my hairdresser about God. I might as well have been talking in a foreign language for all the response I got. Then, one day, as I went in for a final trim before we left to find a house in Boston, she said, "I'm sorry you're moving away. I wanted to have a luncheon for my friends and have you come talk, just like you do in Christian Women's Club." After I retrieved my jaw from the floor, I said, "Oh no problem…we're just going to look for a house, and I'll be back to pack up. So, you go ahead and set up the lunch and I'll call you when I get back."

All went as planned. When I returned, I called and she said all the arrangements had been made. "We'll be meeting in a restaurant. Is that okay?" she asked. "Perfect," I assured her. "That's what we do too." She continued, "…and I thought we would have a special feature, just the way you do." "That's wonderful!" I exclaimed. "What is it?" "It's a wine tasting" she enthused. There was a moment's silence on my end of the wire, and she caught it immediately. "Is that okay?" she asked. "Sure," I assured her, "just give me the directions to the restaurant."

The big day came, and I headed off to a new adventure (perhaps the word "adventure" is a bit dramatic, but at the very least it was a new experience). I drove and drove, getting nearer and nearer to the steel district. The street I was looking for was incredibly dirty, and lined with tired buildings that looked as though one good storm would do them in. I drove carefully looking for the number I had been given. I discovered it was not a restaurant, after all. It was a neighborhood tavern.

I had picked my outfit for the day carefully…a winter white wool dress, white gloves, and a large white fur hat (which, now that I think of it, must have made me look like a lost drum majorette). Every head in the tavern turned as I picked my way through a crowd of men at the bar. I mean every head. As a former actress, it was an entrance I would have died for at one time in my life. At that point, I just wanted to die. I made my way to the bartender and cleared my throat nervously. "Is there a ladies' luncheon here?" "Sure, kid," he rumbled, "in the back."

February 6: The Woman in White (continued)

I tiptoed to the indicated closed door and opened it cautiously. There was a large U-shaped table absolutely awash with wine bottles, a man in the middle and 22 women whose heads also swiveled incredulously at my approach. My hostess approached and guided me to a table for one. Me. Alone. Except for God.

I nibbled apathetically at some Welsh rarebit and was then introduced. The introduction from that day is firmly fixed in my mind. "You got one surprise when you came and we had a wine tasting. Now you're gonna have another" (I shuddered). "I don't know nothing about this lady, but I cut her hair, and she seems real nice."

I thanked the Father I had people praying for me and began to share the story of how I had become a believer. I had barely gotten one sentence out before a girl who had graduated from wine to martinis said in a loud, blurry voice, "My God, she's gonna talk about salvation!"

My knees started to shake, and I could feel the sweat break out under my white fur hat. Everyone was about a joke and a half behind, but I staggered on through, prayed, and then went around the table and gave everyone a booklet.

I sat down amidst a deafening silence. Then a woman got up from the other side of the room and came over to sit down. Big tears were rolling down the wrinkled, tired face of a woman I assumed to be at least in her sixties. "Is what you said really true?" she asked. "Yes," I said, nodding. She continued, "Because I'm 45, and my husband left me this morning for an 18 year old. So if it's not true, I don't have anything to live for." "It is true," I said. "Did you pray to ask Christ into your life?" "Yes," she said. "Then you have everything you need to make a whole new life, and a Savior who will never leave you," I assured her.

And the little woman in white left the tavern thanking God that he had used a weak, shaky vessel, one perspiring over most of her body, who was enabled by the Spirit and the prayers of faithful friends.

"Jews demand miraculous signs and Greeks look for wisdom, but we preach Christ crucified: a stumbling block to Jews and foolishness to Gentiles, but to those whom God has called, both Jews and Greeks, Christ the power of God and the wisdom of God. For the foolishness of God is wiser than man's wisdom, and the weakness of God is stronger than man's strength." (I Corinthians 1:22-25 NIV)

February 7: On Cows

Cows were quite trendy there for a while, although I'm not sure exactly why. Perhaps they just evoke a rural feeling that people enjoy. Whatever the reason, they are included here, because they have had lessons for me.

The first lesson is: I should be content. After all, have you ever seen a cow in a stew? (don't answer that…). It is easy for me to be humming steadily along and then I see a new house, a new dress, a new car or even a new cat, something that brings out that little tickly feeling of "I wish I had that." It may not last long, and it may not turn me into a raving, greedy monster (at least I hope not). The one thing it does do is sneak in and destroy my contentment.

The second thought I have about cows is that, when I study my Bible, I should chew the cud just as the cow does. Many times I race through the Bible as though it were a chore to be finished or a medicine to be swallowed…unlike cows who chew and chew, and get all the good they can without being the first to leave the table. I believe that the more I chew and chew on God's word, the greater my capacity for good digestion, and the more likely I am to remember what I have read. In fact, it is easier to ruminate over one verse than it is to digest an entire book of the Bible all at once. The most marvelous thing about reading the Bible this way is that when I have gotten all the good out of it, the next time it comes up (so to speak) I can chew on it and get something else out of it!

Several years ago, I devised a plan to get the most out of spending time with the Father. I take a book, either in the old or new Testament, and just read slowly, asking God to stop me on the verse He has for me that day. I underline it and then write it out in an inexpensive notebook. Then I ruminate on that verse and just chew and chew and write down anything that comes into my mind (not the grocery list, you understand, I mean things that pertain to the verse and how it may be applied to my life). This is tremendously rewarding and makes my day more purposeful. Even more important, it makes my heart sing to realize that I have been in communication with the God of the entire universe!

"And religion does make your life rich, by making you content with what you have." (I Timothy 6:6 CEV)

February 8: Wool Coats

As a conceited theater major, living in a world of Shakespeare and other more esoteric playwrights, I had always considered Westerns far, far beneath my notice (and I even thought Zane Grey should have called one of his books *Riders of the Purple Stage*). I have recently discovered, however, that while they aren't in the same class as Dickens or Dumas, they are educational to a certain extent, as well as entertaining. Old Louie L'Amour and others have introduced me to men and women of integrity, as well as to villains with no character and black hearts. Happily, the "white hats" always win. This is also the case with the sea stories of Alexander Kent and C.S. Forrester, which we also enjoy.

One of these villains, speaking of someone he considered "easy pickings," called the man "a fat sheep in high oats." I thought that was a fascinating description of how the world, many times, views Christians. Certainly the Lord calls us sheep (with many of their characteristics, such as willfulness and stupidity), but those who think they denigrate believers by calling them sheep are forgetting the most important thing a sheep has: a Shepherd.

We may indeed have the qualities that would make us "easy pickings," but, although we are defenseless to a great degree, the Shepherd is not. I hug these words from John to my heart: "My sheep recognize my voice; I know them, and they follow me. I give them eternal life, and they will never perish. No one will snatch them away from me, for my Father has given them to me, and he is more powerful than anyone else. So no one can take them from me. The Father and I are one" (John 10:27-29 NLT).

So when you feel a little anxious about venturing out, remember the one who holds you in His hand!

February 9: Cat and Mouse

It was a warm afternoon, and we had the windows down in the car as my daughter, Virginia, and I drove to a Mother-Daughter party at our church. For some reason (lost in the mist of time), we were in costume (as we so often were when someone mentioned party or play—or even guests for dinner). Anyway, she was dressed as the Pied Piper, and I was a rat. This had not been my original distribution of roles, but you know what they say about the best-laid plans of mice and men....

We were going through a residential neighborhood and passed two little boys, about four years old, walking along the street holding a kitten. As we slowly drove past, I leaned out of the window to get a better look at the furry animal clutched in their grasp. The boys glanced up and saw me with dawning horror. "Look at the size of that rat, Tommy!" one of them gasped. "We'd better get out of here!" and off they ran, casting nervous looks in our direction all the way to the corner, where they gratefully ran up on a porch. I would have reassured them if I could that I was not a real rat, big enough to drive a car, but I presume they were too frightened to risk any close encounters of an odd kind, so to speak. They had been terrified for nothing and never knew that I was just a nutty mom in disguise.

I get frightened sometimes, too, though. And when I don't stop to investigate, my terror grows like giant rats in the jungle of my thoughts. I love the verse in Psalm 56:3 that tells how David felt: "When I am afraid, I will trust in you" (NIV). The thing that encourages me is that David did not say he would never be afraid, but that he knew what to do when fright came, imagined or real. May I remember this too when I face the giant rats in my life.

"I sought the Lord, and he answered me; he delivered me from all my fears." (Psalm 34:4 NIV)

February 10: Word of Mouth

I have always had the bad habit of saying the first thing that pops into my head. "Put brain into gear before speaking" is advice I have been known to give but not follow.

Many years ago, I was at a party, talking to some of my mother's friends, when my eyes lit on a woman who had owned a nearby camera store. She had owned it forever, and I was of the opinion that it was practically a blight on the landscape. It was as dusty as an Egyptian tomb, without the first piece of decoration. However, I had just that week happened to walk by the store, and when I looked in the sparkling window, I couldn't believe my eyes. There were flowers and wrapping paper and interesting items all vying for attention. I pounced on this woman and told her I had noticed the wonderful job she had done redecorating. "Oh, it's ever so much nicer now," I warbled; and then I noticed the sudden stillness in the group. In the deathly quiet, she said, "We sold the store last month." I choked on my cookie and wondered if I could be transported to China.

A few years ago, when I was speaking in New York, I was invited to spend the night with a girl I had known many years previously at camp. It was winter, and freezing cold, but she told me as I walked in that they had put the thermometer up to 60, knowing that my Floridian blood was probably thin (I ended up sleeping in my bathrobe and topcoat). At dinner that night, I was seated across the table from one of her teenage daughters. As we were chatting, I noticed that one of them had something on her nose. She seemed unconscious of it, and thinking it was something she had missed when washing for dinner, I said quietly, "You have a spot on the side of your nose." "Yes," she answered flatly, "it's a diamond."

Another of my many gaffes was when I was in Germany on a college tour. I quickly grew cranky at not understanding a word anyone said, and I longed for someone with whom I could converse. On a trolley, the man in front of me sneezed, and his companion said, "Gesundheit!" Relieved, I poked my head in his ear and joyfully shouted, "Thank goodness, you speak English!"

My prayer is that as I soak my head and heart in scripture, my tongue, in between the two, will also be saturated. Then I will be able to "Listen twice and speak once."

"Help me to guard my words whenever I say something." (Psalm 141:3 CEV)

February 11: The Sky is Falling!

I was kneeling in my closet when it happened. It surely would have been more spiritual if I had been praying in there, but the truth is, I was trying to get something out of my suitcase, and it was proving recalcitrant in the extreme. The disaster occurred because in my effort to unjam the suitcase, I had managed to get myself entangled in a dress hanging from the knob of a three-tiered cabinet. The cabinets were not locked, hooked, or pasted together. They were only balanced one on top of the other (and evidently not well balanced) because they all three crashed down on my back as I was bent over. It knocked the wind out of me, and made enough noise to bring one of my daughters running in to see if we had had a localized earthquake. Hauling me up, she determined that I only had bruises on my back and not a spine cracked in half (which proves I am not half-cracked as you might have supposed).

I've noticed that when people are crushed by a heavy burden, they often are focused solely on that burden, whether it is a financial disaster, the death of a loved one, the heartbreak over a child, a broken relationship, or an illness. When I am living through a dark time, I also hobble around stiffly, conscious only of my pain. At times like these, I find it hard to believe that God is concerned, or even watching, so I have to force myself to turn from subjectivity to objectivity. Verse after verse in the Bible assures us that God is faithful and loving, day after day, hour after hour.

"Though they stumble, they will not fall, for the Lord holds them by the hand." (Psalm 7:24 NLT)

February 12: A Dillar A Dollar

Every Sunday she came in late for choir, and every Sunday I would squirm and feel grumpy about her tardiness. Didn't she know she was causing a distraction? It wasn't that she made a big fuss about slipping into the choir loft, but I thought it was discourteous. I wondered why in the world she couldn't arrange her time better. Was she over-sleeping? Was she out in the foyer talking to someone? Didn't she care that she was the only one who didn't show up on time?

One day, I very self-righteously mentioned this breach of etiquette to my daughter, Margaret, who explained to me why that woman was always late. It seems she led the opening exercises for the children's Sunday school. I went from five feet to five inches in less than sixty seconds. I felt terrible that I had been so busy misjudging a sister who had been helping where there was a need…and I shouldn't have been concerned about it in the first place!

It's just amazing how quickly I can stick my nose into other people's business. The word "judge" comes into play here, because it carries the meaning of "condemnation," and is entirely different than "to discern." I know about judging because I have been guilty of it, and I also have been misjudged. It's not a happy feeling either way. The tricky thing is that we do not know the hearts of others as our Father does…so, it's really better to stay out of the whole thing!

"Therefore judge nothing before the appointed time; wait until the Lord comes. He will bring to light what is hidden in darkness and will expose the motives of men's hearts. At that time each will receive his praise from God." (I Corinthians 4:5 NIV)

February 13: Little Red Schoolhouse

I assume you know that when Dr. Watson asked Sherlock Holmes where he had attended school, the great man replied, "Elementary, my dear Watson, elementary."

Everyone who starts school has to begin in the first grade, and this is true spiritually as well as physically. Some new believers are not thrilled with this piece of information; it's not fun to be "elementary." It would be much nicer just to pop right into graduate school. However, I have discovered there are no short cuts in the spiritual journey. Anyone can memorize the books of the Bible or the Sermon on the Mount, but these tidbits of knowledge do not help us to become more Christ-like. Naturally, some are faster learners than others, and some courses God has for us are harder than others. However, the Christian experience has similar elements for everyone.

The core of our education is knowing that LOVE is the mark of a Christian (*The Mark of a Christian* is the title of a Francis Schaffer book). Then, it is critical to live out what we have learned in our lives!

No one gets his or her "Master's Degree" without undergoing tests of one kind or another, but we may take comfort in the fact that our Teacher is always present, and He loves His pupils very much.

Prayer: May I be willing to learn from You, Lord!

"Respect and obey the Lord! This is the beginning of knowledge." (Proverbs 1:7a CEV)

February 14: My True Love

A few weeks before our son Allen was born, our two other children came down with chicken pox. I was under the impression I had already had this disease, and I hovered solicitously over our daughter, Lissa, and our son, Will. Unfortunately, the awful truth came out about the same time my spots did (Allen and the pox had evidently been incubating at the same time).

My strange, itchy bumps became redder and larger and spread to every corner of my continent. I was so sick I didn't move from my bed for a week. The day I staggered to the bathroom and looked in the mirror remains photographed permanently in my memory (and thankfully, ONLY in my memory!). My hair, formerly below my shoulders, stuck out at right angles due to the fact that I had been told the itching would stop if I smeared my head with Vaseline. This was untrue, and not only did it not perform the task to which it had been assigned, it caused a petroleum backlash similar to the oil spills in the Atlantic. I was also covered most unattractively with large black scabs that peppered my face with a Swiss cheese look that only a modern artist could have appreciated.

I simply could not imagine that my husband, Bill, had slept in the same room without screaming. Yet, he never mentioned that I looked like someone the Black Plague death wagons had missed picking up, or say "poor thing," or try to hide me in the closet. He simply accepted the situation as if it were a temporary condition. It was, more or less…although I had to wash my hair in Tide seven times to get the Vaseline out. Evidently, his love was not based on how I looked.

God is like this to me. In my present condition, pocked with sin, He still accepts and loves me, for Jesus has cleansed me. When I am ugly with pride or despair, He knows it is only a temporary condition, and that when I see Him face to face, I will be finally and eternally beautiful. But for now, His love is not based on how I look.

"When we were utterly helpless, Christ came at just the right time and died for us sinners. Now, no one is likely to die for a good person, though someone might be willing to die for a person who is especially good. But God showed his great love for us by sending Christ to die for us while we were still sinners." (Romans 5:6-8 NLT)

February 15: Worry Warts

I don't think my mother ever heard about worry beads, but she was up to the minute on worrywarts. A worrywart is someone who has a heavy heart and a broken back from hauling around all the cares and anxieties of life. Their days are miserable because their worries seem bigger than their abilities, and their nights are miserable because, every time they start drifting off to sleep, they start enumerating all the things that have to be done. All in all, this is a no win situation, and Mother wouldn't put up with it.

George MacDonald, who authored some very pithy statements about the Christian life, had this to say about staying awake to worry, "If God is not watching, then worry is useless. If God is watching, then we may sleep in peace."

The wonderful thing is, we may have God's peace at any time, because He is watching. Isaiah 26:3 assures us, "You will keep in perfect peace him whose mind is steadfast, because he trusts in you" (NIV). A minister, commenting on this said, "He will keep him in perfect peace whose mind stops at God." When we stop at God we do not allow any worry wool gathering, but simply stop, because we have a faithful God who cares for His flock.

"Cast all your anxiety on him because he cares for you." (I Peter 5:7 NIV)

February 16: Changed Your (S)oil Lately?

I am afraid I have a great affinity for the kudzu plant (known previously only to crossword and Scrabble fans). It is a plant rapidly taking over much of the state of Georgia and parts of several other Southern states. In case you don't believe me, remove yourself from Interstate 75 when heading south, and start down a side road. To your left and right, you will see a luxuriant vine seemingly growing at the rate of an inch an hour, and completely covering everything it touches: trees, telephone pole, barns and fences. I think if you stood still long enough, it would also cover you. It seems to be impervious to car fumes, insects, and bad perfume, and just goes right on its conquering path. The only thing this plant needs is the right kind of soil, for it only grows in clay.

And, of course, that's the reason I relate to kudzu—for I have feet of clay…it's a wonder people passing by don't see tendrils of green creeping up my legs. I suppose most Christians have this problem, but it isn't terribly fun to admit. I would love to be a hero who jumps over buildings (and shortcomings) at a single bound. The truth is that, most of the time, I can't even make it over a dust bunny.

I don't mean to sin by exhibiting pride and selfishness, but it seems to creep in just when I feel I have conquered all the dragons (humble, and proud of it, you might say....). A true servant does not feel this way; so, Lord, I ask that you would help me to grow in grace, not in green.

"Show your love for me, your servant, and teach me your laws. I serve you, so let me understand your teachings." (Psalm 119:124-125 CEV)

February 17: Picnic Time

In the *Peanuts* comic strip, the dog Snoopy is often pictured writing the first sentence of a book that he does not have the ability or skills to finish (rather reminds me of this book, now that I think of it). Snoopy's novel usually begins, "It was a dark and stormy night."

This story doesn't exactly fall into the same "night" category, but it had the same feeling. My husband's dear mother had been in the hospital for weeks with a terminal case of cancer. It was nearly Christmas and the world seemed to be dancing around, heedless of our stress and heartache, and I just couldn't bring myself to fix a big fancy dinner on the day of Christ's birth. I suggested we have a picnic on the way home from the hospital.

It was about a forty-mile drive and our Florida weather was being very uncooperative. The sun was under several cloud layers, and the wind was whistling louder than the seven dwarfs. All in all, it was not a good day for a picnic. Even so, I had made a picnic pie that could be eaten cold (I didn't realize how cold…), and added a batch of fruit soup.

We came home from the hospital by way of the Sunshine Skyway, for I remembered there were several grassy verges on which to sit and view the scenery. Unfortunately, even the view was hard to come by on that dark, overcast day. To make matters worse, it was so cold and windy that we had to wrap up in large, black garbage bags. People zooming by (in order to get back to their warm houses as soon as possible) stared at us in astonishment.

After the food was laid out on the grass, my husband tasted the soup and asked cautiously, "Are there any prunes in here?" Well, of course there were some—and in my defense, lots of other fruit as well. Bill, however, had those prunes firmly in mind and heart, and who knows where else, and he refused to take another bite. We started all laughing hysterically, thinking of sitting there on the grass, in the freezing cold, wrapped in garbage bags, and eating prunes, so far from civilization. That funny day has lasted many years, not because of the sad occasion that started it, but because of a dear close family that had the freedom to laugh together.

"In Jerusalem, the LORD Almighty will spread a wonderful feast for everyone around the world. It will be a delicious feast of good food, with clear, well-aged wine and choice beef. In that day he will remove the cloud of gloom, the shadow of death that hangs over the earth. He will swallow up death forever! The Sovereign LORD will wipe away all tears...." (Isaiah 25:6-8a NLT)

February 18: I.B.M. Compatible

I am not only incapable of understanding the outer space of the last frontier; I am also incapable of understanding the space between my ears. In fact, there are so many things I can't understand, I can't even name them all, including such seemingly mundane items as how a toaster works and what makes a bridge stay up.

But it's computers that frustrate me on a daily basis. The thing is this: if a child can do it, I should be able to do it. Or perhaps it's the difference of learning a language at your mother's knee and struggling with it thirty years later. Oh, I've made tentative forays, although it took me nearly a week to learn how to turn it on: "Push this button, Mom! Then do that." The whole thing is a foreign language of the first order (if there is such a thing), and I don't speak the same language. In self-defense, I have finally mastered the art of e-mail, and I have managed to put thoughts in the computer for writing devotions and speeches; but I am actually still wallowing in such a helpless menu of bytes that I want to byte the menu.

Christians have a jargon of their own, too, in case you haven't noticed. While all the phrases are precious to those of us who are Christians, there are many listening who have no idea what we are saying. I need to focus on showing others God's love, not on trying to impress people with phrases they don't understand. Those to whom Jesus spoke were drawn by His concern and love. Are they drawn by mine?

Jesus answered them, "He who speaks on his own does so to gain honor for himself, but he who works for the honor of the one who sent him is a man of truth; there is nothing false about him" (John 7:18 NIV).

February 19: On Termites

Contrary to the opinion of some, termites are not related to the Hittites, Amorites or Peruzzites, although it IS true they march in to destroy. The human armies use their arms for their weapons, however, and termites use their mouths. Invading armies of termites can be very destructive, and you don't know they are there until it is too late, as they do their work unseen.

Other destructive work done by mouths is also unseen…and it destroys friendships and ruins reputations. Stan Touissant has said, "The tongue is the slave of the heart; so make sure the heart is a good master." Proverbs 21:23 reminds us that "Watching what you say can save you a lot of trouble" (CEV).

This is as true today as when it was written, but I certainly haven't improved any over the years. Time and effort alone will not keep my mouth shut, however. I must be willing to submit it to God and give him my right to be right. The desire to retaliate and/or defend is so strong that it can literally eat away love and trust, leaving only the shavings of what had been a close relationship. God is the only one who can terminate this destructive force! A book I found helpful on this subject is *Tongue in Check*, by Joseph Stowell.

February 20: It's a Shoe-in!

I travel a great deal and one of the interesting sights is what people wear on their feet. There is a mind-boggling array of footwear out there, including sandals, boots, sneakers, wingtips, and a few high heels that are probably not planning to walk very far. Shoes are as individual as the owners, and they are all taking their owners some place. I have an obligation to any of those hurrying feet that pause to make contact with me, for I may be the only Christian they meet.

I had been ill with flu the day before leaving for an itinerary, and my husband didn't really want me to go. As I was leaving Saturday night and not speaking until Monday, I assured him that I would be recovered. On the way out the door, I happened to look down at my feet, and saw that in my misery I had put on dotted pumps that clashed terribly with my suit. "I have to change my shoes!" I wailed, but my daughter, Lissa, assured me that I looked fine, and she poured me into the car for the trip to the airport.

On the plane I was in the aisle seat. A man was seated next to me, and his wife was seated by the window. Immediately he looked at my feet, and asked me where I got my shoes. "They're the first thing I notice about a woman," he confided. He was a shoe salesman, and we began a conversation that led to me giving him a booklet that told of God's love.

I was beginning to learn that even things that we think are mistakes are things that God uses. So, the next time you go somewhere (whether to the grocery store or to Outer Mongolia), don't worry about your shoes! You never know what kind of appointment God has planned for you!

"How beautiful on the mountains are the feet of those who bring good news of peace and salvation…." (Isaiah 52:7a NLT)

February 21: Service, Please!

I think it was Robert Benchley who remarked, "There are two ways to travel: First Class, and with children." Having done both, here are some of my observations: Traveling First Class is dignified. Traveling with children is dusty, dirty—veering sharply toward drippy, and often dreadful. Traveling First Class is impeccable. Traveling with children is involved, in every sense of the word. Involved in who gets to sit next to the window. Involved in damp peanut butter kisses. Involved in discovering that although M & M's don't melt in your hand, they tend to surrender when left on a car seat in the sun. Involved in despair over a toy dog left at a motel by mistake. Involved in keeping a tribe of children out of the hair of the sweating mechanic who is struggling to fix your car in 90-degree heat. Involved in mediating squabbles that would strain the Wisdom of Solomon. Traveling First Class is being served. Traveling with children is serving—serving with love and patience, when what you really want to do is scream.

I like to think I am a servant of the Lord, but I heard a question that puts it in perspective. Someone asked Lorne Sanny of Navigators how to know if he had the heart of a servant. He replied, "By the way you act when you're treated like one."

Prayer: Father, give me the heart of a servant, that I might be like you.

"Your attitude should be the same as that of Christ Jesus: Who, being in very nature God, did not consider equality with God something to be grasped, but made himself nothing, taking the very nature of a servant, being made in human likeness." (Philippians 2:5-7 NIV)

February 22: Death Valley Days

If you have ever had a filling fall out or a broken tooth, you will remember how your tongue probed in the space, constantly rehearsing the rough edges. I have done this with deep sorrow too, waking up in the dawn and finding painful remembrance flooding back into my mind.

My sorrow was intense—my chest felt as though a knife had cut off my air supply, and I couldn't swallow because of the lump in my throat. My face felt frozen with my feet moving like lead coffins at the end of my body. I wanted to be far away, perhaps in a far off desert, so that I couldn't see life going along merrily without me.

Brokenness is a time to throw ourselves on the God who is sufficient. God is greater than our sorrow. So, when grief or anger or despair floods us, we may choose to turn to the Father and say, "Help me, God. I am your child, but I am so hurt I am crying out against You. I hate what has happened to me! I cannot stand the pain and suffering!"

God understands our rage, and He is a safe refuge. Christ was sent to "…to heal the brokenhearted…" (Isaiah 61:1d CEV), and we may rest our souls in the arms of the One who truly understands. When we give Him our grief and failures, He gives us rest. In His time, He gives His joy. For joy is not the absence of sorrow, but the presence of God.

"The Lord is there to rescue all who are discouraged and have given up hope." (Psalm 34:18 CEV)

February 23: Memory Lapse

I have always been sort of a space cadet, but as the years advance, my memory recedes. I cross the room to get something, and when I get there, I forget what I wanted. An idea will come for a devotion, and by the time I have located pen and paper, the whole thing will have vanished into the outer recesses of my inner resources. As some one aptly put it, "It's hard to be nostalgic when you can't remember anything."

But, *mirabile dictu* (as my mother used to say about her graduation—which apparently is Latin for "wonderful to say"), this is not important to our heavenly Father. An old saint remarked, "I can't remember any of God's promises anymore, but it doesn't matter because God hasn't forgotten a single one!"

When I first became a believer, I heard a story about an elderly Christian whose favorite verse was in the second book of Timothy: "...for I know the one in whom I trust, and I am sure that he is able to guard what I have entrusted to him until the day of his return" (II Timothy 1:12b NLT). Each month more and more of that verse slipped away from her mind, becoming "He is able" and finally just "He." In that one word, she had all that she needed. If you want to be refreshed, even in times of stress and darkness, start memorizing scripture so that you can meditate on it and extract God's strength and love.

"And I am convinced that nothing can ever separate us from his love. Death can't, and life can't. The angels can't, and the demons can't. Our fears for today, our worries about tomorrow, and even the powers of hell can't keep God's love away." (Romans 8:38 NLT)

February 24: Traveler's Aid

An important rule I try to remember when traveling cross country is this: never travel with a child who has just learned either to (a) whistle—as in one song, or (b) read—as in all road signs, bill boards, and shop windows. Either of the above-mentioned skills quickly compels me to install a permanent glass partition right behind the driver's seat.

Why do I let little things like this make my life so hairy? As someone has pointed out, "It's not the big things of this world that put us on the rack…you can sit upon a mountain, but not upon a tack." In feeling stressed out by the tacks of life, I, like David, long for the wings of a dove to escape.

But surely Jesus must have had lots of irritations too: slow-witted disciples, religious leaders who were always looking for a slip that could be turned to their advantage, and people of every size, shape and condition who pressed Him at every turn. Our Lord had no wings to escape the tacks of His life, but He did spend much time in prayer on the mountain to receive strength and guidance from the Father.

Perhaps if I spent more time in preparation for my day, and less time in reactions to it, I might be able to find strength too. Because I am weak and easily irritated by disruptions (even by those I love), I need to prepare for my day by asking the Father in advance for my needs and concerns. Somewhere I read, "Starting my day by hemming it with prayer makes it less easy to become unraveled!"

"Look to the Lord and his strength; seek his face always." (I Chronicles 16:11 NIV)

February 25: What's in Your Hand?

Several years ago, after a conversation with the church secretary when I had given her some items for the church bulletin, I couldn't help hearing her small sigh of desperation (for some strange reason, I often hear this sigh after I talk to people…). As a result, I called back and heard myself asking if she could use some help. She gasped in relief and said she could. So I went to fill a need—not because I knew anything about offices. In fact, the poor secretary had to start at the beginning—the very beginning—to get me going (as in "this is a filing cabinet, this is where we print the bulletins, etc."). I taught myself how to use a typewriter (in a manner of speaking) and although I wasn't very speedy due to the fact that I was always leaving letters out, I did manage to pound out a few things now and then.

After a while, they got a real secretary who knew things, and I put my newly learned "skills" back on the shelf. It never occurred to me that God would use any of that in a different way, but here I am typing these devotionals…and it's all because God used what was at hand.

God took Moses' staff and turned it into a serpent, and He turned Peter's fishing boat into a pulpit (see Luke 5:1-3). I'm sure there are an amazing number of things that we have that God could use if we gave them to Him. Perhaps you are good at cooking, or woodworking, or piloting a plane, or sewing, or plumbing, or photography…or even typing! Have you ever thought that God could do something special with that skill if you gave it to Him? It doesn't matter if you are a novice or an expert. In God's hands, it will turn into something useful for His Kingdom.

"The Lord answered, 'What's that in your hand?' 'A walking stick,' Moses replied." (Exodus 4:2a CEV)

February 26: A Walk in the Dark

I had gotten up in the middle of the night to make a necessary little trip and suddenly found myself absolutely and completely tangled up in a place I did not recognize. I fumbled around in there as I though I had turned the corner into the bathroom, but I kept coming up against what felt like clothes instead of what I was looking for. Hoping for. Needing.

Finally, in desperation, I called my husband, knowing I was waking him up out of a sound sleep, but helpless to the point of almost hysteria. "Bill! Bill!" I shouted. "Come and find out where I am!" (not really the sort of thing you want to wake up to).

Poor Bill turned on the light and started laughing. I could cheerfully have killed him if I had the means at hand. "You've still got your night mask on," he said, "…and you are in your closet."

Well, I do wear a mask because my eyelids don't shut all the way, and my eyes dry out if they are left partly open all night, but I never realized I hadn't pushed it up out of the way. Thus, I turned an incorrect corner and ended up where I certainly had no intention of going. Ordinarily, we have night-lights that keep me on the right path, but I never gave them a chance to show me where I went wrong.

We do this spiritually, too, of course, and most of the time we don't realize we are wearing a mask that keeps us from seeing the light that only Christ can give. Disobedience brings blindness, and we may end up in some place a lot worse than a closet. We must call on the Lord for help, and He will do so, for we are His children and the sheep of His pasture.

"…and I will lead them home with great care. They will walk beside quiet streams and not stumble." (Jeremiah 31:9b-c NLT)

February 27: Undone

Although my mother was beautifully talented at embroidery of every description, I must have slipped a gene somewhere, because I am absolutely hopeless with a needle. When I was expecting our first child, however, I felt an unaccustomed rush of sewing adrenaline. I decided to make an evening dress so gorgeous that I would wear it for years after the baby came (at that point I didn't know you never wanted to see maternity clothes after the baby arrived).

At any rate, I rushed blindly to the fabric store and picked out the most expensive material they had. I also got a pattern that I assumed would unravel the mysteries of sewing in one easy lesson. When I got home, I found incomprehensible instructions about seam A and gusset B—neither of which I could locate. I made a few half-hearted attempts to assemble this project, but it had begun to assume Herculean proportions with which I was not prepared to struggle. Five children later, I still have not planted one needle into that very expensive material.

I am ashamed to say that I also have some projects for God that have been started and not finished. It is so much easier for me to begin a project, than to carry it through to a conclusion. Yet, I should be like Paul who said to Timothy, "I have fought the good fight, I have finished the race, I have kept the faith" (II Timothy 4:7 NIV). If you, too, have a little unfinished project lurking somewhere in your house that the Lord has given you to do for Him, pray and ask for His help on your "unfinished garment," so that you may be a faithful follower without excuses.

"He said to another man, 'Follow me.' But the man replied, 'Lord, first let me go and bury my father.' Jesus said to him, 'Let the dead bury their own dead, but you go and proclaim the kingdom of God.'" (Luke 9:59-60 NIV)

February 28: Orange Blossom Christianity

The fragrance of fresh orange blossoms is wonderfully sweet but not cloying. The delicious quality of it when near a grove is almost overwhelming. However, the artificial smell of orange blossoms is a skunk of another color.

We were leaving the Miami Orange Bowl game early to beat the crowd because the score was so lopsided. In doing this, we were unaware of two things: first, that an artificial orange scent was sprayed over the entire stadium before the end of the game, and second, that our path led directly in front of the nozzle. It let loose just as we were in front of the spray, and we were inundated from top to bottom and from side to side. The smell that emanated from us was so horrific that the first two taxis wouldn't allow us get in, and we had to bribe the third. We had to wash our clothes, our skin and our hair several times to get that smell out…and the only positive thing about it is that I am positive we will never forget it.

There is a big difference between "artificial" and "natural" Christianity, too. Some people act the part quite well, but I'm afraid the smell is artificial. Natural Christianity does not spring from a desire to do good things, but from a real and vital relationship with Christ the Vine; apart from Him, we can do nothing, (John 15:5). The result of abiding in Christ is a sweetness that cannot be duplicated.

"Stay joined to me, and I will stay joined to you. Just as a branch cannot produce fruit unless it stays joined to the vine, you cannot produce fruit unless you stay joined to me." (John 15:4 CEV)

March 1: Days Like a Shadow

I see the wisps of smoke
blown and tattered,
gone by mid-day.

What can I say?

Is it not to be expected?

This ephemeral life—
so quickly passed,
flowers grown and discarded, forgotten.

But my shadow lives:
the Savior gives
the form: stitched and gathered
into eternity…no longer smoke.

I smile because
outside of time I pause
to see a shadow become substance.

March 2: The Pit of Sin

We had a small elevator in my parent's home that was used mainly to haul trunks or furniture up to the third floor. It was only about four feet square, and was lifted not by electricity but by someone inside the elevator heaving on the ropes. I was forbidden to climb in the elevator alone, but I constantly agitated to accompany anyone who used it.

On several occasions, I considered sneaking in to the elevator, but I never screwed up the courage to actually do it. I knew that I was not strong enough to work the ropes, and my fertile mind always imagined the elevator magically descending and then stopping half way between floors, with me unable to raise the elevator by myself. I further imagined an unhappy person climbing down to pull me out, and my even unhappier parents waiting to greet me at the top of the shaft.

I was never stuck in that elevator shaft; but before I came to God, I was in a similar situation. I was not strong enough to climb out of the deep hole into which I had fallen. I needed someone who was not only willing to enter my "slimy pit," but who also was powerful enough to lift me out. Thank God! Not only did He willingly rescued me; He also cleansed me, and put me on the solid Rock.

"I waited patiently for the Lord to help me, and he turned to me and heard my cry. He lifted me out of the pit of despair, out of the mud and the mire. He set my feet on solid ground and steadied me as I walked along." (Psalm 40:1-2 NLT)

March 3: Road Rage

My sister-in-law and I were driving down a narrow two-lane beach road when we were stopped by a long line of cars. Traffic was allowed to flow only in one direction. Way up in the front, we could see a young woman in an orange vest, short (very short) shorts, and not much else. She was slowly revolving a sign in an unenthusiastic manner that had "Slow" on one side and "Stop" on the other. Eventually, it was the turn of our line to inch ahead, but as I started past her, she screamed at me, "Hey! Didn't you see the stop sign?? Back up, Stupid!" I found this situation untenable for two very different reasons. First, since she never seemed to stop revolving the sign, it was impossible for me to see exactly which side was facing oncoming traffic. Secondly, I intensely dislike being screamed at. My dislike was further intensified by the use of the word "stupid" by someone who looked—well, one might say "haphazard."

I had been working on memorizing the first chapter of James, but at that moment, Scripture flew out the window and temper flew in. I completely lost control of myself, rolled down the passenger window and leaned across my startled sister-in-law, and screamed right back, "No, I didn't see your sign; it was twisting in both directions. And, I'm not backing up until you say 'please'!"

By now everyone was hot under the collar. Some people were honking, and others were screaming. Finally, the man in back of me yelled, "PLEASE, Lady!!!" Upon which I ungraciously backed up, ignoring my sister-in-law who was trying to melt into the car frame. I learned that day that memorizing Scripture doesn't do me any good at all if I don't apply it to my life.

"My dear brothers, take note of this: Everyone should be quick to listen, slow to speak and slow to become angry.... Do not merely listen to the word, and so deceive yourselves. Do what it says." (James 1:19,22 NIV)

March 4: Through Glasses Darkly

My husband and I share a somewhat stubborn streak (although I can't imagine where I get it, and I am sure all of our children get it from his side of the family…). This little trait was emphasized when I first bought bifocals and bobbled a lot going up and down curbs. Bill thought this was amusing—until the day the doctor told him he needed bifocals, too. Bill had never worn glasses in his life (and he never gets cavities or headaches, he hits tennis balls and golf balls with hurricane force, and is just disgustingly healthy) so he was unprepared for what he viewed as a sign of old age (I was delighted…).

At any rate, Bill announced to the ophthalmologist that he was not going to get bifocals, and the doctor would have to think of something else. After a short struggle, the doctor gave two prescriptions: one for distance and one for reading. The next day, we went to church, and Bill wore his distance glasses to drive. Things were a little blurry when greeting people, so he switched to reading glasses. When he sat down, he couldn't see the minister clearly so he put on distance glasses. Then, he couldn't see the hymns and had to put on reading glasses. During the sermon, he wore distance glasses, unless he was looking up Scripture, and then he had to wear reading glasses. On Monday, he got bifocals.

Sometimes we get so caught up in what we feel is best, that we refuse to see other's opinions or viewpoints (and I'm not just discussing Bill here—it's all of us!).

Today's scripture comes from the book of Esther. Esther's older cousin, Mordecai, convinced her that she had to admit to the King that she was Jewish. (The King had just signed a law that all Jews, young and old, must be killed.) Mordecai said to her, "Don't think that you will escape being killed with the rest of the Jews, just because you live in the king's palace. If you don't speak up now, we will somehow get help, but you and your family will be killed. It could be that you were made queen for a time like this!" (Esther 4:13b-14 CEV). Queen Esther was smart enough to take advice from Mordecai, because she trusted him and his Godly wisdom.

It's not easy for me to follow advice, but may I become more like Esther, and listen carefully to wisdom from others.

March 5: Trees and Temples

"The stones used in the construction of the Temple were prefinished at the quarry, so the entire structure was built without the sound of hammer, ax, or any other iron tool at the building site." (I Kings 6:7 NLT)

Sometimes I feel overworked, under compensated, overwhelmed, and even under-slung. When this is true, I should consider the very un-stressful activity of watching a tree grow. It's quite hard to detect its growing, of course, because there's no noise and no discernable effort on the part of the tree. Yet, there is evidently a lot of undercover work going on, with sap and photosynthesis and fibers all busy.

At the temple in Jerusalem, it must have been pretty quiet, too, since no tools were heard there—or even allowed. But, there was a lot of activity, for it took a lot of muscle work to fit all those blocks together into a perfect building for God.

God is still in the building business, in case you hadn't noticed…but if anyone is watching us grow as temples of the Holy Spirit, it must seem as though not much is happening. Even so, as with building blocks, God is fitting us together with others and scraping off all the rough edges and smoothing us down to fit His plan and direction. His ways are not our ways, so we must learn to submit with grace to His blueprint. We should not be discouraged if we do not see as much progress as we would like: it takes time to grow a tree, and time to build a temple.

March 6: The Jumping-off Place

My five older brothers were "five little stair steps" (at least, that's what my parents called them) who loved to get away with as much as possible. One summer, when the family was leaving for their summer cottage at Mohonk Lake, the boys were taken to the train station, accompanied not only by adults who were charged with retention and restraint, but by a confusing collection of trunks, bags, and hat boxes (my mother was a great believer in hats on any and every occasion…). All of this created a great to-do, with porters rushing hither and yon and the boys creating as much hilarity as possible.

These young boys were all dressed alike in their Peter Thompson suits (which no one born after the 1940's would remember), and my paternal Grandfather had been pressed into service to make sure that the actual entrainment went smoothly. They found their car, and Grandpa kissed the first, and put him into the Pullman; he was followed by the second, third and so on. What he didn't realize (after all, he only had one son), was that the boys, seeing the immediate opportunity for pandemonium, were racing to the end of the car, jumping off, and then getting back in line to be kissed and put back into the car. Poor Grandpa was kissing and lifting for quite a while before he started counting.

God is not so easily fooled. Not even if his children dress alike, talk alike, or look alike. God, our Creator, made each of us, and He knows us intimately. So, when we are foolish children, jumping off the place where He has placed us, He allows us our free will, but He draws us back to Him with loving-kindness. No matter where we are or what our situation is, God is there, and we may serve Him with a joyful heart.

"Not even a sparrow, worth only half a penny, can fall to the ground without your Father knowing it. And the very hairs on your head are all numbered. So don't be afraid; you are more valuable to him than a whole flock of sparrows.." (Matthew 10:29-31 NLT)

March 7: Blessed Assurance

My brother, George, had been a faithful member of his church, but when he divorced his wife, he was excommunicated. He never recovered from it, I think because his relationship had been with the church, and not with God. Not long after this, I gave him a Stonecroft Ministries booklet, written by a physicist. Since George was an engineer, perhaps he was impressed that someone intellectually gifted had become a believer. He was thrilled with that booklet, and showed it to several people saying, "My sister gave me this, isn't it great?"

A short time later, George became ill and was confined to his bed. When I visited him, I was appalled to see how thin he was. A few days after my visit, his new wife called to say he was in the hospital.

Very often when I send flowers, I wait three or four days until the recipient is well enough to enjoy them. But this time, I felt an urgent need to go directly to the phone and order a bouquet to be delivered that very day. I thought of a Bible verse I wanted to put on the card. Since I wasn't sure that he had a Bible with him, I asked the florist to include the whole verse.

When the flowers arrived, George's wife said, "Your sister sent you some flowers. Do you want me to read what it says on the card?" He nodded, and she read these words to him: "The Lord himself watches over you! The Lord stands beside you as your protective shade...The Lord keeps watch over you as you come and go, both now and forever" (Psalm 121:5,8 NLT). His wife told me later that these were the last words my brother heard before he died.

Prayer: Thank you, God, for watching over us, now and in the future.

March 8: Small Comforts for Small People

The color of the walls were a depressing gray. I lay on my gurney in the basement of the large hospital and looked around at the controlled chaos (at least I hoped it was controlled). I was not enjoying my state of near-nakedness, covered only by a sheet.

I was there to have an angiogram. I had a badly infected toe that had managed to turn rather blue and then black, and the doctors thought it might be a sign of a clogged artery. That wasn't the only thing that was clogged—my breathing was coming in small gaps and gasps, and I felt we should be doing something to unclog that too. No one there knew me. My husband had been with me, but he was told to go back to work: he couldn't be with me during all the cutting and sewing, anyway.

Since I knew God was still there, I asked Him for a verse to comfort me, as I was feeling lonely. The verse that came to me was "…Do not be afraid, for I am with you…" (Genesis 26:24b NLT).

I began to think about the parts of that verse. First, the "I" meant God himself, not an angel or any other heavenly messenger, because He is the eternal "I am." I thought about the "I am." That means not "was" or "will be" but I am with you now—in the present. Third, He was "with" me, not against me, so I did not need to fear. Unlike doctors and nurses, He doesn't go off duty.

When the doctor got around to me, I was grinning foolishly. I suppose he wondered if I had somehow raided the drug cabinet. I just couldn't help smiling and even joking with the nurses because I knew that, no matter what the results, I would be in God's presence. As it turned out, the angiogram turned into an angioplasty, and they found a large clot in my leg. That was manhandled out, turning my toes into a lovely shade of pink. Pink is now my favorite color!

"With this news, strengthen those who have tired hands, and encourage those who have weak knees. Say to those who are afraid, "Be strong, and do not fear…." (Isaiah 35:3-4a NLT)

March 9: The Bruiser

The young boy and his father were already seated at a table when we walked into the restaurant. The boy was in a motorized wheelchair decorated with stickers and decals of every description. I couldn't see the boy's face from where I was sitting, but I could tell he was pitifully thin with arms the size of matchsticks. He was also evidently very weak because he could barely feed himself. Every bite was accomplished only with effort.

In the middle of the meal, the father excused himself to make a quick phone call. He said casually to his son as he left, "Be right back, Bruiser!" Bruiser! That kid couldn't have swatted a comatose cockroach. He knew it of course, but I thought he sat just a little straighter in his wheelchair. His father's love and acceptance of him as a worthwhile person (coupled with a name which assured the boy that his dad was looking at his character and not his physical condition) must have been a real boost to his moral. I don't imagine it stopped at that restaurant. His father probably reached out with love and encouragement every day.

Isn't that what God does for us? He overlooks our disabilities, whether physical or mental, and says, "I love you just the way you are." We can also follow in His steps as we reach out to encourage those who may be weak and tired or worn with worry. By caring, we can show others a glimpse of our Father they may never have seen.

"May our Lord Jesus Christ himself and God our Father, who loved us and by his grace gave us eternal encouragement and good hope, encourage your hearts and strengthen you in every good deed and word." (II Thessalonians 2:16-17 NIV)

March 10: Present and Accounted For

"God is our mighty fortress, always ready to help in times of trouble. And so, we won't be afraid! Let the earth tremble and the mountains tumble into the deepest sea.... The Lord All-Powerful is with us. The God of Jacob is our fortress." (Psalm 46:1-2,7 CEV)

At the girl's college I attended my freshman and sophomore year, we received demerits when we were late for night check in (you can tell this was back in the days when Arthur did not include women at the Round Table). After a certain number of demerits had been earned for not being on time, one received the honor of waiting tables for a week. I had to do this many times: I was much more interested in having a _good_ time than being _on_ time.

In spite of all this practice at carrying food back and forth, I was lamentably lacking in waitress skills. I spilled water, dropped dishes of peas (and in case you were wondering, a dish full of peas covers a lot of territory!), but, worst of all, I dumped red Harvard beets down the white dress of the Dean of Women. People seated at my table soon began wearing raincoats or slickers for protection.

What do I do when unexpected events crash upon me with surprising force? God wants me to remember that He is always with me, and always ready to help in times of trouble. That means nothing ever takes Him by surprise, nothing is unexpected, and nothing is beyond His ability to overcome. So, even though I may not be aware of His presence, by faith I rest in the promise that His presence is indeed present and accounted for.

March 11: Wash Day

It's a mystery to me, how I can put (almost) perfectly clean clothes in the washer and end up with a lint filter filled with an ugly assortment of icky things I'd rather not touch without gloves. I am talking here about normal adult clothes that do not have anything hanging on them that would make you scream for help. Why then all this stuff in the filter?? Could it be I am carrying around more dirt than I am aware of? That deep in the cracks and crevices of my sanitary-appearing outerwear, there are things lurking that might have crawled out of a green swamp?

What about the person inside those sanitary appearing clothes? Have I got any smeary blotches of pride or envy that I haven't exhibited? What about a few black strings of hatred or lust or even nasty stains of resentment or bitterness—to say nothing of fuzzy webs of indifference to others' problems or heartaches?

Thank goodness that God washes the dark and spotted places in my heart! God's detergent is not only strong, it is also gentle. Moreover, He can make me purer than even Ivory Soap, which, as they always used to say, was "99 and 44/100 percent pure!"

"Have mercy on me, O God, because of your unfailing love. Because of your great compassion, blot out the stain of my sins. Wash me clean from my guilt. Purify me from sin." (Psalm 51:1-2 NLT)

March 12: Elephants and Flies

In a recent study done in Nepal on Asian elephants, it was found that they employ fly swatters just as we do. Grasping a branch in their trunk, they swish it around their bodies with a corresponding forty percent drop in flies. Swatter use increased as the rising temperature brought more flies, and some elephants saved swatters for later use…I suppose in case the rising temperature brought a corresponding rise in fly population after the general swatting had subsided.

Fly swatters are handy to have when insects bother us, but what should we use when we are bothered by pesky people? It doesn't help to bite back or buzz belligerently.

Situations like these call not for our natural reaction but for God's supernatural reaction. Christ loves this person, and He is willing to accept him or her (with buzz intact!). Because Christ lives in us, we may do this too.

Prayer: Lord, help me not to be critical. Help me to see others with your eyes of love.

"Accept one another, then, just as Christ accepted you, in order to bring praise to God." (Romans 15:7 NIV)

March 13: Toupee Tape

I don't suppose toupee tape is something that the average American woman thinks much about. However, I have come to regard it as an essential part of my traveling equipment. A friend of mine in Maryland introduced me to this little gem, and I have been carrying it in my suitcase ever since. It's not just toupee wearers who benefit from toupee tape, you understand; it may be pressed into service to re-hem a dress that has come unraveled, keep a fractious shoulder pad in place, close an envelope that has lost its stickiness, or to affix a schedule to the inside of your suitcase (unfortunately, it will not keep one's mouth shut).

There's a possibility that today could be one of your "I'm not much use to anyone days." If so, consider the toupee tape. It's not really attractive, nobody notices when you use it, and there are very few who have even heard of it, but it does serve a purpose.

We may be assured that our worth to the kingdom of God is not measured by attractiveness or by the applause and attention of others. Your worth to the kingdom is this: God made you the way you are. You are His, and what He would like from you is faithfulness in being a vessel (or some tape) for Him.

"In a large house some dishes are made of gold or silver, while others are made of wood or clay. Some of these are special, and others are not. That's also how it is with people. The ones who stop doing evil and make themselves pure will become special. Their lives will be holy and pleasing to their Master, and they will be able to do all kinds of good deeds." (II Timothy 2:20-21 CEV)

March 14: Workshops

Although never prim, my mother was both proper and dignified (we're not much alike…). She was born in the late 1800's, so she was what might be termed a "Victorian Innocent." She took an almost childish pleasure in going places and meeting people, and she had the lovely gift of extending love in equal measure to everyone.

One of her drawbacks, freely admitted, was her packrat collection of items both large and small. Her specialties were photographs, ribbon and wrapping paper, and letters. There were also other items we discovered later, such as a box labeled "string too small to be used." Furthermore, she wasn't picky about adding other *impedimenta* to a room that was known in the family as "the Workshop of the World." Unlike Santa's Workshop, however, the piles never grew any smaller, and she could be found at almost any hour, when not scouring antique shops or attending DAR meetings, adding to her acorn supply.

I expect we all have our little gathered treasures of one kind or another: books, fishing lures, stamps, decoys, coins, etc. It could be, however, that our collection is not quite so innocent. We might be hoarding envelopes of envy, bottles of bitterness, sacks of selfishness, pouches of pride, ampoules of anger, or other unattractive items that have crept into the workshops of our hearts. We should be as ruthless in discarding the junk we have accumulated as if it were on display (it really is!) and give God the key to our heart and ask Him to do the cleaning.

Prayer: Father, may my collection be of eternal things: love, kindness, generosity, graciousness and mercy. Help me to illustrate the person of Christ in all that I say and do today.

"There are six things the Lord hates—no, seven things he detests: haughty eyes, a lying tongue, hands that kill the innocent, a heart that plots evil, feet that race to do wrong, a false witness who pours out lies, a person who sows discord among brothers." (Proverbs 6:16-19 NLT)

March 15: Night Train To London

C.S. Lewis is said to have been on a walking tour of England, and as he boarded the train for his return journey to London, his unkempt appearance startled an old dragon in the First Class compartment. "Do you have a First Class ticket?" she demanded. "Yes, madam," replied Lewis, "But I'm afraid I'll be needing it for myself."

This is the kind of delicious comeback I can never think of until I've left the train. But by his quick wit, Lewis demonstrated that the lady had made rather a fool of herself in her righteous indignation. The only way to avoid this kind of position, where one falls flat on his or her face, is to remember that we are not here to judge one another.

This doesn't mean we should be slovenly just to prove that someone who goes "all out" for Christ should look "all in"—but it does mean we have to stop comparing ourselves to others. You can nearly always find someone who looks worse than you do, but that doesn't make you any better than they are.

"Stop judging by mere appearances...." (John 7:24a NIV)

March 16: Close Encounters of the First Kind

In my twenties, I traveled on a ship from New York to Rotterdam. Trying to keep students off the decks and out of the water must have been a full time job for the crew, and they came up with some form of entertainment every night. The evening we had a costume party, I inveigled seven of my friends to put their arms above their heads in white pillowcases (suitably painted with faces) so that we could appear as Snow Dwarf and the Seven Whites. Even with such a close dwarfish encounter, I cannot reel off the names of all Snow White's dwarfs, nor can I recall all the names of Santa's reindeer despite the fact that I've lived through many Christmas seasons. Worse yet, I can get tangled in the names of the Twelve Disciples.

In spite of that, I am not dreading a pop quiz in heaven on how to spell Nebuchadnezzar or how to put all the Minor Prophets in chronological order. These after all, are just facts. Facts are important, of course, but if that's all we are holding on to, we are grasping the wrong end of the stick. Notice in the Scripture below, the command is to "obey"—not just to sit around and memorize.

Prayer: Father I know I have not been as obedient as I should be. Make me willing not just to learn facts, but to listen and obey.

"You must stop doing anything immoral or evil. Instead be humble and accept the message that is planted in you to save you. Obey God's message! Don't fool yourselves by just listening to it." (James 1:21-22 CEV)

March 17: Knowing Christ

"As a result, I can really know Christ and experience the mighty power that raised him from the dead. I can learn what it means to suffer with him…." (Philippians 3:10a-c NLT)

I was a fairly new Christian when a friend of mine showed me this verse in Philippians and told me it was her prayer for me. I was unfamiliar with Scripture, and as I read this verse for the first time, I was thrilled with the idea of knowing Christ. Yes! That was my goal!

Then, I read further and saw "and experience the mighty power that raised him from the dead." It seemed wonderful, although I didn't really understand what it meant.

Then, I read even further and came to the words and "I can learn what it means to suffer with him…" I frowned. Good night! Why would she be praying something like that?? I thought it sounded quite unattractive and even scary, if you want to know the truth. With the exception of the loss of my father shortly after our marriage, I had never suffered a thing, and I thought the hymn that talks about going to heaven "on beds of flowery ease" seemed the perfect way to go.

But, evidently, my friend kept on praying for me, for all three things in that Scripture. I want you to know, that the suffering part has been the best of all; I have learned more of the Lord and His care than I ever could have if I had not been through physical and emotional pain. So, thank you, dear friend! And thank You, Lord, for teaching me with faithfulness and love!

March 18: Shoulder Your Boulder

Some of our northern states have large boulders scattered everywhere, deposited eons ago by glaciers. I discovered, when visiting one state, that they can be found in yards, on college campuses and even in office complexes. Some homeowners had cleverly incorporated the boulders into their landscape (one actually had a house built around part of one. They must have read the story about the unfortunate house built upon the sand). Most of the homeowners, though, seemed to act as if the boulders weren't there. This is quite hard to do, as these are substantial boulders, not just big rocks. The boulders sat forlornly in their yards, looking as though someone (well, a very LARGE someone) had forgotten to put away their toys when they were through.

I also have boulders in my life. I can do the same things the homeowners did. I can either turn them into something worthwhile or pretend they are not there. God allows these boulders so that my faith can deepen, but that will never happen if I spend my time studiously ignoring them. Instead, I must accept them with grace (I'm trying to practice!) and I must give my worries and uncertainties to Him again and again. Like the pearl formed over an irritation, I have the opportunity to turn problems, tragedies, or trials into things of great beauty.

"These have come so that your faith—of greater worth than gold, which perishes even though refined by fire—may be proved genuine and may result in praise, glory and honor when Jesus Christ is revealed." (I Peter 1:7 NIV)

March 19: A Little About the Ephod

"Put two onyx stones in gold settings, then attach one to each of the shoulder straps. On one of these stones engrave the names of Israel's first six sons in the order of their birth. And do the same with his remaining six sons on the other stone. In this way Aaron will always carry the names of the tribes of Israel when he enters the holy place, and I will never forget my people." (Exodus 28:9-12 CEV)

Everyone knows about peas and pea pods. Peas grow in their little pods and stay snuggled there until they make their debut on the banquet circuit. Ephods, on the other hand, are not really the topic of everyday conversation, even at banquets. But they were an important part of the priestly garments worn in the temple. Although they are no longer in use, I think they have a lesson for us.

The ephod was a beautifully embroidered vest on which a gold breastplate was attached. The breastplate had an inset of precious stones with the names of the twelve tribes of Israel. As he served, the High Priest wore the ephod. It was a symbolic way of keeping the twelve tribes of Israel before God.

In a spiritual sense, those who are Christians are children of Abraham through Christ ("And so, you should understand that everyone who has faith is a child of Abraham" Galatians 3:7 CEV). Jesus Christ, who is our High Priest, now carries our names before the Father.

So if you are feeling lonely and forlorn today, remember that you are remembered by Christ, who intercedes for you. You are one of God's children. He will never forget you!

March 20: The Fallen Woman

Most of our family had gathered at our son's house in Raleigh for the Christmas holidays. The first morning after our arrival, I picked out fresh clothes and made a start for the bathroom to take a shower. I carefully locked the door because we had a good many little bittys who would never be fazed by a door that was just closed. I whisked off my nightgown, ran the water in the shower to the correct temperature, and took a big step in over the tub edge. Before stepping in, however, I did not look carefully at the tub or its slick, pristine surface. And thus came a crash that echoed through the house.

I had skidded, gracefully, I am sure, across the entire length of the tub and ended up smashed bloodily on the built-in soap dish. I must have yelled on the way down: almost immediately, I heard loud knocking on the door. Unfortunately, due to my careful forethought in locking it, no one could come in.

Eventually, my husband was able to strong-arm his way in, only to see me sitting in the bottom of the tub with blood streaming down my face, water splashing far and wide due to the downward removal of the shower curtain, and tears mixing nicely with everything else.

It was another (admittedly painful) lesson in the never-ending task of teaching myself to be more careful. I am forever dashing ahead, only to remember, often too late, that care taken before an action is not only beneficial; it often saves time in the long run!

Prayer: Lord, please help me to think before I act.

"If you think you are standing strong, be careful, for you, too, may fall into the same sin." (I Corinthians 10:12 NLT)

March 21: Alien-Nation

When we took our three oldest children to Mexico and started through customs on our arrival, we were faced with two lines under two signs: one read "Citizens" and the other "Aliens." I immediately got in the line that said citizens, because while I don't mind being considered weird or off-beat, I certainly was not going to be considered an alien. Eventually, I was forcibly ejected from the incorrect line, and after several patient explanations, it finally penetrated my head that while I was indeed a citizen of the United States, I was considered an alien in Mexico because I was only there temporarily.

Many years later, when my daughter and I went to Europe, I had to laugh every time I saw those signs. In the intervening years, I had become a Christian, and now, I am even an alien in my own land, for I am just here temporarily.

We are not only aliens, but also strangers and pilgrims in a foreign land, and our "tents" are frail and quickly pulled down. I must remember not to get too settled or attached to things, so that I am ready to move on to higher ground at a moment's notice. The day is coming when we will see not only the true King, but also the land of our birth. Our citizenship is in heaven.

"By faith he made his home in the promised land like a stranger in a foreign country.... For he was looking forward to the city with foundations, whose architect and builder is God." (Hebrews 11:9a,10 NIV)

March 22: Fire Drill (Almost)

I had a two-hour trip ahead of me, and the seats beside me on the plane were marvelously and mysteriously empty, so I stretched out and prepared to doze. After a short time, I heard a crackling noise that seemed to grow louder. I thought, at first, that it must be rain on the roof of the plane, but after a moment's reflection, I realized that we must be above the clouds, so that really didn't seem a possibility. The crackling seemed to sort of ebb and flow around me in various directions, and I wondered if I should open my eyes and be the very first to shout, "Fire!" By this time, I was sure the flames were eating away the interior of the plane's shell, and I was the only one who could hear it because I had my head against the bulkhead. My eyes finally flew open to see if anyone else looked panicky, and I saw that everyone was placidly undoing the cellophane wrapping around their box lunches.

More often than I like to admit, my thoughts trigger emotions, which, in turn, trigger actions. My misguided intention of shouting, "Fire!" and getting everyone organized to evacuate was fortunately nipped in the bud when I opened my eyes. But I have known other times, the details of which I will mercifully spare you, when my eyes were open physically but closed spiritually, and I, therefore, jumped precipitously into an action that reflected not God, but only self-interest. So, the next time I am tempted to spring into action to save the world, I plan to stop first and ask God to open my eyes to what His plan for me is.

"Our Lord and our God, I turn my eyes to you, on your throne in heaven." (Psalm 123:1 CEV)

March 23: Cue from Fescue

While visiting our daughter, Margaret, who lives in the farmland of Missouri, I learned a lot of things about crops, cattle and countryside. As one who grew up in the city (and whose idea of camping out is a motel with no room service), my farm knowledge is pitiful in the extreme. However, as time went by, I did manage to garner a few facts.

My biggest discovery was that fescue was a type of grass that, although it is not classified as crabby, is definitely picky. It seems there is only a very short time when fescue should be harvested—that is, when the heads of the grass may be cut off by the combines to obtain seeds. If this short window of opportunity is lost, the seeds dry out and blow away, never to be recovered.

I, too, have been given seed to sow, waiting for God to make it grow. I must be about His business while there is still time. In Isaiah, God compares His word to the seed: "It is the same with my word. I send it out, and it always produces fruit. It will accomplish all I want it to, and it will prosper everywhere I send it" (Isaiah 55:11 NLT).

"A time to plant and a time to harvest." (Ecclesiastes 3:2b NLT)

March 24: A Fungus Among Us

Many parts of the United States don't struggle with mildew; unfortunately, Florida does. Heat and humidity combine to produce the perfect environment for this unwelcome guest. I've noticed the prevalence of mildew is never mentioned in advertisements encouraging Florida vacations. This is understandable, since most visitors are not interested in a mildew encounter (you'd have to look long and hard to find a road side attraction advertising both "Swim With the Dolphins" and "Meet Some Mildew"). But I'm not worried about truth in advertisement either, because most tourists are only here for a week or so, and they often spend their time swimming and walking on the beach. Mildew doesn't grow well on things that keep moving. It prefers things cozily quiet, and when an object is still, and the temperature and humidity are high, mildew can put its bloom on anything within you can think of, including framed pictures and fancy shoes.

Unfortunately, Florida is not alone in having a high M.Q. (Mildew Quotient). When I sit cozily still in the dark, with greenhouse-heat all around me, mildew easily blooms on my heart. I've noted (much to my sorrow) that I have never, ever come across a verse in the Bible that encourages me to "Loll around." Quite the opposite: I am asked to love, seek, obey, take care of, pray, meditate (which, by the way, has nothing to do with gazing at my navel—no matter how fascinating it may be), and follow, to name a few. It takes spiritual energy to follow God, but even when I'm sick in bed, my heart may run to Him. The M.Q. in my house may be high, but may I spend so much time serving God that mildew never has a chance to bloom on my heart.

"I hold fast to your statutes, O Lord; do not let me be put to shame. I run in the path of your commands, for you have set my heart free." (Psalm 119:31-32 NIV)

March 25: Looking Ahead

Children are a comfort in your old age, as the saying goes, and they help us reach it faster, too. They can be exasperating, entertaining, and exhausting. Older mothers used to tell me that the childhood days would go by all too quickly, but deep in diapers, don'ts and discipline, I simply couldn't believe it.

Looking back now, it's a wonder I didn't get skin burn from the speed of those days zipping past. Bill and I enjoy our children as adults now, and try to look wise and remember the right answers when questions are asked (sometimes, now, we can't even remember the question…). But we are pleased when they ask, just as though we were the founts of wisdom they thought we were when they were under six.

The important thing about children, though, is not the warm fuzzies we get when we are together, but the fact that we are passing on the torch of a spiritual heritage. We're not here just to work, play, and re-cycle glass. We're here to pour out God's love to others.

Children, whether ours by blood or choice, are what the world will be tomorrow. So, pass your spiritual heritage on to those who are our future. If you don't have children, pass God's love to the children in your neighborhood, your church, and your extended family.

"You must be very careful not to forget the things you have seen God do for you. Keep reminding yourselves, and tell your children and grandchildren as well." (Deuteronomy 4:9 CEV)

March 26: Hiding

Staying with Ben and Stephen, the sons of our daughter, Lissa, was truly a learning experience (she was in the hospital having her third child). I gave it my all, and tried to remember to stay alert and not let anyone run away from home or decide to burn the house down. I did pretty well in those departments (by the end, we still had two boys and one house) until one night around dinner time. I sent the boys into the bathroom to wash their hands, but unlike MacArthur, they did not return. I called, but there was no answer. I called again (I'm a slow learner…). Finally, I went to the door and turned the handle. It was locked. I rattled the knob and spoke in my most menacing tone: "Open this door!" I screamed.

Much 3 and 5 year old scurrying took place, and then the door swung open to reveal the floor covered by every towel and washcloth in the house, with remnants of water leaking ominously from all the corners. "Don't you ever do that again!" I admonished with beady eyes. Back came the quick answer without losing a beat, "Not while you're around, we won't!"

This little scene, makes me wonder if there are times when I wait until I think God isn't looking to plan something I know would not be pleasing to Him. Although I know that nothing is ever hidden from His sight, sometimes I ignore that fact in my everyday walk, and I just stroll haphazardly without careful thought as to the consequences or the probable quenching of the Spirit.

Prayer: Lord, help me to give my wayward thoughts to You before I act.

"The Lord looks down from heaven and sees the whole human race. From his throne he observes all who live on the earth. He made their hearts, so he understands everything they do." (Psalm 33:13-15 NLT)

March 27: Rain

There were five brothers at our house when I grew up. One night, my two youngest brothers decided to camp out in the yard for the night and set about rigging up a tent.

When it got dark, they settled down to enjoy their adventure and then noticed that it was beginning to rain. They thought if it didn't rain too hard they would wait it out, but the water poured down more and more, nearly washing their flimsy shelter away.

They finally gave up and dashed from beneath the tent to the house. The door was locked. Noticing that the rain seemed to be coming at a strange angle, they looked up and discovered our father spraying garden hoses in their direction and laughing. He didn't play many tricks on us, but those he did were well thought out!

Has there been rain on your parade today? Whether it's local or widespread, the best refuge is your Father's house. His door is never locked, and you can flee there for safety and protection when you feel drenched and unhappy.

"God is our refuge and our strength, an ever present help in trouble." (Psalm 46:1 NIV)

March 28: Buttons (and no Bows)

Seated at the head table as a luncheon started, I was startled to see one of the gold buttons on my jacket drop off as I reached for my water. I was getting ready to give a speech, so I was happy to note that the button was next to the lowest one, and, thus, might not be noticeable behind the lectern. A few minutes later, I bent to get something out of my purse, and another button popped off (note to self: if you're sitting at the head table in front of an audience, there's a lot to be said for remaining motionless). This button was higher up the ladder, so to speak, and when I stood up, the last one dropped off with a large clang of doom. I was left clutching the podium with one hand and the front of my jacket with the other, looking rather like Napoleon before he got all the way into his coat.

When the ordeal mercifully ended, the audience having graciously ignored my state of disrepair, I retired to the Ladies' Room to examine the problem. To my amazement, all that was left was one thread dangling maliciously down the inside of the jacket. All those buttons had been sewn on with one thread! When the wind blew and the cradle had rocked…well down came nearly everything.

My steps in the Christian life are not to be like this! Because my world is constantly unraveling, I need to be anchored in Christ. Examination of my life's thread is essential. If it is not prayerfully and carefully done, it is likely to come undone in a time of crisis.

"God cannot tell lies! And so his promises and vows are two things that can never be changed. We have run to God for safety. Now his promises should greatly encourage us to take hold of the hope that is right in front of us. This hope is like a firm and steady anchor for our souls. In fact, hope reaches behind the curtain and into the most holy place." (Hebrews 6:18-19 CEV)

March 29: Caution: God at Work

Road construction drives me crazy, especially on streets I travel frequently. There I am, in a big hurry, and I seem to come across the same torn up old road, with the same people, leaning on the same shovels, who look as though rigor mortis may be setting in any moment. Then my plans are changed, and I must either sit in a long line of cars, all going two miles an hour, or detour through unfamiliar streets. I am not happy doing either. I understand that the end result of all of this construction is to make the road in question wider or smoother, but it's easy for me to lose sight of the long-term benefits because of short-term inconveniences.

The same thing happens when my spiritual journey is interrupted by "construction projects" in my life. God is at work leveling out mountains of pride in my life, along with valleys of inferiority, and gullies of greed. Unfortunately, I have not planned for these interruptions, so it's easy for me to lose focus on the long-term benefits. May God give me the grace to leave each and every day in the hand of the One who builds for a purpose.

"'My thoughts are completely different from yours,' says the Lord. 'And my ways are far beyond anything you could imagine. For just as the heavens are higher than the earth, so are my ways higher than your ways and my thoughts higher than your thoughts.'" (Isaiah 55:8-9 NLT)

"As for God, his way is perfect." (II Samuel 22:31a NLT)

March 30: Lesson from the Laundromat

The man who came into the Laundromat was obviously in an alien environment. He did have soap, but had neglected to bring bleach, fabric softener, hangers, or a basket. The directions for using the equipment seemed to cause some distress, but his Waterloo came when he least expected it. He had manhandled the things from the dryer into a formidable mound onto the folding table, and he started making little, darting forays into the interior of the pile. Children's socks refused to be mated, underwear bunched, and shirts were recalcitrant about turning right side out. He grew more and more frustrated, and ended by squashing it all into a shapeless wad and crushing it back into the bag he had brought. He had, no doubt, been doing what his wife was momentarily incapable of performing, perhaps because of illness or a new baby, but she was going to have a bigger task at unraveling all the snarls in that good deed.

This episode reminds me of my attempts at telling others of God's love for them. I go only partly prepared: no prayer and no love. I have a hard time screwing up enough courage to speak, and when my vocal cords actually produce a sound, I make little darting forays around a subject that is probably incomprehensible. Eventually, I jam as much Scripture as I can remember down someone's throat, and leave them gasping for air and hoping for someone to come along and unsnarl the mess of my intended good deed.

Witnessing should not be an alien environment! It should be an outflow of God's love, explaining how our relationship to Him gives us strength for the day and bright hope for tomorrow.

"For the grace of God that brings salvation has appeared to all men. It teaches us to say 'No' to ungodliness and worldly passions, and to live self-controlled, upright and godly lives in this present age, while we wait for the blessed hope—the glorious appearing of our great God and Savior, Jesus Christ…." (Titus 2:11-13)

March 31: Ship to Shore

On my trip through Europe with my college classmates, I received a package from my father when we got to Rome. I have explained elsewhere that my father, being an engineer, was big on details. The package proved it beyond a doubt, for inside was a pack of balloons and a detailed set of directions. In short, as our ship sailed into the New York harbor, I was to go up on the top deck, blow up the balloons, and search for my parents who would be on the crowded pier. They would also be holding balloons. This way, we would be able to locate each other easily in the crushing mass of people.

There were several pieces of information that neither of us knew, however. One was that, since we were on an immigrant ship, all the other passengers (except for me and my classmates) were leaving the ship when we docked in Nova Scotia. The second was that, since all the other students were from the Midwest, none of their parents were driving all the way to New York.

The day of our arrival, I dutifully followed my father's instructions. As we entered the harbor, I staggered up to the top deck and blew up all my balloons, surrounded by the nineteen other students. It was a big ship and we didn't take up much room. As we neared the pier, I saw that my parents had also blown up their balloons. They were standing by themselves, alone on the large dock. Needless to say, we saw each other right away.

Have you realized that God knows every one of His children by name? And He doesn't need to resort to balloons to find us. In Psalm 139:1-4, David says of God, "You have looked deep into my heart, Lord, and you know all about me. You know when I am resting or when I am working, and from heaven you discover my thoughts. You notice everything I do and everywhere I go. Before I even speak a word, you know what I will say" (CEV).

April 1: April Fool

When my husband and I were in the dating stage, I was very inquisitive about everything he liked, did, and thought. I found out that his favorite color was brown, which I never imagined to be anybody's favorite color, least of all the man I was going to marry. I found out that he played tennis, golf, and chess, none of which I had ever tried. I found out that he read encyclopedias and the *Wall Street Journal*, neither of which I had ever poked my nose into. And, I found out he thought about me, which I felt was very good indeed, because I certainly thought about him.

At this point in my life I didn't think much about God; my focus was firmly anchored on *terra firma*—and mainly on our wedding. It's astounding how much time I spent thinking about that wedding, and how little time I spent in thinking about what might happen later. Or even later. Or later, later…as in fifty years later.

When I did picture my future, it was draped gauzily in clouds of light pink and crimson, and never held disaster, desperation, or despair…all of which land heavily on everyone at one time or another. Thankfully, God showed Himself to me and filled me with His Spirit, so my heartaches weren't faced alone. My husband is wonderful, but he can't be with me all the time (although he certainly has shone, through "sickness and health, richer and poorer!"). But God can.

I am a wiser now than I was before our wedding 50 years ago (some would say not much wiser!), and I know that my future will hold even more sorrow and despair. But I am comforted, because I know God will always be with me. I also am thankful for my dear husband, and am grateful that, because of the death and resurrection of Christ, we will be with each other forever.

"The angel showed me a river that was crystal clear, and its waters gave life. The river came from the throne where God and the Lamb were seated. Then it flowed down the middle of the city's main street. On each side of the river are trees that grow a different kind of fruit each month of the year. The fruit gives life, and the leaves are used as medicine to heal the nations. God's curse will no longer be on the people of that city. He and the Lamb will be seated there on their thrones, and its people will worship God and will see him face to face. God's name will be written on the foreheads of the people. Never again will night appear, and no one who lives there will ever need a lamp or the sun." (Revelation 22:1-5a CEV)

April 2: Are You Lumpy?

"These are the instructions regarding the grain offering. Aaron's sons must present this offering to the Lord in front of the altar. The priest on duty will take a handful of the choice flour that has been mixed with olive oil and sprinkled with incense. He will burn this token portion on the altar, and it will be very pleasing to the Lord." (Leviticus 6:14-15 NLT)

I find the word "lumpy" fascinating for some reason. Perhaps it's because I have put several strange and lumpy "offerings" on the dinner table.

I created one memorable lumpy culinary dish not long after we were first married. I had heard a lot about how difficult piecrusts were to make, so I solicited a recipe from a friend. "It's foolproof," she assured me (she didn't realize whom she was dealing with.)

I set out to make an apple pie, so I started on the crust. I mixed the flour and other ingredients and rolled it out. Unfortunately, when I tried to put it in the pie pan, the crust fell apart. I threw everything out and started over. Same result. I decided the dough needed to be really thick in order to make the transfer to the pie pan, so I rolled out a crust so thick it resembled a round, white brownie. Needless to say, it did not fall apart when I moved it to the pan. As a cooking novice, I had no idea there were recipes for pies as well as for crusts, so I simply cut up an apple and arranged the slices artistically on the lower crust. I finished up with another hefty crust on top of the cut-up apple.

I'll say this…Bill didn't recognize anything familiar when it was served.

If I had not given up so quickly and if I had taken the time to roll the dough out properly, my crust would not have been so pale and lumpy (and I'm sure the pie would have tasted better if I had used a few more ingredients!). The above verses from Leviticus talk about the flour given in the offering; it was not not coarse or "lumpy." Christ came to earth and he allowed himself to be crushed as an offering for our sins.

I want to follow Christ's example. May I continually give up the right to myself; may I do and be what God wants—even if it means being crushed in the process.

April 3: Signs and Wonders

"After leaving Succoth they camped at Etham on the edge of the desert. By day the Lord went ahead of them in a pillar of cloud to guide them on their way and by night in a pillar of fire to give them light, so that they could travel by day or night. Neither the pillar of cloud by day nor the pillar of fire by night left its place in front of the people." (Exodus 13:20-22 NIV)

Some highway signs are clear and concise: "Last exit before 20 mile bridge" (clear, but usually too late). Some highway signs are somewhat clear: "All you can drink for $1.00" (who knows? Perhaps one glass is all they will allow you!). Some highway signs are ambiguous: "You will never forget our orange juice" (you've got to admit—that one makes you stop and think!).

But where are God's highway signs? I long for a visible signpost from God every time I reach a crossroad in my life (where's that fiery pillar, Lord?). Not only do I have to journey without clouds and fire, I don't even have a clue to my destination (now I have an inkling of how Moses felt those 40 years wandering around in the desert!). Whether I like it or not, God only shows my road step by step.

It may be true that I don't know my destination, but thankfully, I know my Guide, and I know He is trustworthy. So, instead of concerning myself with possible destinations, may I instead relax and focus on each step of my journey, and rejoice that I am in the company of the King of Kings Himself.

Prayer: Thank you, Father, that we may all walk with you, and that we may know your loving guidance day by day.

April 4: Advance Preparation

Explo '72 was a 5-day conference put on by Campus Crusade (held in 1972, obviously). I don't know exactly how I got talked into going to it, since it was advertised for young people, but since there were three of those said people going from our house, I hated to miss any of the fun.

There had been a lot of advance preparation for this crusade. Every person on every page of the Dallas phone book had been prayed for, and huge ads were placed in the papers saying that people from Explo would be coming to visit door to door. I thought this was a great idea, until I found out that I was going to participate in this little exercise.

I searched the room I was in when I heard this announcement, hoping to find a way to escape gracefully. Then I heard that we had each been assigned to a partner, and mine found me before I could rip off my nametag. She looked normal enough, and assured me that she had done this before. I made her promise to go first so I could watch (I was supposed to be praying), and I followed her reluctantly up to an apartment.

I had forgotten that God makes advance preparations. At one address we were assigned, a young man answered the door and asked us in. I gaped as we entered his living room. There were pictures of butterflies on every square inch, including one worked into his rug. Since I was busy trying to match them up with the ones in my stomach, I almost missed what my partner was saying. It seems her father was one of the world's most famous lepidopterists, and she knew nearly everything about butterflies, too.

The Lord was busy that day in Dallas, and I had the opportunity to see Him at work. Not only did this man pray to become a Christian, God reminded me that He really does go before us, and that He can handle butterflies in timid children!

"An important Ethiopian official happened to be going along that road in his chariot. He was the chief treasurer for Candace, the Queen of Ethiopia. The official had gone to Jerusalem to worship and was now on his way home. He was sitting in his chariot, reading the book of the prophet Isaiah. The Spirit told Philip to catch up with the chariot. Philip ran up close and heard the man reading aloud from the book of Isaiah. Philip asked him, 'Do you understand what you are reading?' The official answered, 'How can I understand unless someone helps me?' He then invited Philip to come up and sit beside him....So Philip began at this place in the Scriptures and explained the good news about Jesus." (Acts 8:27b-31, 35 CEV)

April 5: A Rainy Lesson

At Explo, it rained nearly all the last day. When I stopped at the hotel to meet a friend who had kindly arranged a ride for me, her roommate was in bed with a bad cold and feeling very puny. I urged her to come on and go to the last meeting anyway, because I was positive the rain would stop. After all, there were eighty thousand of us there, and we had prayed the rain would stop by the time the meeting started. When you have over eighty thousand people praying, I felt God was surely bound to answer with clear skies and light hearts. My friend's roommate shocked me when she calmly asserted the rain would not stop. Privately, I thought this showed an amazing lack of faith.

She was right, of course. The rain did not stop. It not only rained, it poured.

It rained all the way to the stadium, all through the singing and all through the preaching. The amazing thing was, it didn't seem to dampen anyone's spirits; and we had "more joy in Mudville" than when Casey was at bat. The joy just went on and on, through the laughter when the closing hymn "Oh, for a Thousand Tongues to Sing" was announced. As the service ended, the clouds lifted and we saw a glorious rainbow, telling us that God had been there all along.

I missed the main point of all this rain business, however, until I saw a newscast of the event that showed all the crazy believers singing their heads off with water dripping from every angle. The news story was visually interesting and thematically arresting. It was a heavenly lesson for Dallas that they never would have noticed if the day had been sunny. It was one for me, too. I began to learn that faith doesn't hang on the answer, but on God.

"Whatever is good and perfect comes to us from God above, who created all heaven's lights." (James 1:17a NLT)

April 6: Alligators and Crocodiles

Although these two reptiles operate (scary word there) in different areas, they are closely related. They certainly share their method of attack. Both alligators and crocodiles lie just beneath the surface in swampy locales with only their half-closed eyeballs showing, doing their utmost to look as much like floating logs as possible. If a bird or land animal comes near (this includes humans, unfortunately), the log explodes into a furious frenzy of gaping teeth and slashing jaws.

I find all of this quite unattractive, especially since I have a strong aversion to being dragged under water by reptiles with large teeth. But, when I stop to think about it, alligators and crocodiles have something in common with Satan, who coasts along, quite concealed to my eye.

This would be downright frightening if it weren't for the fact that I can remain safe simply by staying on the path God has set for me. Unfortunately, I don't always walk where I should. Why do I resist following God's instructions? Why do I court temptation? The more I inch toward what I know is wrong, the more I am likely to stray too close to the murky water and meet up with a log that's up to no good.

Prayer: Lord, please guide my footsteps and keep me on your path.

"For the Lord watches over the way of the righteous, but the way of the wicked will perish." (Psalm 1:6 NIV)

April 7: A Happy Medium

When I was in college, I asked a friend to come to Florida with me for spring vacation. My mother warned her about the dangers of over-exposure to the sun, but my friend just laughed and said she always got a little red, but that it didn't mean anything.

We set out to prove this point by going to the beach at ten in the morning and staying until four o'clock in the afternoon. We also stayed in agony for the next few days. Passing a barbershop up town, we had the idea (unfounded, to be sure) that they might have something to ease the pain, and we were given a bottle of green liquid. It did look cool, but when we slathered it on, people began retreating in all directions. Take my word for it: "Lucky Tiger Hair Tonic" is no cure for sunburn.

Philippians 4:5 urges us to "Let your moderation be known unto all men" (KJV), and I'm sure this applies to more than beach going. Some people out-scrooge Scrooge; others buy a new Rolls Royce every March. Some people look as if they have their jeans painted on, while others wear so many layers of outsized clothing they look like stand-ins for the Abominable Snowman. Some folks can't bear to bypass anything remotely edible without a sample, while others take pride in looking skeletal.

None of these extremes are the moderation Paul thought best. May I do my best to stay in the temperate zone!

April 8: Little House on the Freeway

Today, with so many motels, it's difficult to remember a time when the roads were not littered with them. When I was a child, a motel was almost unheard of.

One winter, my father announced that we would launch into those heretofore-uncharted waters, and stay at one of the new-fangled motels or "tourist cabins" as they were then called. It was a freezing snowy afternoon in Virginia when we, huddled like cattle against the wind, pulled up in front of six cabins. A sign flopping on a pole assured us we had reached our destination. We were sorry to hear it.

We found each cabin had two beds and one chair adjoining a tiny bath with a shower stall too small for human occupation. We shivered our way through the night, and in the morning my mother insisted on trying to take her shower. She weighed only about 135, but she somehow got herself wedged in the door, and we had to call the manager's wife to come and extract her even though my mother was in nothing but her birthday suit. Poor mother would have given anything to help herself out of this embarrassing predicament, but it just wasn't possible. She had to accept help from someone outside her situation.

"Self help" just doesn't hack it in the Christian walk either: we must constantly be aware that we are not sufficient in ourselves. If I try to take over control of my life, there's a good chance I might get stuck.

"Yes, I am the vine; you are the branches. Those who remain in me, and I in them, will produce much fruit. For apart from me you can do nothing." (John 15:5 NLT)

April 9: Presence, Not Presents

When I first started speaking, I would usually be gone for just one meeting. Then, as time passed and the children got older, sometimes I would be gone overnight. By the time the top three were in high school, I was taking itineraries. I tried to hold this to once every other month, so that the kids knew whom the face at the door belonged to, but when the four oldest left to get married and go to college, I made a bad mistake. Our youngest was in ninth grade, and I guess I was forgetting there wasn't a whole household filled with company. When I was away she would be on her own until Bill got home from work (teenagers need hugs too!).

One day she came to tell me that she had the lead in the school play. Unfortunately, all the dates the play were to be performed conflicted with a speaking engagement: the itinerary had been set long before. There was nothing I could do about this, short of dropping dead, which would hardly be helpful. I had to go ahead and try to make up for not attending an event I knew was important to her. I wrote a long funny poem and arranged for it to be delivered backstage with a big bunch of balloons, and I prayed for her the whole time I was away. But it wasn't enough. When I saw that face as I got home, I knew that the Lord was telling me not to take any more itineraries until she had graduated. The strange thing was, that once I had made this decision, I never got another invitation to speak until that time came.

It was an important lesson for me to learn: my family comes before work (or ministry in this case!).

"These commandments that I give you today are to be upon your hearts. Impress them on your children. Talk about them when you sit at home and when you walk along the road, when you lie down and when you get up." (Deuteronomy 6:6-7 NIV)

April 10: Accent-u-ate the Positive

In Bermuda, there are some beautiful birds called long tail swallows. They swoop around that island in great numbers, and they are very popular. They are painted on pictures, plates, pocketbooks, and nearly anything else standing still. For many years, people were unable to find out where they nested. They would seem to disappear near the cliffs in the pale evening light. Finally, a scientist was able to net one of these birds and attach a tiny transmitter to its leg, so that he was able to trace it home to one of the caves in the shore cliffs.

I have a transmitter too. As I fly though life, I am constantly emitting signals of one kind or another. Sometimes they are a positive witness for the Lord, and sometimes they are not. But positive or negative, they are there for the entire world to see and hear. They are my actions and reactions.

What kind of a message do I transmit when the food checker in the grocery store makes a mistake, when my car is dented, when the waiter spills gravy in my lap, or when my child makes muddy tracks on a clean floor? Since there's not much time to think, my reaction is going to emerge from what is in my heart and spill over onto the person who is with me. There are lots of reactions I wish I could take back. Since I can't, I guess I need to begin filling my heart with the milk of human kindness instead of sour grapes.

"You are like a letter written by Christ and delivered by us. But you are not written with pen and ink or on tablets made of stone. You are written in our hearts by the Spirit of the living God." (II Corinthians 3:3 CEV)

April 11: Scarlett and God

God is always doing wonderful and unusual things isn't He? At a meeting in Alabama, I had the fun of seeing Him touch someone's life in an amazing way.

When I was closing the meeting and getting ready to give an invitation to receive Christ, I said something I have never said before or since. It's almost as if God took over my vocal cords and put words in my mouth that I had no intention of saying. I heard myself say, "Don't be like Scarlett O'Hara and say 'I'll think about it tomorrow.'"

As I stood by the door saying goodbye, a young woman came out with tears streaming down her face. One never knows exactly what to say to someone in this condition, but I thought perhaps she had made a commitment and it had been an emotional experience of some sort.

"Did you pray to receive Christ today?" I asked gently.

"No," she said, "I have been a believer for some time, but I have been away from the Lord for the past three years. My friend kept encouraging me, and she kept inviting me to come to luncheons, but I always put her off. This month the luncheon fell on my birthday, and she said she wanted me to be her guest as a birthday gift. It would have been awkward to refuse." Then she added, "I have been putting off coming back to the Lord, but my name is Scarlett, and today God cared enough to call me by my name."

Indeed He did care for her, just as He cares for each of His children. He never has called my name out loud, but I know He knows it!

"And the Lord replied to Moses, 'I will indeed do what you have asked, for you have found favor with me, and you are my friend.'" (Exodus 33:17 NLT)

April 12: Word Stuck

Entering the main terminal at the airport of a distant city to speak at a conference, I saw a huge banner stretched across the width of the entrance to baggage pick up. It said "Welcome, Word Stuck Authors!" I thought, "Wow! How did they know I was coming?"

As I got closer, however, I saw that I had jumped to a false conclusion based on faulty observation. My beady little eyes had once again led me far astray. The sign actually said "Welcome, Word Struck Authors!" I suppose it was an organization that was also having a conference in that city, and I wondered briefly if I should make a detour to see if they knew what to do if you're stuck instead of struck. The thing is, I have a nagging fear I will run out of ideas, and find myself with the world's worst case of writer's block. Everyone pooh-poohs this of course, but I notice they're not the ones writing.

Objectively, I know there is no danger of this because I am writing about our living God, and He is a real source of ideas great and small. Since He is always with me, He will impart if I will listen.

Everyone has a gift, and we need to use it as God intends, so that others may see our progress and give God the glory for what He is creating. So, writing is of no greater consequence than showing mercy, or giving, or teaching, or any of the other gifts. We all contribute to the Body, and since God is the "Author and Finisher of our faith," we may count on Him to give us the zeal (and words!) to do the task at hand.

"We have different gifts, according to the grace given us. If a man's gift is prophesying, let him use it in proportion to his faith. If it is serving, let him serve; if it is teaching, let him teach; if it is encouraging, let him encourage; if it is contributing to the needs of others, let him give generously; if it is leadership, let him govern diligently; if it is showing mercy, let him do it cheerfully." (Romans 12:6-8 NIV)

April 13: Castles in the Air

My husband and I were visiting our daughter in England, and she and her husband volunteered to take us to Scotland for the weekend. I always thought a castle was a castle, until I saw the one at Edinborough. It was a castle, of course, but it is also practically an entire city perched up there on the huge rocks. Perhaps there are other castles like this one, but since this is the one I wandered through, I was more than impressed. It has everything you would ever need for a battle or a siege, including an armory, a hospital, a chapel, and (naturally) a place for the inhabitants to sleep.

When people shut themselves up in that castle, all their needs were provided for, because it was both a battleground and a safe refuge. It is wonderful to know that in God we have both a place to battle the enemy of our souls and a safe place in times of danger or distress. We may hide in Him, having all the provision we need for sustenance, rest, healing and worship. We may also make use of the armory, which gives us the protection of truth and righteousness, the shield of faith, the helmet of salvation, and our all important weapon of defense: God's Word, which is the sword of the Spirit.

I have run to God's castle many times, and He is always there. Thank you dear Lord, that You are truly a present help in times of trouble!

"The Lord is a mighty tower where his people can run for safety...." (Proverbs 18:10 CEV)

April 14: Time on Your Hands

My style of packing could be (and has been) called haphazard, but my mother's was the exact opposite. She turned packing into a fine art that required long nights of study and rearrangement. Articles of attire for each day were assigned to a layer and placed in the suitcase on a long, ironed linen towel. This towel could then be lifted out with everything in place, and of course it was never wrinkled because everything was stuffed with tissue paper. Toilet articles were relegated to a leather case all their own, with bottles, vials, jars, and boxes of every description ready not only for makeup, but to succor any traveling companion who might need medication, bandaging, or swabbing. Then, of course, there were the silver toilet articles from her bedroom dresser (comb, brush, mirror, clock, hair container, photographs, and many other various items). All these would be placed neatly on the dresser in the hotel where we would spend the night.

Mother was not trying to be ostentatious; heaven knows, she was the least ostentatious of anyone I have known. It was partly the way she was raised, I suppose, and partly the result of the time in which she lived. In the 1800's and early 1900's, people packed with trunks, trunks, and more trunks, whether they were going abroad or up to the mountains for the summer. It was understood that any place outside the city was wilderness, and so, it was necessary to carry everything with you.

My darling mother made use of her time, but I often wonder if it were really the best use when all that was involved was packing a suitcase. It is wonderful to be organized, and even devoutly to be wished, but it is possible to spend so much time organizing, that people or the important things of life get lost in the shuffle.

May I not be so busy packing that I am insensitive to the Holy Spirit and have no time for love. May I never forget, as I formulate the plans for the day's activities, to leave room for God's opportunities of interruptions (which are often inconvenient, messy, and even undesirable!). Since I don't know what God has in mind when He allows an interruption, it is good for me to practice "flexible packing" and leave some room for unexpected items that may turn out to be invaluable.

"So be careful how you live, not as fools but as those who are wise. Make the most of every opportunity for doing good in these evil days." (Ephesians 5:15-16 NLT)

April 15: Mexican Sunday

When my husband and I, with our three oldest children, were in Mexico City, we made plans to attend a church. We knew there was a church of our denomination because we had looked it up in the Yellow Pages, but the taxi driver seemed very dubious. He scowled at the address and mumbled as we swerved through crowds of other racing, honking cars. The ad had said that the service started at 9:45 a.m., but when we arrived, the doors were locked.

Deposited like sacks of meal and left to our own devices, we felt like waifs in a Dickens's novel huddled in the chilly (was this really Mexico?) morning air. Eventually, someone came with a key and we trooped gratefully into the small sanctuary. Soon, a few more came, and then a few more. We could tell they didn't have much in the way of material wealth. They were dressed rather poorly, but they were warm and welcoming. After a few minutes, they started the service.

Do you know what kind of a service it was? It was a prayer service for the Sunday School and the Worship service to follow. What a wonderful idea! There were probably 30 or 35 people there, and they prayed with great earnestness. Although we couldn't understand a word they said, somehow we had the feeling we could. It didn't matter anyway, as they were praying to the God who not only understands every language, but also the unspoken words of the heart.

It is so important to pray for our brothers and sisters in other lands, especially those who are going through times of persecution. We also need to pray for those who need God and have no idea of His love. May we never forget to pray for all God's children throughout the world, and may they know His love for them.

"The heavens declare the glory of God; the skies proclaim the work of his hands. Day after day they pour forth speech; night after night they display knowledge. There is no speech or language where their voice is not heard." (Psalm 19:1-3 NIV)

April 16: Leaf it to Beaver

While on a recent trip up north in the fall of the year, (for me it's not north, but nawth) I noticed that there were lots and lots of leaves on the ground. Some of the more industrious homeowners had raked their lawns, but very few had been able to get everything out of their shrubs and low bushes. The leaves didn't seem to mind this lack of attention. They just rested there, seemingly composed while decomposing.

The word "composed" means to put your mind in a state of tranquility or repose, a little lesson I could learn from the leaves. Leaves don't get rattled, even though they do rattle in the wind now and then. Leaves have no selfish ambition that I know of—this certainly puts them ahead of me in the peace and rest category.

I have a hard time submitting to the cold times in my life, and, when I'm torn from the safe haven I've carved out for myself, I'm anything but pliable. The opposite should be true: I must be willing to submit to the process that is conforming me to the image of Christ (even if it seems to involve a time of rot and decay), because only in accepting the will of God for my life day by day will I find that I have true "composure."

"I pray that the Lord, who gives peace, will always bless you with peace." (II Thessalonians 3:16a CEV)

April 17: Provision

When I was about twelve, my mother had an outfit made for me from some beautiful glen plaid material she had bought in Canada. It consisted of a coat, a suit, and a hat, and I wore it until I went to prep school. By that time, I had grown some (although not enough to scare anybody), so my mother had the bottom of the coat cut off and sewed onto the top of the suit coat. The material wore like iron, and I was still wearing it when we got married (although not at the wedding!).

By that time, we were living in Florida, and there was not much demand for a forty-pound winter outfit. During a cold snap, however, I dragged it out and discovered that moths had made hefty inroads into it—too many to make it worthwhile to be re-woven. Reluctantly, I said goodbye to an old friend, and gave it to the Salvation Army. When we moved a year later, I found a roll of nearly two yards of that beautiful material which my mother had kept in a box for just such an emergency.

I had not realized (in this case, at least!) that my mother knew what lay ahead. God always does; and He not only knows, He has made provision for any emergency we might face. He has provided not only "materially" but also spiritually. He not only goes before us, He is behind us, beside us and most wonderful of all, IN us. His abiding is the most precious provision of all, for He remains with us always,

"…He is the one who keeps every promise forever." (Psalm 146:6b NLT)

April 18: Perspective

Perspective can mean several different things, but I am fascinated by the following quotation by Dick Larson of MIT: "By manipulating perception, companies and industries can help 'line waiters' be more satisfied." He cites a case in which passengers at the Houston airport complained about the luggage delay. Here was the situation: travelers would get off the plane and take a one-minute walk to the luggage carousel. There they had to wait for seven minutes. The complaints continued even after airport officials conducted studies and hired additional baggage handlers.

The solution, in the end, was simple: the disembarking location was moved from the main terminal to a distant location, so that the passenger walk-time to the baggage carousel was increased from one minute to six minutes. They picked up their baggage not long after they walked up to the carousel. The baggage arrived at the same time as before, but passenger perceptions were altered. Complaints dropped almost to zero.

I need this sort of perspective in my life circumstances. Sometimes I have the impression that I am alone and uncared for because I am tired of the waiting in my life. But what would happen if I were to take heart and concentrated instead on my walk? Even though I may be more aware of God's absence than His presence, I must not forget that He has the solution. The perspective I should take is to trust God, because, as Paul says, "Now we see but a poor reflection; then we shall see face to face (I Corinthians 13:12 NIV). Thus, I can believe that God is acting to do what is best, and that He loves me.

"Oh, the depth of the riches of the wisdom and knowledge of God! How unsearchable his judgments, and his paths beyond tracing out! Who has known the mind of the Lord? Or who has been his counselor? Who has ever given to God, that God should repay him? For from him and through him and to him are all things. To him be the glory forever! Amen." (Romans 11:33-36 NIV)

April 19: I'll Take Vanilla

I used to specialize in wild and exotic flavors of ice cream. I started, calmly enough, with sherbet, because, when I took a spoon and filled it with water, nestled it deep in the scoop and left it there, it froze into a perfect spoon shape, much to the surprise and amazement of my friends.

I soon progressed on to chocolate, thence to strawberry, and then I bounded joyfully into the world of butter pecan, pistachio, tutti-frutti and Quarter Back crunch. I never liked vanilla. It was too dull, too ordinary, and too everyday. Lately, however, I have reconsidered vanilla. Although, it is true, it is not as flamboyant as pralines and cream, there is something about its flavor I find appealing. It's like life in a way, because our everyday lives are not flamboyant either (unless, of course, you happen to be a tight-ropewalker). I don't think we were meant to have the most intense emotions every day—whether peril or pleasure.

I agree with the quotation from Piet Hein: "We on whom God's light does fall, see the great things in the small." We were meant to find contentment in the ordinary occurrences of life. We were meant to see God's hand in the everyday, to enjoy His presence in our daily tasks, to feel His strength and comfort as we minister to family and friends. This is God's vanilla. I'll take it with delight.

"'Go out and stand on the mountain,' the Lord replied. 'I want you to see me when I pass by.' All at once, a strong wind shook the mountain and shattered the rocks. But the Lord was not in the wind. Next, there was an earthquake, but the Lord was not in the earthquake. Then there was a fire, but the Lord was not in the fire. Finally, there was a gentle breeze, and when Elijah heard it, he covered his face with his coat. He went out and stood at the entrance to the cave. The Lord asked, 'Elijah, why are you here?'" (I Kings 19:11-13 CEV)

April 20: Ground Work

We have a huge pine tree in our yard that is called a sand pine. According to a nurseryman friend of ours, this tree drops cones that break open and spread seed only when it is burned. If there is no fire, there is no way for the seed to germinate.

Many know the story of Joni Eareckson Tada, who as a teenager dove into shallow water and broke her neck. She endured many months in an iron lung and, later, many months in a bed that rotated her body upside down so she wouldn't get bedsores. Her progress was extremely slow, and she had many days of despair and rebellion against God. Eventually, however, she came to the place where she committed her life to Him. She taught herself how to paint with a brush in her mouth, and, with the help of her husband and friends, she has written several best-selling books about her struggles and victories. She is an amazing illustration of God's love and grace. I am sure that after her accident Mrs. Tada thought her life was effectively over. Instead, her life has brought forth hundreds of thousands of sprouts of faith from those who have had the opportunity to read her books or hear her speak.

When I face a time of fire (literal or not!), I pray I will remember that, like the sand pinecone, I will find that there will be new growth, not only in me but also in others. Sometimes the seeds of God's love can be spread in a way that would not have been possible had the fire not come.

"The truth is, a kernel of wheat must be planted in the soil. Unless it dies it will be alone—a single seed. But its death will produce many new kernels—a plentiful harvest of new lives." (John 12:24 NLT)

April 21: The Man in the White Suit

The author, Tom Wolfe, known for his penchant of making appearances only in white suits, was probably unknown at the time of the incident I am about to relay to you. I have no doubt he was alive and well at the time, but I seriously doubt that he wore white suits in his childhood.

I had a distant cousin who showed up (unannounced and unexpected) wearing a white suit, looking remarkably like someone ready to be announced at court. I never was really sure of the reason for this royal visit, but I must confess, the rest of us looked fairly shabby in contrast. Whether this was his intention, I don't know; I will give him the benefit of the doubt and just say perhaps he considered it *de rigueur* for trips to the South.

I hastily made some coffee and scraped the bottom of the cookie jar so we could have something to do besides examine our fingernails. Conversation was lagging a bit, when one of our children, about seven at the time and full of steam, came careening around the corner and slammed into my relative's legs, which were draped gracefully over the side of the couch. Unfortunately, my cousin was enjoying a cup of coffee at the time. "Good to the last drop" would not be appropriate here. I wiped, he wiped, we all wiped. He left promptly in a whirl of apologies on my side and several versions of "Perfectly all right, my dear" on his.

This story has two morals for me. The first is to never, ever wear an all-white outfit when visiting a house with small children. The second is for me to consider my motive when I do visit someone. Am I visiting to show off a new purchase or to drop a word about a wonderful promotion? Am I visiting to show love to someone who is home bound? Am I visiting to offer friendship to a newcomer in my neighborhood? Am I visiting carrying my cleaning rags to help a friend who has been sick in bed and would love some housecleaning help? May I examine my motives, so that I may be a living light that shines with His light to those around me.

"Love must be sincere." (Romans 12:9a NIV)

April 22: A Message in Flowers

People say spring and fall are the prettiest times to visit Scotland because of the yellow gorse in May and the purple heather in September. My husband Bill and I were there in May, and enjoyed seeing the bright yellow gorse on roads, lakesides, and golf courses. We enjoyed it, that is, until Bill hit a golf ball into a clump of it. When he tried to reach his golf ball, he was severely scratched, because the stems are covered with thorns.

We could see heather too, but it certainly didn't look very promising at that stage in its career. The moors looked dispirited and dull, with an olive brown, lifeless complexion. Even so, while wading through some heather to pick up one of my golf balls (which I couldn't believe had gone so far off course), I picked up a small piece. Even though the heather wasn't in bloom, it was perfectly lovely. It was a dark brownish green, ferny stem with just a blush of pink at the tip. What had been ugly from a distance turned out to be enchanting up close and personal.

Sometimes people are this way too. Some who look very glamorous turn out to have a great many thorns, which make a relationship hard going. On the other hand, the seemingly drab and colorless creature that is passed over at first glance may turn out to be a truly beautiful person. A lot of the time, I get so busy majoring on trying to improve the outside image, I forget the more important qualities that lie underneath and will bloom in the fullness of time and reflect the beauty of the Savior.

"Don't depend on things like fancy hairdos or gold jewelry or expensive clothes to make you look beautiful. Be beautiful in your heart by being gentle and quiet. This kind of beauty will last, and God considers it very special." (I Peter 3:3-4 CEV)

April 23: Foxes

Many people think of foxes as sly, but adaptable might be a better term for them. They can live in a wide variety of terrains, including America, Europe, and Asia (and the woods in our back yard). They are omnivorous, meaning they will eat anything that strikes their fancy—from chickens to candy bars. Farmers, as a rule, are very protective of their chickens, and I am very protective of my candy bars, so I suppose foxes sometimes have pretty slim pickings.

Oddly enough, the fox's diet may also include grapes. They can deprive growers of their juicy crop almost before they can wake up and smell the Welch's. In this country, we are accustomed to seeing grapes grown in arbors or on high wires strung between poles. I noticed in Switzerland they were grown quite close to the ground, and in ancient Palestine, it is thought they were probably grown around a supporting stick. Since these were also close to the ground, even baby foxes could nibble quietly away until the farmer saw that underneath the vines there was widespread destruction—and it was too late to do anything about it.

This has an unpleasant lesson for me; I'd rather not identify the little foxes that may be nibbling away in my own vineyard. Unfortunately, I have lots of foxes to choose from: self-indulgence, intolerance, self-pity (always the sneaky one!), touchiness, stubbornness, pride, poor priorities, self-will, petulance and, oh dear, I'm afraid many more. When I allow these foxes in my arbor, without putting up the gate of constant examination before the Lord, I may one day wake up to find that I am no longer "fit for the Master's use." May I remain so close to the vine of Christ that I am aware the moment a little fox touches me!

"Quick! Catch all the little foxes before they ruin the vineyard of your love, for the grapevines are all in blossom." (Song of Solomon 2:15 NLT)

April 24: Golden Oldies

I don't suppose anyone is really thrilled at the onset (or continuance) of old age. Florida, along with California and Arizona, are filled with people who are not only retired; they are just plain tired. Tired of serving God, tired of new adventures and experiences, and tired of life. They don't seem to contemplate anything deeper than their golf or shuffle board scores, and their final word on anything in the church is "Let the young folks do it. I've served my time." Well, to quote a well-known curmudgeon, "Bah-Humbug!"

It's interesting to me that no one in the Bible makes a statement like that. Both Moses and Caleb, for example, were going strong into their eighties, and they were valuable men who made strong contributions even in their old age.

Of course, I'm not advocating doing something to amaze and stun the world when you qualify as an "aged parent" as Charles Dickens expresses it. Although I can't leap over tall buildings at a single bound, that is no reason to fold my hands and rock my rolls. There is very little call for the high jump in Christian service anyway. As long as I can still breathe, God can use me (even in little ways!) if I am willing to be used.

"Never be lacking in zeal, but keep your spiritual fervor, serving the Lord." (Romans 12:11 NIV)

April 25: Mountain Sights

Mountain tops are usually associated with the high points of our lives: the peace in times of stress, the thrill of answered prayer, the joy of seeing someone begin their relationship with God. Unfortunately, however, there are mountaintop experiences that are not those of fulfillment and delight.

Some of the heights that we must cross are peaks of pain and sorrow, alps of disappointment and rejection, ranges of failure and despair. While we are crossing these mountains, we are only able to stumble onward, limping in self-pity and in an absence of understanding. But later, these same mountains may stand out in our mind as revealing God in a new way. The knowledge that we can fail, and still be loved and accepted is a great balm to the soul. The knowledge that He is with us in all places and circumstances is strength to the heart. The knowledge that He and He alone is our source of comfort is an incentive to set our hearts on things above (see Colossians 3:1).

Moreover, these experiences give us greater compassion for others on the mountaintops, and we are able to point them to the God of all comfort. A famous minister once said, "God does not comfort us to make us comfortable, but to make us comforters."

"Praise God, the Father of our Lord Jesus Christ! The Father is a merciful God, who always gives us comfort. He comforts us when we are in trouble, so that we can share that same comfort with others in trouble." (II Corinthians 1:3-4 CEV)

April 26: Body Language

I was in a new town, and knew nothing about the people, places or things...least of all the doctors. Or hospitals. Just before I went for the delivery of our fifth child, I learned that the doctor I had chosen was affiliated with a hospital of a different religion. I was already feeling lonely, and to this I now added belligerent. I stared scornfully at the hospital staff, resented the nurses, and generally made myself miserable.

Perhaps because the baby was six weeks early, or because they were expecting complications, I was given a very heavy sedation. Since, at the time, I was more or less a 98-pound weakling, it didn't take much to knock me out, and they had a hard time getting me back to the future, so to speak.

Three days later, I was still only semi-conscious when I heard soft footsteps come in my room. A cool hand was laid on my forehead, and a sweet low voice asked, "Are you feeling better today?" I knew instantly that she had asked in love, ignoring my attitude of dislike and self-pity. Tears spilled down my cheeks in repentance, washing away the ugliness of my heart. I had been armed against argument, and ready for rhetoric, but I could not close my heart against love.

"In this new life, it doesn't matter if you are a Jew or a Gentile, circumcised or uncircumcised, barbaric, uncivilized, slave, or free. Christ is all that matters, and he lives in all of us." (Colossians 3:10 NLT)

April 27: White/White

WINTER:

Snow falling gently, quietly—
covering the ugly dirt and rubble.

The white mounds and drifts sweetly rounding the angularity of life
bringing an exhilarating sense of freshness.
A temporary blanket of atonement
glistening and white and clean…

But underneath beauty, the hardness is unchanged.

SPRING:

Fuzzy halos of green and gold,
appear as silently as snow.

But this is change within,
responding to the sun—
and from the inner heart, there pulses life.

How wonderful that God would touch the winter of my heart
and give me life from love and light—
new life to serve the One who made the seasons.

April 28: The Scientific American

Our youngest daughter, Margaret, can make a dessert superb enough to make a strong man weep, but at the time of this story the more mundane aspects of cooking did not have her undivided attention.

The morning of her father's birthday, she suggested that since we had leftover creamed spinach, we could have Eggs Sardou for breakfast. As far as she was concerned, the "Sardou" part was not a mystery…but the egg part was a little vague. She asked me about it, so that she could get the proper gourmet approach. "You just poach them in this pan over boiling water," I explained. "And how do you know when they're done?" came the query. "Well, you just look." "Oh," was the disappointed response from someone who measured out cakes and crepes with careful precision. "Not as scientific as I thought."

Later this statement came back to me as I thought about life in general. Life is not scientific either, in spite of all attempts to make it so. Some times the scientific spirit can hinder us. Consider the beauty of the sunset, for example. Science can explain why the sun turns red, but that explanation does not help us appreciate the beauty of God's creation.

"All of you nations, clap your hands and shout joyful praises to God. The Lord Most High is fearsome, the ruler of all the earth." (Psalm 47:1-2 CEV)

April 29: Coming Home

Shakespeare wrote, "Uneasy is the head that wears the crown."

I'll bet if Shakespeare were living today, he would change the above quotation to: "Uneasy is the head whose teenagers are out at night." When our children first started this nocturnal prowling, we asked them to come and wake us up so we would know they were home in one piece (and at the designated hour).

As the years went by, and we got tireder, we hit upon the idea of setting an alarm clock ten minutes later than the proposed arrival. They then had that ten-minute leeway to get into the bedroom and push in the stem. If the stem was not touched, the alarm rang. When that happened, as the song goes, there was "trouble right here in River City."

I think all parents feel uneasy when their children are away from home. Some parents have to live with the knowledge that their child is in a far country, indeed. Some parents have to live with the knowledge that their child has not left home, but has strayed from God.

But God is still in the business of bringing back those who have strayed. Matthew 18:12 assures us, "If a shepherd has one hundred sheep, and one wanders away and is lost, what will he do? Won't he leave the ninety-nine others and go out into the hills to search for the lost one?" (NLT). So, we can take comfort that our Good Shepherd cares for our children even more than we do, and He loves them.

April 30: Stop, Look and Listen

Our present, presidential resident cat is named Micah (we had bred his mother and expected a major profit—but it turned out to be only a minor prophet). Like all cats, he is his own eccentric self, so he fits in well with his owners. Many cats will leap up in your lap if they feel the urge, but Micah, although well acquainted with lapdom, has never made such a leap in his life. He has the most cautious overture this side of burglary, and will only lie on your lap if you are on a bed, with a large approach area. First, one paw is tentatively extended toward the chest of the prone participant. Then, it is placed very lightly so that it may be removed without loss of face if danger threatens, war is declared, or someone breathes. Finally the other three feet are s-l-o-w-l-y moved to the landing pad, his stomach is then gently lowered and the purr box is activated.

I wonder if I show the same caution when approaching a delicate situation. Often, I am so sure of myself that when something goes wrong, I have the tendency to think, "Oh, yes, I have faced this before. I can fix it."

Joshua made a serious mistake when he eliminated the cautious approach that includes looking to the Lord in prayer (see Joshua 7), and I must not follow his example. He zoomed ahead thinking that because God had given him one victory, God would do it again. Well, of course, God could have done it again and again. But, Joshua (like me, I'm afraid), got to thinking that he didn't need to pray for directions: he assumed that what worked one time would just keep on working.

May I always remember to <u>pray</u> before I <u>act</u>!

"After leaving them, he [Jesus] went into the hills to pray." (Mark 6:46 NIV)

May 1: Slip—Not

When we lived in Detroit, our church group took a trip to Cedar Point, an amusement park in Ohio. One of the rides was a large cylinder that was reached by climbing a long flight of stairs. After entering, we were instructed to array ourselves around the inner wall, and we were told that when the cylinder revolved, we would be held in place by centrifugal force. Never having experienced centrifugal force, I was blissfully unaware of what was to come. I laughed as we started to turn. Faster and faster we went, and sure enough, we did seem to be pressed against the walls.

Suddenly, however, the floor dropped completely away, and I screamed, wondering how long it would be before we slid into the relentless, turning gears below. I remembered Edgar Allen Poe, and thought despairingly of "The Pit and the Pendulum," knowing it was only a matter of minutes before getting geared into eternity. I tried clinging tenaciously to the revolving wall by my fingernails, certain that, since the Velcro had lost its stickum, I would only be a memory when everyone else left to go home.

That was my subjective view. Later, when I found out I was still among the living, I was given the objective view. I had never moved an inch, because a force greater than I had held me in place.

Sometimes, I feel the bottom of my world has dropped away, too, and I feel I am slipping downwards. But objectively, my great God holds me, and I may rest even while revolving, for He will never disappoint me.

"The Lord is your protector, and he won't go to sleep or let you stumble." (Psalm 121:3 CEV)

May 2: Driven by Distraction

My husband and I had picked up our children from camp, and we were intending to make the road trip home together. Unfortunately, he had to fly home unexpectedly, so I was left with the task of driving homewards all by my lonesome (if you can call being in a car with five children lonesome). Our station wagon was filled to capacity with seven suitcases, five trunks, two golf bags, an antique piano bench that we had picked up at an auction, and, for some unknown reason, many helium balloons.

It takes about twelve hours to make the trip from Asheville to Tampa; it took us twelve hours, too. The only difference was my comfort factor: I don't like to drive for more than a few hours at a time. Thus, we only drove four hours a day, and in so doing, managed to stretch out our trip to three days. My schedule called for two hours of driving in the morning, a long lunch break, and then, two hours more in the afternoon. After that, we stopped at a motel with a pool for the children and a quiet, padded room for their mother.

I managed to make this trip a three-day seminar of misery because I was lazy and unwilling to discipline myself. In my insistence on immediate relief, I concentrated only on sinking into as many soft mattresses as I could.

I have forever been unwilling to put forth effort and patience to get a job finished. Instead, I put off tasks that could be completed to my satisfaction and pleasure with just a little perseverance. My father used to prod me, by saying, "Finish the job!" And, naturally, the more I heard this as a child and teenager, the more I hated it. Actually, as fathers often are, he was right.

In the years since, I have learned that my father was trying to instill in me the qualities (found in the book of Hebrews, among other places) of faith and patience. These are not natural reactions (at least not for me!), but both can be supernatural reactions when I am looking to the Lord for the fruit of His Spirit.

"But when the Holy Spirit controls our lives, he will produce this kind of fruit in us: love, joy, peace, patience, kindness, generosity, fidelity, tolerance, and self control...." (Galatians 5:22-23a NLT)

May 3: Ants in the Plants

Each area of the United States has it own particular flora and fauna, but ants seem to be ubiquitous. It's true that the Bible commends them for their industry, but, to my mind, they go overboard on the busy business.

I had been to a seminar north of our home in Florida, and since I had originally been unable to find a parking place close to my room, I went out to move my car after everyone was settled. It was very dark, but I managed to park by the rim of grass circling the lot. I got out, hitting the automatic door locks. Then, I remembered I had left my notebook inside the car. Since everything I know, think, or need to be reminded of is in that notebook, I didn't want to leave it outside in the car, so I fumbled in the dark for my keys.

All of this did not take long (I'm a fast fumbler), but it was long enough for me to feel a burning sensation on my legs. I opened the door, turned on the lights in the car, and looked down to see my lower limbs covered with fire ants, biting and carrying on for all they were worth. I brushed and jumped and scraped and hollered: fire ant bites are really painful! It was not a great way to start a seminar.

I was in the dark, and I stepped in the wrong place. When I am out of fellowship with God and not walking in His light, I am apt to find trouble waiting that will sting and cause anguish that could have been avoided.

"This is the message we have heard from him and declare to you: God is light; in him there is no darkness at all. If we claim to have fellowship with him yet walk in the darkness, we lie and do not live by the truth. (I John 1:5-6 NIV)

May 4: A Listening Heart

Someone I love once told me that I have a listening heart, and it was one of the dearest things I ever heard. One night, as I was lying in bed trying to overcome jet-lag from a recent trip by will power and won't power (as in "I won't let all this travel get to me…"), this statement of a listening heart came back to me. I thought, "I'm glad I have a listening heart for people, but do I have a listening heart for God? Do I really listen to God with all my attention? Or am I distracted and uncaring when He is speaking to me?"

If I love God, I should be focused on Him. A listening heart involves action; it is not only soaking up information. If I did this, I would quickly become a swollen balloon that is either so proud of itself that it pops with pride, or a Dead Sea with no outlet that becomes salty and useless, or, even, a theological fountain that spouts endless details that evaporate without satisfying the one who is thirsty.

I saw a sign in a local business the other day that pretty well sums this up: "People don't care how much you know, until they know you care." The writer to the Hebrews reminds us: "Through Jesus therefore, let us continually offer a sacrifice of praise—the fruit of lips that confess His name. And do not forget to do good and to share with others, for with such sacrifices God is well pleased" (Hebrews 13:15-16 NIV). Plan to put into action the loving concern you have received from listening to God; don't let it just get filed under good intentions.

"Words can bring death or life! Talk toomuch, and you will eat everything you say." (Proverbs 18:21 CEV)

May 5: It's Hard to Look Impressive (When You're Not!)

I do a lot of speaking—here, there, and everywhere, and in all kinds of settings: seminars, church retreats, conferences, and at Christian Women's Clubs. But it's strange; no matter where I go or what I wear, if no one in the group knows me, someone will inevitably come up and blurt out, "You don't look like a speaker!" It's a little discouraging, and I have tried various methods of trying to look like a speaker—even going so far as to consider pasting an "S" on my forehead. But I was afraid people would think it stood for "Stupid" or worse, "Senile," so I abandoned the idea.

I've heard many women say they want to be beautiful, but I haven't heard many bemoaning the fact that they don't look impressive. I'm not actually interested in impressing anyone with my impressiveness, but I really could use a little of whatever it is that makes others think—"Boy! I can't wait to hear what she has to say!"

Perhaps it will come with old age, when I have to totter in and be helped up to the platform (which will have to be raised so I can see over the podium). I must confess I have not been patient about this…but I was helped greatly when I saw a sign the other day that said, "Have patience, it takes time for grass to turn into milk." So, I am asking the Lord to watch my green, and make it milk in His time. Meanwhile, I am practicing on just standing straight, if not tall, for Him.

"My times are in your hands." (Psalm 31:15 NIV)

May 6: Fireside Chat

Some years ago, my husband took me along on a business trip to Oregon. With the gift of a free day, we decided to go skiing, although, perhaps "skiing" is too optimistic a word because I was not in very good shape (I had a shape, just not a very good one). Despite this, we rushed in and rented boots and skis. My boots were very, very, very heavy—much more so than I had remembered from several years earlier (when I was fitter and several years younger). By the time I clumped over to the bunny hill (with four year old skiers zooming by me), I was totally exhausted. So I immediately gave up and staggered back to our hut, without even putting the skis on my booted feet.

I'm sad to say that I have been known to stagger along like this in my spiritual life, ready to give up at any moment. Thankfully, I also know that when I am willing to walk, Jesus says He will help me with what I must carry. Why do I sit inside, when I should be skiing?

"Then Jesus said, 'Come to me, all of you who are weary and carry heavy burdens, and I will give you rest. Take my yoke upon you. Let me teach you, because I am humble and gentle, and you will find rest for your souls. For my yoke fits perfectly, and the burden I give you is light.'" (Matthew 11:28-30 NLT)

May 7: In Nonessentials, Charity

Some people are becoming strangely militant about food and drink: for example, bread (white or wheat), coffee and tea (regular or decaffeinated), our choice of cholesterol (butter or margarine), and meat (red, white, or blue). We seem to have turned into a nation of nutrition nitpickers, patrolling each other's eating habits to search out and destroy any that might be out of step with our (correct, of course) ideas.

Unfortunately, this attitude has a tendency to leak over into other areas, too. I have seen people get positively glassy-eyed over one particular version of the Bible, clutching it tightly lest someone venture a verse from a different translation. Stained glass seems to be essential for some worshippers, while others pooh-pooh this as so much frippery. Congregations have come to blows over the color of choir robes, and churches have split over the spending of their money.

Should we not recall that we are one Body but with many parts? It's true we are at war, but it shouldn't be with each other! Paul reminds us in his letter to the Ephesians, "We are not fighting against humans. We are fighting against forces and authorities and against rulers of darkness and powers of the spiritual world" (Ephesians 6:12 CEV). May I remember to concentrate on the union I have with others in the essentials and not demand uniformity in anything else.

May 8: The Greatest of All….

"James and John, the sons of Zebedee, came up to Jesus and asked, 'Teacher, will you do us a favor?' Jesus asked them what they wanted, and they answered, 'When you come into your glory, please let one of us sit at your right side and the other at your left.' Jesus told them, 'You don't really know what you're asking! Are you able to drink from the cup that I must soon drink from or be baptized as I must be baptized?' 'Yes, we are!' James and John answered." (Mark 10:35-39a CEV)

"When the ten other disciples heard this, they were angry with James and John. But Jesus called the disciples together and said: 'You know that those foreigners who call themselves kings like to order their people around. And their great leaders have full power over the people they rule. But don't act like them. If you want to be great, you must be the servant of all the others. And if you want to be first, you must be everyone's slave. The Son of Man did not come to be a slave master, but a slave who will give his life to rescue many people.'" (Mark 10:41-44 CEV)

Some friends of ours baby sit occasionally for their grandchildren. One day, the little three-year-old discovered that her granddaddy was at work in the garage. Earlier, he had told her that she was not allowed to join him in his work area because she might get hurt. He looked up in surprise to see her march inside. "I told you that you cannot come in," he reminded. "Yes, I can," she announced. "I can do all things through Christ."

James and John were full of self-confidence, too, when they assured the Lord that they could drink from his cup of suffering. They were willing to suffer with Jesus because they imagined that joining with him would help them achieve their goal of greatness.

Our friend's toddler was in good company with James and John; she also tried to use a "spiritual method" to get what she wanted! May I remember instead to be a "servant of all,"—someone who changes focus away myself to the needs of others.

May 9: Family Business

A sign advertising a business not only struck me as funny, it also led to further amused speculation. The business was called "Family Pest Control." As I have a rather skewed sense of humor, I wondered how they proposed to control the pests that are found in families. Keep them on a long leash? Lock them up in boxes, and let them out only on holidays? Farm them out to distant relatives until they reform? I could go on, but with mercy aforethought, I shall not.

Actually, nearly every family has pests of one kind or another. I have heard them called the "irregular people" of our lives. There is no easy answer for how deal with them, but if we remind ourselves that God loved them enough to die for them, we can concentrate on controlling ourselves (rather than controlling the "pest"!)

In Romans 15:7 we are told, "Honor God by accepting each other, as Christ accepted you" (CEV). Unconditional love is not easy; but God never said it would be. After all, look at how He loves even me!

Prayer: Dear God, help me to love those that are difficult for me to love. Help me to pray for them, and may I continually be reminded of your deep love for them.

"Don't be hateful and insult people just because they are hateful and insult you. Instead, treat everyone with kindness. You are God's chosen ones, and he will bless you." (I Peter 2:9-10 CEV)

May 10: A Mother of Love

When Bill and I got married, I bet my mother-in-law went into her closet to pray for a week, maybe two. Mother Edith and I were completely different in nearly every way possible. She was from the country; I was from the city. She ate things like black-eyed peas and sausage; I ate things like artichokes and escargots. She was patient; I was impatient. She loved everybody she saw; I loved, well, actually, myself. Doesn't sound too promising, does it? But the amazing thing is, she loved me and accepted me as I was. Mother Edith never did anything that the world would say was important; she just loved God and loved people. You won't find a statue to her, but there's one in my heart. Her love drew me closer to the Savior.

When she got cancer, and it grew worse, she went to the hospital to die and step into God's presence. He didn't take her right away. So for nearly four months, she lay there, not being able to do anything. At least, that's what she thought.

I was in her room one day, and asked her if she had ever heard about the museum in heaven, a concept from Edith Schaffer's book entitled *Affliction*. In heaven, she says, there is a great museum, and in it are all the pictures of people who suffer. Some suffer a little, and some suffer a great amount; but they are all there, for God watches over them. Satan strolls in there once in a while, and, often, he will point to one and say, "Look at that one! She doesn't really love you; she's not doing a thing!" And God replies "Oh, yes. We're in a spiritual battle up here…and every time someone trusts in me in the midst of suffering, that's a victory for Jesus." After I told her this story, Mother Edith smiled.

The last time I saw her, she said weakly, "Still trusting—a victory for Jesus." Then she left us and went to see her Savior face to face.

"And I heard a loud voice from the throne saying, 'Now the dwelling of God is with men, and he will live with them. They will be his people, and God himself will be with them and be their God. He will wipe every tear from their eyes. There will be no more death or mourning or crying or pain, for the old order of things has passed away.'" (Revelation 21:3-4 NIV)

May 11: Listen Up

I was in the beauty parlor getting my hair cut, and listening (albeit reluctantly) to the music coming over the loudspeaker. I had considered wearing my earmuffs, but felt it would be a problem getting the scissors around that metal band at the top. It was a morning talk show that seemed to be mostly screams and hyena-like laughs, with two disc jockeys vying for the primary sound waves. They had some celebrity with them on this particular morning. She was in town to promote a cause, and I was only listening with half an ear (taking into account the volume, this was quite a feat!).

Suddenly, I heard one of the DJs ask the movie star why she was involved with this particular illness (which happened to be Alzheimer's), and she said quietly that her mother was very badly afflicted. There was a little silence and then the disc jockey said, "Yeah, I can identify with you. My mom has it, too. It's really hard, isn't it?"

You could have knocked me over with a bobby pin. I so often think of people like this as being deaf and dumb to the problems the rest of the world faces. I forget that there are hurting hearts and those who are poor and needy in spirit in every corner of the world. Even people who put on professional faces of laughter can sometimes be hiding broken dreams and broken hearts. I need to look around and realize that I should be kind, showing mercy and compassion in thought and deed to all. The neediest hearts are sometimes in the most unexpected places.

"This is what the Lord Almighty says: Judge fairly and honestly, and show mercy and kindness to one another. Do not oppress widows, orphans, foreigners, and poor people. And do not make evil plans to harm each other." (Zechariah 7:9-10 NLT)

May 12: I See What I See

Evidently my mother's parents had a sentimental fondness for crabapple blossoms, for each May they would make a special trip to the woods to look for the first full branch of flowering beauty. My mother was born in 1888, and as soon as she was able to totter along, she became part of this tradition. One year, she and my grandfather decided to surprise my grandmother by bringing her a branch they had found themselves, and it, thus, became a traditional twosome of father and daughter each year.

I became a part of this special father-daughter time when I reached the age of five or so. I remember many years of going through the woods (not so nearby now!) and trying to be the first to spot the pink blossoms among the new green of the trees. Part of the ceremony was the fun of taking it home to a dutifully surprised mother.

We found the blossoms because that was what we were looking for. People (and animals) usually do find what they look for: the hummingbirds find flowers, and vultures find carrion. As I examine my plans for the day and think about these two birds, I apply the lesson to my life. Am I looking for the joy of Christian fellowship? Or do I seek questionable things that should be passed by? The choices I make day by day not only influence others, they also mold my own life.

"Finally, brothers, whatever is true, whatever is noble, whatever is right, whatever is pure, whatever is lovely, whatever is admirable—if anything is excellent or praiseworthy—think about such things." (Philippians 4:6 NIV)

May 13: Standing Firm

In *Gulliver's Travels*, one of the stories tells of a court that was divided because they could not decide on the correct heel height. One group favored high heels, and the other favored low. The animosity among them was so great, they would neither eat nor drink nor talk with one another. Their silly prince tried to please both sides by adopting a high heel for one foot and a low one for the other. He was what, in my family, we used to call a "mugwump," meaning someone who was sitting on a fence, not wanting to take a stand either way.

In Ephesians 4:14 it says, "We must stop acting like children. We must not let deceitful people trick us by their false teachings, which are like winds that toss us around from place to place" (CEV). Actually, I AM often influenced by other's opinions, especially if I don't know much about a subject. I know nothing about astronomy, for instance, and could probably be convinced that the moon is made of cheese if an expert chose to convince me.

I want to avoid wobbling about on mismatched heels, to be led hither and yon by one group or another. Instead, I want to "...stay deeply rooted and firm in [my] faith" (Colossians 1:23a CEV).

May 14: Hope Chest

Back when the earth was without form and void (remembered by those 60 and older), young girls had hope chests. It didn't matter whether they had any hope or not, they still had hope chests. The ones I was familiar with were huge bulky chests made of cedar to keep the moths at bay, and took up a lot of room.

The idea was that, at a very tender age, girls would be taught to sew, embroider, crochet, and knit. Then the fruits of her labor would be placed lovingly in the aforementioned chest to be dreamed over until her hope was fulfilled and the prince came to carry her off to the castle where she would stun the peasants with her handiwork. I never got the hang of this very well: I was too impatient to learn anything, especially if a needle was involved. My mother saw to it that I did have a hope chest, however, and she did her best to fill it up for me. I discovered after I got married that this consisted mostly of doilies, linen towels, and napkins, none of which got a big play in our castle, OR stunned any peasants (though I did see some pheasants in a zoo once).

However, There is a different kind of hope chest that is constantly being used. It is our hope stored in heaven, and the passage below from Colossians tells us that our faith and love come from that hope (and this hope is a sure hope with an iron-clad guarantee from the Manufacturer!). So, the next time I use my faith or love, I want to remember to thank the King who keeps our hope chest. It is His Person and character that have made provision certain for the church universal—the bride of Christ.

"This same Good News that came to you is going out all over the world, changing lives everywhere, just as it changed yours that very first day you heard and understood the truth about God's great kindness to sinners." (Colossians 1:6 CEV)

May 15: Special Delivery

"Thy word is a lamp unto my feet, and a light unto my path" (Psalm 119:105 KJV). Children in Pioneer Clubs across the land chorus this little verse each week because it is their motto. They say the words easily, but perhaps they have trouble understanding the wonder of its application to their lives. In fact, I venture to say that this is also true of us even as adults: I often rattle off verses without taking the time to delve into their meanings.

Many years ago when I was in London on a college tour, I struck up an acquaintance with an elderly gentleman who was also enjoying afternoon tea in the lobby of my hotel. He had had an interesting life, and in the course of the conversation, pulled a tattered old letter from his breast pocket. Carefully he unfolded it, and brushing the crumbs from his moustache, he read me the contents. It was from one of Queen Mary's ladies-in-waiting, and in it she thanked him on behalf of the Queen for an occasion when he had performed a heroic deed while in her Royal Guards. He leaned reminiscently over the letter to make sure I was getting the full import of this. "She signed it herself, she did," he murmured reverently, "and I'll always treasure it."

We have a letter we should treasure even more because it is God's letter to us. It is not only signed by him, but also written by him. Do I treasure it and read it as a personal letter from the one who is not only the King of Kings, but also our Savior and Lord? Do I spend time reading and studying it? Do I apply its truths to my everyday life? Do I share its contents with evident enjoyment? Do I prove my love for the Lord by obeying His commands to love each person He created? Thank the Lord that, unlike the letter from the Queen, His word will never become old and tattered: like dew to our souls, it is new every morning.

May 16: Night Flight

It was late at night and we were hurtling over the plains of New Mexico (well, perhaps droning over the plains might be more accurate). Our cigar-shaped cylinder held two pilots and ten passengers on slippery seats that lined an aisle meant for the seven dwarfs, but not Snow White. Because there were no arm rests, I had to clutch my kneecaps when we bounced; and because there was no parachute, all I could do was hope we landed safely.

There was no sign of life on the dark planet below, and the only light in the sky was the intermittent weak blink on the end of the wing. It was like the pulse of someone who wasn't going to make it. With the roar of motors, and the imprisonment of our seat belt, we were held incommunicado as effectively as though we were all in separate planes. I wondered if the blackness and the isolation held some of the elements of hell.

How wonderful that God promises that His children will live in a place He is preparing for them, where there is no darkness because God Himself will be our light! May we also remember to show God's love to those who are walking in darkness and pray that their eyes will be opened to see what Christ has done for them.

"Abraham said 'Moses and the prophets had warned them. Your brothers can read their writings anytime they want to.' The rich man replied, 'No, Father Abraham! But if someone is sent to them from the dead, then they will turn from their sins.' But Abraham said, 'If they won't listen to Moses and the prophets, they won't listen even if someone rises from the dead.'" (Luke 16:29-31 NLT)

"We know that the same God who raised our Lord Jesus will also raise us with Jesus and present us to himself along with you. All of these things are for your benefit. And as God's grace brings more and more people to Christ, there will be great thanksgiving, and God will receive more and more glory."(II Corinthians 4:14-16 NLT)

May 17: Open Doors

When I visited Germany a few years after WWII, there was still much rubble left from the Allied bombing. In some places, they had not begun rebuilding yet. This was forcibly brought home to me when I stayed at a small hotel near a ruined area. I was on the fourth floor of the hotel, and going down the hall, I found a closed door. Forgetting that curiosity killed the cat, I opened it, expecting to find stairs or perhaps another section of the hotel—but the door opened onto empty space (four-floors-high-empty space). If I had been going faster (unlikely in my case, of course), I would have catapulted onto a pile of bricks, and that would have been the end of this cat.

Another door incident occurred while I was on a speaking itinerary. I had arrived late at night at the home of my hostess and I hadn't really looked around for anything except my bed. Getting up in the middle of the night to find the bathroom (and thinking it was a good thing I wasn't at that hotel in Germany), I found a closed door and cautiously turned the knob. The door was locked! I waited patiently (well fairly patiently) and then knocked. Suddenly, in the dim light, I noticed another door around a corner. I realized that the light was coming from the bathroom. I had been knocking on the door of someone who was, thankfully, a heavy sleeper, and who had (also, thankfully) locked the door.

Unlike these doors, God's doors do not open onto empty space, and we may enter with full confidence. If the door in front is closed, God will show you another in His own time.

"The Lord will always guide you...." (Isaiah 58:11a CEV)

May 18: One-Way Signs

"As for God, his way is perfect; the word of the Lord is flawless. He is a shield for all who take refuge in him." (II Samuel 22:31 NIV)

It was the era of the hippies, and the car next to us was packed full of them…beards and hair flowing in the breeze. It was dark, and we were on our way home from church. I could see them plainly in the streetlights, but I couldn't hear what they were saying because our air conditioner was on. "Look! They must be Christians!" I announced to the children, and we watched the small group gesticulating wildly and pointing at us. This was the era of the "One Way" signal among Christian believers, and so, we pointed upward and grinned broadly, at which they all laughed delightedly.

We had to turn off just then, so we left them behind, and talked about the excitement of a chance encounter with such an unlikely group of saints. When we got home, we found that one of our headlights was out. They had been pointing and waving to let us know. We felt very foolish at misunderstanding their attempts to communicate!

Sometimes, I misunderstand God; it's especially easy to feel that God doesn't care about me when I am going through difficult circumstances. But God is and has always been a God of love. His love didn't start suddenly in the New Testament. It is all through the Old Testament too.

I Chronicles 16:34 reminds us of His loving care: "Give thanks to the Lord, for he is good; his love endures forever" (NIV). Each day, may I grow to understand more fully who God is.

May 19: A Near Glimpse of Eternity

Once in a while, when our children were small, we would throw caution to the wind and take them out to dinner. Usually, this would mean a hamburger even if we had thought of dining at the Waldorf Astoria (which we never did). When our daughter Virginia was about five, we made one of these sorties into the adult world of gourmet cuisine, and she, being true to all childhood tenets, ordered one of the aforementioned hamburgers.

The hamburger was evidently a wee bit gristly (which is hard to believe considering the price we had to pay for it), and she made heavy work of it. When we walked out to the parking lot she was still chewing. We urged her to swallow. She chewed some more. We begged her to swallow. She rolled her eyes and chewed some more. She chewed all the way home where upon it was forcibly removed. It was a little gray rubbery wad that would no doubt have lasted from here to eternity if it had remained in her mouth.

Not really, of course, for only God and the things belonging to Him are eternal. In fact, as C.S. Lewis said, "All things that are not eternal are eternally out of date." So we are blessed beyond measure that our God is eternal, that His kingdom and domain are eternal. Daniel 4:3 says, "His miracles are mighty and marvelous. He will rule forever and his kingdom will never end" (CEV). The things of this earth are only temporal—may I instead focus on what only God can give.

May 20: Packin' It In

"Therefore, since we are surrounded by such a huge crowd of witnesses to the life of faith, let us strip off every weight that slows us down, especially the sin that so easily hinders our progress. And let us run with endurance the race that God has set before us." (Hebrews 12:1 NLT)

When I pack to go on a trip, I know I take excess baggage. I cram in everything I can, just in case. Somehow, I seem to have a subconscious idea that I will be stranded in the dark of Outer Mongolia without a store in sight. So, I laboriously squeeze in a hot water bottle, extension cord, light bulb, tea, lemons, and all manner of really unnecessary stuff. This results in a great deal of huffing and puffing on the part of anyone who lifts aforesaid luggage, who have, no doubt, snapped backs as well as snapped tempers.

On my spiritual journey however, I am exhorted to forget all these hindrances to progress. I am in a race, as the author of Hebrews reminds us, and I would look pretty silly trying to run with a couple of suitcases bumping along (even if I could lift them). Yet isn't that what I try to do sometimes? I carry all manner of *impedimenta* that slows me down, and then I wonder why I become so discouraged and tired.

Whenever I think about the excess weight I may be carrying, such as little sins or habits that have begun to take up my thought life, I try to remember, "little sins, like little habits, soon will multiply like rabbits!" I need to be very careful how I pack the corridors of my mind, or I might find it is a weight too heavy to cast off!

May 21: Open Window

"Before they call I will answer; while they are still speaking I will hear." (Isaiah 65:24 NIV)

Our first three children were all born thirteen months apart, and life in those days was lived on the ragged edge, you might say. It was almost like having triplets, except that some could escape faster than others. They all slept in the same room, so the noise could be contained and the possibility of destruction limited.

One night, after everyone had been kissed and watered for the last time, and we thought sleep was not far away, there came a tremendous crash. Bill and I raced into their room and found only one child. The other two were lying outside amidst shards of broken glass and screaming their heads off. Later we found out they had crawled up on the high jalousie window and leaned so hard that the panes fell out. The children fell on top of the glass, with the bottom child having the opportunity to contact the most glass.

I ran to the phone, prepared to call my mother and ask for a ride to the hospital. As I picked up the receiver, my mother walked in the front door. Living only a block away, she had come over to tell us to look at the sunset.

To me, this is a beautiful illustration of what God does for every one of us. The founder of Stonecroft Ministries used to say that Isaiah 65:24 was "God's phone number;" how comforting it is to know that the God who holds the world is near to those who are in need!

Prayer: Thank you God, for loving us and hearing us.

May 22: An Old Injury

When I was about seven, my parents sent me to a camp in the Adirondacks. It must have been the world's smallest, as there were only five other people, and two of them were sons of the owner. The camp consisted of three cabins on Lake Saranac. Since my parents wanted me to be away from the Pittsburgh smog for a month, it seemed a good solution. There was no real schedule of course, as we mostly just ate, slept, and swam, but I had a wonderful time.

The one exception was the day I was roughhousing with the two sons who were about 18 and 20 (and who seemed about 18 and 20 feet tall). They were throwing me back and forth like a basketball (which I closely resembled), and then, one of them dropped me and I skittered across the wood floor and ended up against a dresser. It hurt, but nothing was broken, and life went on. The injury was forgotten, and I returned home tanner and rounder than ever.

Many years later, when I began to develop arthritis, it was determined that one of the places where it developed was that old injury. Old injuries have a way of cropping up, don't they? And, they're not all physical. Sometimes, words that were spoken to hurt and wound loom up as fresh and new as if they were just hatched. And if we brood on them, they will become even bigger! This little trip down Memory Lane is not one we are meant to take.

It has been wisely said, "Write injuries in sand, benefits in marble." I must determine to forgive injuries (both old and new) as completely as I have been forgiven; and I must dwell not on the extent of my hurt, but on the extent of God's love and mercy in forgiving me.

"You must make allowance for each other's faults and forgive the person who offends you. Remember, the Lord forgave you, so you must forgive others." (Colossians 3:13 NLT)

May 23: Flying High

My brother, Hugh, was quite a character (he fit in well with the rest of the family). He was also extremely cocky and self confident, sure he knew everything worth knowing. When he was in his teens he was asked one day if he knew where the encyclopedia was. "No," he said. "What do you want to know?" He was a dear brother, and grew to be a generous and thoughtful man, even if he was a little smart alecky when he was younger!

This quality actually fitted him admirably as a fighter pilot, and he flew a P51 fighter plane in Italy during World War II. He dressed for the part with goggles, scarf, and riding crop (no, I don't know why the riding crop—perhaps he was imitating Rommel). One morning, he and his squadron leader were returning from a mission when the leader radioed from around the side of a mountain that a German convoy was beneath him. He was already too far past to strafe, so he told Hugh to watch for them. Hugh flew close to the mountainside, and got ready to fire as soon as he spotted the convoy. As soon as he saw them, he fired his guns, but they didn't work. They had been working, so he couldn't understand the problem. He squeezed harder and jiggled switches, but nothing happened. By this time, he was on top of the convoy and looked down. The trucks were filled with American POWs.

Hugh did not come to know the Lord until several years later, but that day he saw God's power and protection in action…I think it was then he began to realize that life is not all smart answers and quick reactions.

There is a sequel to this story of God's sovereignty—one that thrills me each time I think of it. Some 55 years later, I met a woman at a leadership conference who had read of this incident in a magazine. With tears in her eyes, she told me that her husband had been a prisoner in Italy at that time, and was transferred across the Alps from one camp to another. She feels that even though she is not sure of the date, it was possible that God used His power in stopping Hugh's guns to save the life of her husband. So, remember with joy and gladness, that no matter what our circumstances, "My life is in [God's] hands…" (Psalm 31:15a CEV).

"You saw what I did in Egypt, and you know how I brought you here to me, just as a mighty eagle carries its young." (Exodus 19:4 CEV)

May 24: Sight and Insight

"I do regret each day that passes," comments a wag, "that insight isn't helped by glasses." The truth is, I think I see well, but, most of the time, I do not. For example, when I see someone homeless, I might think, "Here is a candidate for heaven because he has so many needs." Conversely, when we meet someone in furs and jewels, I might decide it is no use witnessing to her because she doesn't have any needs.

I could be wrong on both counts. The homeless person could be someone whose heart is hard and bitter, and the socialite might realize that her position and wealth have not provided the peace and joy she seeks. John 7:24 reminds us, "Stop judging by mere appearances, and make a right judgment" (NIV).

Another mistake I sometimes make is to cross people off when a certain stage is reached in their life. I may feel they are too far gone when they fall into blatant sin; but until that soul steps into eternity, it is not too late for God.

Even though I majored in weekends at college, I'm glad God didn't give up on me when I was 22 and a major flibbertigibbet. I'm glad He didn't give up on me when I was 30 but not much better. I did not come to know God in a personal way until I was 31. If He had crossed me off His list as being hopeless, I would, in reality, have BEEN hopeless, and my life would have remained without purpose or significance.

Since God does not give up on us, we must not give up praying for others! Their salvation may be just ahead, and imagine how you would feel if you had not continued to pray for them! Nothing is too hard for God!

"So God said to him, 'Since you have asked for this and not for long life or wealth for yourself, nor have asked for the death of your enemies but for discernment in administering justice, I will do what you have asked.'" (I Kings 3:11-12a NIV)

May 25: The Only Proper Dress

"He made the church holy by the power of his word, and he made it pure by washing it with water. Christ did this, so that he would have a glorious and holy church, without faults or spots or wrinkles or any other flaws." (Ephesians 5:26-27 CEV)

My husband looks with an understandably jaundiced eye toward any ideas I put forth about the proper dress for various occasions. The reason for this is found in two events that remain fresh in my mind, although they happened about ten years after we were married.

The first was a Garden Party. The words "Garden Party" conveyed to my mind a very dressy affair—the more so as the hostess had borrowed some silver platters from me. We arrived dressed to the hilt—and found everyone else in shorts for a backyard barbecue. We hurriedly explained we had just stopped by, as we were on our way somewhere else (bed).

The second was an invitation that we received to a beach party. We were staying at the beach at the time, and when Bill came back from town and started to change into his suit, I told him that a suit would be unnecessary because this was a beach party, and I was planning on wearing shorts. Reluctantly, he let himself be persuaded, and we arrived at the house to find that not only was it semi-formal, but that there was a receiving line! (I now have permanent instructions to inquire as to the exact dress expected).

The one time I won't have to worry about what to wear is when I arrive in heaven. God has found me worthy (no matter what I wear!) because He looks at me through the righteousness of Christ. We will all be without spots, wrinkles or flaws, not because of anything we have done, but because of the love and mercy of God and the worthiness of Jesus Christ the Lord. He will clothe us in His righteousness, and it will be the perfect clothing for an eternity of worship.

May 26: S.O.S.

After living in the south for many years, we were excited to be transferred to Pittsburgh, way up in the snowy north. Our new house was on a hilly street, and a heavy snow fell while we were inside helping the movers unload. Later, when we were about to leave, I saw that the driveway looked like a downhill ski jump. I doubted that I would be able to get to the top of our street even after a zooming start, and so decided to go the other direction: down the hill. I thought we could make it up the other side if we gathered enough momentum going down the hill first. I was mistaken. We sat locked in snowy splendor halfway up the hill, not knowing one person within 1000 miles (which happened to be the distance back to Florida). Of course, my husband was in the same city, but I had no idea where. As this was BCP (Before Cell Phones), there was no way to contact him. I was wondering if there would be six stiff bodies in a car so covered with snow he wouldn't recognize it when he came home from work. That is, of course, if he actually could make it home from work.

Our sons were then about 11 and 12 and weighed a probable combined total of 130 pounds. We were in a station wagon that weighed several tons, but I didn't stop to put those two facts together. I told the boys to hop out and push us up the hill. They pushed valiantly, but we only slipped alarmingly sideways as I pressed the accelerator. I had visions of sitting there until the spring thaw. Suddenly, a big truck pulled up beside us. "We'll put down some ashes to get you up the hill!" they yelled. Our daughter, Lissa, said quietly, "Good. I was praying for someone to rescue us." I was astounded. Prayer had been the furthest thing from my mind…which shows you how distracted mothers can be sometimes. And also shows you that God's ear is open to the call of His children. This particular child of His grew up to be a beautiful mother with children of her own. She prays with joy and expectancy…even when it snows.

"For he is the living God, and he will endure forever. His kingdom will never be destroyed, and his rule will never end. He rescues and saves his people…." (Daniel 6:26b-27a NLT)

May 27: Jaws

I have always been extremely, in fact inordinately fond of chewing gum. One year, my parents decided to cure me with an overdose and strung our Christmas tree with hundreds of sticks of gum. It was an awe-inspiring sight for someone who lived and breathed for something to keep her jaws moving. My brothers challenged me to see how many sticks I could get into my mouth at once—this was a challenge I promptly accepted. I was able to cram in sixty-eight, as I recall, and although I couldn't chew or move my jaws in any direction at that point, I did manage a triumphant snort.

Thus the attempt at a cure failed, and I continued to masticate anything within reach. At night, I would "load up" and chew until I fell asleep, at which point the gum would fall out and tangle in my hair. Everyone was initially patient, but, finally, I was forbidden to chew in bed. I immediately disregarded this, and smuggled in a hefty supply for use that night. The next morning, I found a large wad stuck in my bangs…so I took scissors and cut off the offending side of my hair.

What a relief! I imagined that, since the gum was no longer clinging obstreperously to my hair, my disobedience was well hidden. I was amazed to find that the entire household immediately knew of my little escapade, and I had to endure weeks with a most unusual haircut.

I finally learned the lesson taught in Numbers 32:23, "…you may be sure that your sin will find you out" (NIV). In fact it was such a vivid lesson, I have never chewed gum in bed since. Unfortunately, there have been many other sins that I have tried to hide and rationalize, but God is faithful to shine His light on them and convict me of walking in the dark.

"For it is shameful even to mention what the disobedient do in secret. But everything exposed by the light becomes visible, for it is light that makes everything visible." (Ephesians 5:12-14a NIV)

May 28: Be prepared

When our son Will was first married, he came home from Chicago for Christmas and the wedding of our daughter Lissa. His wife was in line for the washroom at the back of the plane with a toothbrush in her hand, and the man behind her (who just HAD to be a dentist!) said appreciatively, "I'm so glad to see you brush your teeth after every meal." "Oh no," she said. "I'm just going in to polish up my diamond ring!"

It was the hilarious start of a wonderful week for all of us, but when the smoke cleared, and we were putting Will and Marsha back on the plane, I noticed he didn't have an overcoat. Being a mother, I immediately pointed this out. Breezily, Will informed me his in-laws were picking them up at the airport and with only the need for a quick dash to the car, there was no need for an overcoat.

To those not in love, Chicago presents a fearsome picture in the winter. O'Hare was socked in when they flew over there, and they had to go on to Minneapolis, where they stayed for three days…without an overcoat. I said what every family member loves to hear: "You should have listened to your mother!"

I may not be flying anywhere, but I, too, must prepare for the winters in my life. There are cold bleak days that come without warning, and if I have not shielded the walls of my heart with Scripture, I will be open to the bone chilling winds of dissension, doubt, and dread. So, I'm going to follow my own advice and insulate myself before I get caught in the cold.

"You lazy people can learn by watching an anthill. Ants don't have leaders, but they store up food during harvest season." (Proverbs 6:6-8 CEV)

May 29: Balloons

Since we live "in the country," and what some refer to as the outer edge of civilization, some people feel they have to pack a lunch when they come to visit. Thus, we very seldom have company. When friends are brave enough to venture out this way, we have found the best way to steer them is to put helium balloons on the mailbox (which does tend to distract the mailman).

Our last balloon showing was for a wedding day brunch, and the mailbox looked very festive when Bill put them up. After the party, he brought them in the house to recover from all that fresh air. They were all tied together, so he left them that way, and 2 of the 3 stayed up, but the third was definitely not well. It started getting smaller and, then, sagged gradually to the floor. Nothing is sadder than a drooping balloon! By the end of the day, it had fallen so low that it pulled the others down with it.

Did you know that we were meant to defy gravity and be so filled with the Spirit that we, in a manner of speaking, float? When I reject another person, however, not only do I sink, I may also drag others down with me.

Prayer: Help me to walk in Your light, and help me to always see others (even people whom I don't like or appreciate!) through Your eyes of love.

"If we claim to be in the light and hate someone, we are still in the dark. But if we love others, we are in the light, and we don't cause problems for them. If we hate others, we are living and walking in the dark. We don't know where we are going, because we can't see in the dark." (I John 2:9-11 CEV)

May 30: Salads to Desserts

I used to hear the expression "Salad Days" now and then, but I guess it has gone the way of the roc and the dodo. I never knew exactly what it meant, anyway, except that it did connote a certain greenness. Well, I guess I'm up to my "Dessert Days," meaning not only that I love desserts, but also that I have become as soft and fluffy as a marshmallow pudding. Dessert is the best part of the meal (ask anyone who knows me!), and it also means that this time of my life is very sweet.

Of course, no one's circumstances are all sweet. That would be like having three meals a day of nothing but hot fudge sundaes. But our reactions to even difficult circumstances can be sweet, if we choose them to be so. Someone has said that by the time you reach 60 you look like where you're going, and I pray that those I meet will sense a delicious taste of heaven. This will happen only as we anticipate with joy the pleasure of God's companionship each day, and treat those around us as His special creations…not tossed together carelessly but lovingly mixed and formed by a Master Chef. When we view others as assets and not liabilities, as those to whom we can minister, as those who have a place reserved for them at the Supper of the Lamb, then we are starting to grasp the menu plan, so to speak.

It doesn't matter whether you are at the appetizer stage or the dessert stage of life: we are never classified as leftovers! God means for us to make those we meet hungry for the food of the soul that only He can provide. I want to be willing to be used as God wills.

"Taste and see that the Lord is good; blessed is the man who takes refuge in him." (Psalm 34:8 NIV)

May 31: Lesson from a Boat

At one time or another, we owned three small boats (thankfully never more than one at a time). Each time, we would go through the same routine, evidently not learning from our mistakes. Before the boat was purchased, we would talk about how wonderful it would be to have a boat. Then, when we got one, we would go out every weekend for about a month. Then, we'd go out maybe twice a month. Then, we'd go out once in a while. Then, we would talk about what we could do with the money if we sold the boat, and we would set about the task of getting rid of it.

The best thing about owning a boat (next to making islands available) was the fact that the motor was loud enough that we couldn't hear our children squabbling. The most aggravating thing (next to being bounced around by every wave bigger than a bread box) was the chore of cleaning the boat; it seems they don't go well when their bottoms are covered with barnacles. Therefore, it is constantly necessary to scrape those little beasties off in order to insure a swift passage (and—let's face it—a quick sale).

I accumulate barnacles in my life also, and they definitely slow my progress. They accumulate so gradually, I hardly notice anything until one day I discover I'm not moving. I need to check occasionally for crusty barnacles of impatience, touchiness, discontent, bitterness, jealousy, and a critical spirit. So, let me do a little review work on my life today—I may have to do a little scraping!

"May the words of my mouth and the thoughts of my heart be pleasing to you, O Lord, my rock and my redeemer." (Psalm 19:14 NLT)

June 1: The Maine Thing

One June day as we left a holiday resort in Maine, we brought provisions for a picnic lunch. We drove down an old road and soon found a grassy meadow beside a little stream. Gleefully unpacking everything and spreading it on a blanket, we had hardly had a mouthful when we were attacked by swarms of big mosquitoes. We decided they must be making up for time lost during the long winters because the dive bombing was so intense we had to throw kids and picnic in the car and drive wildly to safety.

Usually it's not mosquitoes that bug me, it's people. Since we are not all going in the same direction or at the same rate of speed, I suppose it's inevitable to occasionally scrape elbows with others. As Lucy, in the comic strip "Peanuts" said, "I love mankind…it's people I can't stand."

People aren't mosquitoes; I can't always run from them. They are everywhere: at work, at play, and even at home. How do I handle this? Do I allow my human nature or Christ's life in me to control my reactions? Because the Holy Spirit dwells in me, I have both the possibility and the power to accept and to love those who irritate me. But I must choose to do so, and I must will to do so. God will not do it <u>for</u> me, but <u>through</u> me.

Prayer: Father, give me the mind of Christ, that I may love people in your name, and for your sake, because you died for them.

"Since God chose you to be the holy people whom he loves, you must clothe yourselves with tenderhearted mercy, kindness, humility, gentleness, and patience." (Colossians 3:12 NLT)

June 2: The Road Not Taken

There I was, zooming down the road when I saw a sign just ahead of the coming exit that said, without a trace of apology, "Detour." Do you think that made me smile? I'm afraid not. In fact, I felt angry, frustrated, and just plain out of sorts. Grumpily, I turned off and found I had to go many miles to get on at the next entrance.

Thinking about it later, in the cool, calm, collected way I have of being spiritual after the fact, I realized that the detour sign had not been put up there to make me angry. It had been put up there to protect me from harm. Detour signs are not erected to upset us, irritate us, or waste our time. Rather, someone is looking after our safety.

I do this with God, too. Just when I am zooming along in what I consider a hassle-free condition, God closes a bridge, shuts down a ramp, or takes me completely off my planned road. I need to remember that God is protecting me from dangers that I cannot see, and that He has not stopped guiding me just because I am not on the road I expected to take.

In thinking about some of the life detours that I have taken, I can see how God has kept me from harm, and I have discovered that worry, stress, and anxiety do not get me to my destination any faster. Those Maalox Moments (which sometimes seem to stretch out into hours when you are trying to make an appointment on time or catch a plane) add ulcers and bitten fingernails, but not much else. It only seems to be later, after I have arrived, that I remember that God is never surprised by detours, and that His eye never leaves me.

"Aren't two sparrows sold for only a penny? But your Father knows when any one of them falls to the ground. Even the hairs on your head are counted. So don't be afraid! You are worth much more than many sparrows." (Matthew 10:29-31 CEV)

June 3: A Gifted People

It's strange, but sometimes a gift that is not particularly welcome at first, turns out to be just what is needed.

When I graduated from prep school, my parents gave me a three-piece set of leather luggage. I was not at all thrilled with this, ungraciously comparing my gift to girls who got diamond rings, cars, and trips to Europe. I felt "all stressed up and no place to go," if you will pardon the pun!

As the years passed, though, I began to appreciate the gift more, and I even added a matching trunk (I was pretty much into luggage by that time).

Sometimes, I must confess, I have felt dissatisfied with the spiritual gifts God has given me. But Paul says, "All these [gifts] are the work of one and the same Spirit, and he gives them to each man, just as he determines" (I Corinthians 12:11 NIV).

May I be thankful, and remember that my gifts were chosen with love.

June 4: The Love of God

After putting our three oldest children on a plane for camp, I got on a plane the next day headed for Pittsburgh. The man in front of me was reading a paper and the headline read, "Plane Crashes in North Carolina: All Killed." I turned to my companion and said rather casually, "Sort of scary to read that just when we're taking off, isn't it?"

When we arrived at our destination, I was met by one of my brothers, who looked distressed. "Did you hear about the plane crash?" he asked sadly. When I nodded, he continued, "I'm sorry, Ciddy. I checked the flight number. That was the plane your kids were on." The floor rose up and smacked me in the face. I found out later that I had fainted.

I will never forget coming to and the feeling of being frozen over with shock. Someone left to inquire further. Some time later, he rushed back to my brother and me. He had discovered that our children were still alive; the plane had crashed during take-off, immediately after our children had gotten off in Asheville. For us, it ended happily. For the families of those who died in the crash, it did not.

Was their trust in the omnipotent God misplaced? No. He did not save their loved ones from death, but I do know that His love never left them. May I remember in times of terrible suffering and tragedy that nothing can separate me from the love of God.

"For I am convinced that nothing can ever separate us from his love. Death can't and life can't. The angels can't and the demons can't. Our fears for today, our worries about tomorrow, even the powers of hell can't keep God's love away." (Romans 8:38-39 NLT)

June 5: Buckle Up

A friend of mine has an older car with inoperable seat belts. She, unfortunately, has not had them repaired, because she was quoted an exorbitant sum to have them fixed (of course, most car repairs seem to fall into that category these days). When I first rode in her car, I was vaguely uncomfortable without a seat belt, and definitely felt something was amiss. The next time I rode with her, I also had a similar feeling, but it did not bother me nearly as much. In fact, I sort of enjoyed not being squashed in the throat (I realize most people are squashed in the chest, but I'm a lot shorter than most people).

After a while, I got really used to her car and felt quite grumpy when I had to use my car and buckle up. Sin is a little like this isn't it? When I first sin, I feel very guilty and uncomfortable, but if I continue, it is all too easy to become accustomed to it.

Let me be aware of what I am doing, and buckle my seat belt, or I may find I have crashed headlong into disaster.

"You know my foolish sins. Not one is hidden from you." (Psalm 69:5 CEV)

June 6: Golf Tips

Quite a few years ago, Virginia, one of our daughters, took an interest in golf. She and her husband got some secondhand clubs, received a subscription to a golf magazine for Christmas, and set out to learn all the aspects of the game (although unasked, I felt my advice was quite succinct: "stay out of the rough").

Needing a little more than this, one of her co-workers lent her a video called *How to Develop a Good Swing*. Virginia practiced assiduously for several weeks before returning the tape. "Let me see how you're doing," her friend suggested. There was a glow of a job well done as Virginia proudly exhibited her new skill.

"Are you left handed?" the owner of the video queried.

"Why, no!" was the mystified reply.

"Well," pointed out her friend, "your grip is fine, but I'm sure it must have felt a little stiff because you're doing it backwards!"

Virginia had forgotten that she had been looking at a mirror image, and she had carefully learned to place her hands in the opposite position from where they should be. I, too, am apt to get things backwards when I base my actions on what I see in others rather than in looking to God.

"Do not conform any longer to the pattern of this world, but be transformed by the renewing of your mind." (Romans 12:2 NIV)

June 7: Field Hand

When I string green beans for supper, I often think of the summer when I became rather intimately acquainted with them. I was at a summer camp, and because of the labor shortage during World War II, it was decided by the directors that we should do some volunteer work. We were told that our morning classes would be canceled for the next month so that we could spend that time picking beans for nearby farmers.

Initially, we were all excited about this and piled happily into our bus. Arriving at the field, we were given buckets and went to work. After 30 minutes, I was tired of beans. After an hour, I was disgusted with beans. As the sun rose and my back sagged, I vowed I would never look at another bean again. But, much to my sorrow, we had to keep going back until those fields were picked. I was lethargic and grouchy, and picked slower than a man facing his first piece of needlepoint.

God is the owner of the field of my life, but He has neither scourge nor whip. No punishment motivates me to work, no stern looks keep me focused on my task. Quite the contrary, I willingly work for God because of His great love for me.

"Whatever you do, do it well. For when you go to the grave, there will be no work or planning or knowledge or wisdom." (Ecclesiastes 9:10 NLT)

June 8: Built to Specification

I am not always thrilled to my socks at the prospect of walking in the morning, but I do it because it is good for me. It is also a great time to talk if you are with a fellow traveler.

One day, while on the west coast, I puffed past a lot filled with mobile homes. Outside the lot, there was a huge sign that promised, "These homes were designed with YOU in mind." Actually, nothing could have been further from the truth: they knew nothing about me. They didn't know that I would be walking by at that moment, that my favorite color was blue, or that I have never considered being a brain surgeon.

I do have a home that is being designed with me in mind, however, and, when I get there, at the end of my journey, it will be perfect. I remember coming home to a house that was brightly lit and filled with family fun and laughter. The welcome was so wonderful that I forgot all the troubles of my journey!

It will be so with our heavenly home. We may be travel-stained and weary, but we will find love and laughter, and the city will be bright with the light of the Lamb. We will give joyous service because we will not tire, and we will worship our God. I'm so glad that heaven (even if nothing else is!) will be "as advertised."

"Then I heard all beings in heaven and on the earth and under the earth and in the sea offer praise. Together, all of them were saying, 'Praise, honor, glory, and strength forever and ever to the one who sits on the throne and to the Lamb!'" (Revelation 5:13 CEV)

June 9: My Father's Whistle

"The man who enters by the gate is the shepherd of his sheep. The watchman opens the gate for him, and the sheep listen to his voice. He calls his own sheep by name and leads them out." (John 10:2-3 NIV)

Years ago, a well known advertisement showed a dog cocking an ear toward a Victrola with a listening device shaped like a trumpet. The title said, "His Master's Voice." Our family used to reenact this scene regularly because of my father's whistle.

His whistle had a very sharp sound, made by blowing through the teeth somehow. My brothers could make it work, but, for some reason, I could not (something in the Y chromosome, perhaps). He could make several different sounds, so my father used one whistle sound for my mother, and a different one for the six of us. This came in handy when we were in crowds (although some might argue that with eight in our family we WERE a crowd). But if someone were missing, or Daddy needed us for anything, he would whistle the sound that was meant especially for us, and we would come running to where he was.

In John 10, we read that Jesus cares for His sheep and that they know His voice because they are attuned to its sound, just as my family knew my father's whistle. We did not always receive good news, but we knew better than to disobey. God does not always have "showers of blessings" for us when we answer his leading either, but if we are wise, we will follow. He is the Good Shepherd, and we should follow Him wherever He goes.

Prayer: Dear Father, I do not always hear and follow when you speak to me. Help me to listen for your voice.

June 10: Ravens

"Elijah obeyed the LORD, and went to live near Cherith Creek. Ravens brought him bread and meat twice a day and he drank water from the creek." (I Kings 17:5-6 CEV)

Ravens are not really the subject of much conversation (unless you happen to be talking to an Edgar Allen Poe fan). They interest me, though, because when the ravens fed Elijah, they were not acting as they normally would. Their natural action would have been to eat the food themselves, but instead they performed a service for God and fed a man living in the wilderness.

People, like the ravens in this story, also can experience something similar and truly out of the ordinary. I call them "raven actions," and they are when we do or say something out of love; when we do or say something very different from our normal actions. These experiences don't happen often (at least not to me!), but when they do, they are quite extraordinary.

I had a "raven action" experience during a very sad time in my life, and it was amazing to watch myself do something out of love that I never would have ordinarily done. After my mother died, one of my brothers had more or less appointed himself in charge of the world. While we were planning the funeral, he heard that I was thinking of having some of Mother's favorite hymns sung. He became practically apoplectic (I think he practiced this a lot, as he was very good at it—or as we used to say in the family, he "had a short fuse"). The general idea that he managed to get across was this: no hymns. Period. Ordinarily, I would have matched him fuse for fuse, but…I heard myself say, "That's fine, John." God helped me to love him.

I was amazed by my "raven action," for I knew the love I felt for and showed my brother certainly did not come from me, but from God.

Surprisingly, the story doesn't end there. We had a funeral in Bradenton, and then we went to our church in Pittsburgh for another. At the funeral in Pittsburgh, without any direction from me, the organist played both of those hymns. My brother never realized what was being played, but I did. I cried and thanked God for his love and mercy to me.

June 11: Reigning Cats and Dogs

Cats have their owners completely under their thumb (or paw, as the case might be); to them people are the servants of a reigning monarch. As has been said, dogs have owners, cats have staff. Just so. There is no similarity between dogs and cats when it comes to obedience. When a dog is called, it will bound up and look alertly at you as if to ask, "Yes? What can I do for you?" A cat on the other hand, will usually only yawn and flex its toenails. The idea is this: "Leave a message, and I'll get back to you."

What is my response when God calls? Am I anxious to obey and do whatever He asks? I may not go so far as to yawn, but I can somehow find something else that needs to be done or put it off until a more convenient time.

Prayer: Dear God, thank you for Your great love for me. Please help me to listen for Your voice, and help me to obey You.

"Do not be like a senseless horse or mule that needs a bit and bridle to keep it under control." (Psalm 32:9 NLT)

June 12: Charge Account

My husband used to call me Teddy Roosevelt because I was always yelling, "Charge!" But one time I went too far. Bill was going to Atlanta on business and I was tagging along. It was winter, and I suddenly realized that I didn't have a heavy coat. A friend generously agreed to let me use her charge card for a particular store, and when we arrived I set out to do just that. Once in the store, I saw some mittens and hats that were on sale, and I decided to get some for the children. The clerk asked for my card, and after I gave it to her, she said, "And what is the address, Mrs. Rood?" Well, to tell the truth, I wasn't too sure of the address, and I stuttered around saying 4091 9th Avenue…no wait…4109 9th Avenue and several other numbers before the clerk grew very frosty. "Do you have other identification?" I admitted I didn't. "Wait here," she said sternly, I'll have to go check with security." I had no intention of being checked out with security, and, with cheeks aflame (and hot enough to go outside without a coat!), I dashed out of the store as fast as a thief.

I had the correct card all right, and the permission to use it, but the account was not in my name. In the letter Paul wrote to Philemon, he said, "So if you consider me a partner, welcome him as you would welcome me. If he has done you any wrong or owes you anything, charge it to me" (Philemon 17-18 NIV).

When Paul said, "Charge it to me," he had the right to say it because it was his account. Our sins have been charged to Christ's account—and that charge was accepted because Christ paid in advance (and He was the only person who could do so!). We may be poor in a financial sense, but those who follow Christ will always be children of the King. We have spiritual wealth that cannot be taken away.

June 13: Fat of the Land

Since I am built straight up and down like a tube sock, I envy people with waists. I used to have one, of course, but that was B.C. (Before Chocolate). I lost all control at a Hershey, PA conference where there were bowls of Hershey kisses at every fingertip. In fact, I not only lost control, I went absolutely bananas. I left a trail of silver wrappings behind me in every room. Unfortunately, this didn't stop when I returned home. I just kept pigging out and gained 20 pounds faster than you can say "Join Weight Watchers." When my clothes began to creak under the strain, I decided to take some steps. Since I had put it on, I had to take it off, and no one could do it for me.

I discovered, sadly enough, that a quickie diet wasn't going to cut the mustard. Losing weight and keeping it off meant a change of lifestyle that will last until I get my new body in heaven (I'm counting on not only being tall, but also ethereally thin).

Most worthwhile things take time, and the Christian life is no exception. I don't mean we have to prove ourselves to God or live up to a set of rules. But, if we are new creatures in Christ, we need to live like new creatures, and that takes discipline. My disciplined regime at the moment requires me to get fat on God's word, feeding diligently on the manna He has provided…and I don't have to count those calories!

"Everyone who is victorious will eat of the manna that has been hidden away in heaven." (Revelation 2:17b NLT)

June 14: A Rabbit Tale

I do believe we have had nearly every pet available, with the exception of a cheetah (cheetah's never prosper), but one of our favorites was a rabbit named Dandelion. We had him in a cage in the back yard, but every time we would inch open the cage door to put in food or water, he would squeeze through and be off and running. He would be gone for two or three days, and then in the midst of fears and tears, he would show back up. But only briefly—as soon as that door was opened wide enough, he would be up and away again.

We decided to try an experiment since he liked freedom so much, and was obviously fending for himself. Besides that, we were going crazy trying to figure out where he hid out all the time (Bill went door-to-door asking about a big white rabbit so often he felt people were comparing him to Jimmy Stewart and Harvey).

The next time the rabbit came home, we didn't put him in the cage, but just let him run around the yard. When he got tired, he tried to come into the house. We closed the door, but there he sat. And sat. And sat. We couldn't get rid of that rabbit! He was under our feet the moment we opened the door, and never left. He responded to love where he had resisted law!

Before I became a Christian, I too wanted to disobey God's law. In Galatians 3:23, Paul says, "The Law controlled us and kept us under its power until the time came when we would have faith" (CEV). When I came to God through Christ and learned to love God, I responded to His grace and wanted to obey because of His love for me.

Prayer: Father, I know I could never have been saved by keeping your law, for I could not keep it! So, I am grateful with all my heart that you made me one of your children by grace. Thank you.

"I want to know only one thing. How were you given God's spirit? Was it by obeying the Law of Moses or by hearing about Christ and having faith in him? (Galatians 3:2 CEV)

June 15: Tick Talk

My husband is sometimes direct in his instructions—and sometimes not. One summer, he and our daughter, Virginia, made plans to look at some property in Georgia. They were going to walk around the boundaries to do some measuring. If you are familiar with Georgia in the summer, you will know that it is very hot and steamy. As they were packing, Bill said he was going to be wearing dungarees and a long sleeved shirt. Virginia was not sure exactly what dungarees were (they are jeans or overalls, in case you're not sure either!), but she knew it was going to be hot. So, she brought along shorts and a short sleeve shirt.

At the end of a long hot tramp around some of Georgia's "innards," they gratefully made for the air-conditioned motel. As they entered, Bill said, "Be sure to check for ticks." "Ticks?" echoed Virginia with more than a trace of disbelief. "Well, yes," said Bill. "You didn't have on long pants and a long sleeved shirt…you've probably got a pretty good crop. Go take a hot bath and look around very carefully."

So, Virginia got into a hot tub and, sure enough, she found ticks, lots of them. She squeezed each one to kill it and then placed the little miscreants in a line on the edge of the tub. When she went into the bathroom the next morning (presumably to gloat over her tidiness), there was not the first sign of a tick anywhere. You can't kill ticks by a simple squeeze—another lesson learned.

I've noticed that sin can jump on me unnoticed, like a tick—and no amount of squashing will get rid of it. Unless I am willing to die to self, I will most probably see my unwelcome sin again.

Prayer: Father God, keep me from giving into what I know is not like Christ.

"Who is wise and understanding among you? Let him show it by his good life, by deeds done in the humility that comes from wisdom…. For where you have envy and selfish ambition, there you find disorder and every evil practice. But the wisdom that comes from heaven is first of all pure…." (James 3:13,16-17a NIV)

June 16: How to Put Hair on Your Chest

As the youngest in a family with five boys, you can readily imagine that I was not only spoiled rotten, but rotten to the core. As a child, people would ask if I were spoiled, and I always said no, because I thought that spoiled people screamed and stamped their feet a lot (screaming and stamping were never necessary—I already had everything). One thing I didn't have however, were other girls to play with because we journeyed south for the winter and north for the summer. I was such a conceited little somebody, it's no wonder people stayed away from me in droves.

I adored my brothers, however, and they went along with most of my outlandish ideas (maybe they didn't want me to try out my screaming or stamping feet). At any rate, I decided the thing I wanted more than anything was to have hair on my chest, just as they had. So, very seriously, they told me that if I ate oatmeal every day until I was thirteen, I would start growing hair on my chest. I had not taken any Biology classes, and since my female hormones were nowhere to be seen at this point, it seemed like a real possibility. From that day on, I religiously stuck to the oatmeal routine (easily obtained as my father also ate oatmeal every morning, and he was glad to see I was taking an interest in a healthful eating program).

The morning of my thirteenth birthday came and I threw down my covers, pulled up my nightgown, and I found that my brothers had glued hair all over my chest (I was elated until it all washed off in the shower).

In my prayer life, I also can get led astray by remaining focused on the answer I want or think is best. Sometimes God's answer appears disheartening, or disappointing, or even dreadful. At those times, may I always remember that though God does not always do what I expect or want, He always does what is best.

"Beg as loud as you can for good common sense. Search for wisdom as you would search for silver or hidden treasure. Then you will understand what it means to respect and to know the Lord God." (Proverbs 2:3-5 CEV)

June 17: Dressed to Kill

When we were fairly new Christians, my husband and I were invited to a Gideon banquet. The only thing I knew about the Gideons was that they put Bibles in hotels, so I was happy to go and learn what they were all about. When we formerly attended banquets, we got dressed up, so, I put on a green lace cocktail dress with no back, and we sailed off into the sunset. I noticed my hostess did sort of keep backing me into a corner during most of the pre-dinner conversation, and that I did seem to be the only one wearing a cocktail dress, but I thought that since most of them had been all day at a convention, they just hadn't had time to go home and change.

On the way home, my friend said casually, "Do you ever pray about what to wear when you go someplace?" "Why, no," I admitted cheerfully, "I've never thought about it!" It took a good three weeks for that comment to penetrate (I guess I'm a pretty slow thinker!). At any rate, it suddenly occurred to me that someone in a green lace cocktail dress must have looked like a parakeet that got mixed in with some wrens and sparrows at a bird show. However, my friend, who had clothed herself with compassion, kindness, gentleness, and humility (sewed together with love), had told me what to do in the future. We have remained friends ever since, because I knew she had bravely tackled what could have been a sticky problem and turned it into a lovely lesson of what God could teach. She had corrected in love, with wisdom and insight, for the sake of the one whom she was teaching, in order that I might grow.

"Since God chose you to be the holy people whom he loves, you must clothe yourselves with tenderheartedness, mercy, kindness, humility, gentleness and patience." (Colossians 3:12 NLT)

June 18: Addiction

"You lie on beds inlaid with ivory and lounge on your couches. You dine on choice lambs and fattened calves. You strum away on your harps like David and improvise on musical instruments. You drink wine by the bowlful and use the finest lotions, but you do not grieve over the ruin of Joseph. Therefore you will be among the first to go into exile; your feasting and lounging will end." (Amos 6:4-7 NIV)

My addiction started at a very young age. In fact, I think, I was only about seven.

I had a bad case of measles and had to stay in bed in a darkened room, so my eyeballs wouldn't dry up, or for some such reason. After you hear *Raggedy Ann and Andy* read to you for the hundredth time, life seems very dull, indeed. Then to my great joy, I discovered radio. Eureka, and all that! I discovered a whole new reason for my existence. *Jack Armstrong, The Green Hornet,* and other radio serials occupied the bulk of my bed-ridden day, but my favorite was *Little Orphan Annie*. After each day's exciting episode was over, someone would read out a new Orphan Annie message to decode. Decoding the message was not possible without her "secret decoder ring," and to get one of those little marvels, you had to send in labels from jars of Ovaltine, a powdered chocolate you added to milk. I cajoled my mother into ordering cases and cases of the stuff. I never drank any of it, though: I thought it had a horrid taste. Despite my dislike of the product, I happily went about ripping off labels and left the de-labeled jars molding in the basement.

My father naturally hit the roof when this was discovered, and he quickly put an end to any further buying until our current supply was used up. I grew up and got married, and as far as I know it never WAS used up (maybe it was willed to the next owners of the house). This was a tremendous waste of money, of course, but money meant absolutely nothing to me. As I grew up, I kept right on spending (not on Ovaltine, however). I wasn't exactly lounging on beds of ivory or strumming harps, like the wicked people that Amos describes, but the principle is the same: "Give me what I want so I can be happy and make my family happy."

The cure for Israel was exile; the cure for me was a severe business reversal when money dried up. It's too bad I wasn't following the advice given in Philippians 2:4: "Each of you should look not only to your own interests, but also to the interests of others" (NIV). I was not thinking of anyone else's interests, nor was I looking to God to understand what He might want me to do with our resources:

I was just buying what caught my fancy (and I'm sorry to say some of it was pretty fancy…). It was a hard lesson, and one I should have learned years and years ago. I have discovered that sometimes lessons learned the hard way are lessons that are not forgotten.

June 19: A Light in South America

Visiting my daughter Virginia and her husband Clint in North Carolina, I heard the testimony of a man at their church. He was from Columbia, South America. He spoke very little English, so there was a translator. It was a stirring story. He had been heavily involved in drug trafficking. As a Communist, he rose high in Government circles until he was one of seven men surrounding the President. A friend talked to him of Christ once or twice, but he did not listen. He laughed off any stories of people who had met the Savior.

One day, there was a revolution. He was trapped in the palace while men with guns and tanks stormed the building. He knew he had no chance of escaping with an arsenal like that facing him, but he remembered the witness of his friend, and he said a prayer in his desperation, "Help me get out of here!" He did escape, and made it across town to his apartment. He said he sat on the bed in amazement, and then said aloud, "I am an atheist, and a Communist—but I am not stupid." And he asked Christ to come into his life and free him from the dominion of darkness that surrounded him. Today, he tells the good news of a God who pardons sin and delights to show mercy.

Prayer: I know You are the one who holds the world in place Father, and I know You hold the hearts of all men. Give me the desire to touch the lives of those I have not met, and yet who have as much right as I do to know the fullness of Your forgiveness and love.

"Our God, no one is like you. We are all that is left of your chosen people, and you freely forgive our sin and guilt. You don't stay angry forever; you're glad to have pity and pleased to be merciful. You will trample on our sins and throw them in the sea." (Micah 7:18-19 CEV)

June 20: Linkage

This story is not about the "missing link," but the "middle link." The middle link is someone who is the middle of a series of witnesses for our Lord. When a person yields His life to God, it is usually the result of the witness of many people. Someone has called this the golden chain that draws a person to Christ. We can't all be the final exciting link, and many times we aren't the first. But, the possibilities are great for us to be "middles." And middles are important, for without them, the chain would not be complete.

On one of my speaking trips, I was seated next to a sailor on an airplane and gave him a booklet describing how one can become a Christian. "Thanks," he said casually, and stuck it into his *Playboy* magazine. That didn't worry me, because I knew he would be looking at that magazine again, and that he would find that booklet!

I was in the mall the other day, watching a wretched-looking teenager working at a coffee kiosk. He wasn't really dirty, but he was scary enough to startle anyone over 20, with earrings, tattoos, and assorted dangling material. I felt the Lord wanted me to give him a booklet, but I couldn't think how to get into it. Finally, as I watched him, it came to me. I was very careful to make sure that I was the last person in line. When he served me I said, "I want you to know you are very efficient." He broke into a smile that would have warmed the heart of a cobra…and thanked me most sincerely for the little book that would tell him how he could know God.

I once returned home from the Boston airport in a taxi. The driver was very chatty, and immediately began to ask where I had been and what I had been doing. It was a heaven sent opportunity for me to tell him how I had come to know Christ in a personal way. He listened intently. When I got through, there was a moment's silence, and then he said gruffly, "You sound just like my sister-in-law!" I knew immediately that his sister in law must be a Christian, and that she had been telling him the good news of Christ.

Someday, when we are in heaven, we will be able to rejoice with all of the links that have been a part of our chain! May we also be a willing link for someone else!

"Faithful messengers are as refreshing as snow in the heat of summer. They revive the spirit of their employer." (Proverbs 25:13 NLT)

June 21: Hanging On

A friend recently shared a story with me about her father. Her dad is a tomato farmer, and last year when he sprayed his crop, the plants grew and grew, but there were no tomatoes. Sick with worry, he contacted the manufacturers of the spray, and found out that a mistake had been made at the factory in the chemical proportions. They assured him that he would be reimbursed, which was a great relief, as he had mortgaged his house to build the greenhouses. Time passed with no communication from the chemical manufacturer, and when he contacted the company again, he was offered only a small amount of compensation. And, of course, there were no tomatoes to sell.

The farmer is a Christian, but he became utterly consumed by the thoughts of this injustice, and the disaster lurking around the corner. It was literally all he could think about and talk of. One night, as he was tossing sleeplessly in his bed, the Lord began to deal with him. He realized that although he thought he had committed this situation to the Father, he was grimly hanging on to the tail of it. Finally, however, he was able to let go, and God's peace returned to his heart.

Am I hanging on to the tail of something that needs to be given to God? It would be best if I followed the advice given in I Peter 5:7: "Cast all your anxiety on him because he cares for you" (NIV).

I am weak, Lord, but You are strong. Give me the grace to put my burdens on Your shoulders and leave them there.

June 22: Fire Man

"The three men (Shadrach, Meshach and Abednego) replied, 'Your majesty, we don't need to defend ourselves. The god we worship can save us from you and your flaming furnace. But even if he doesn't, we still won't worship your gods and the gold statue you have set up.'" (Daniel 3:16-18 CEV)

My childhood days were spent in Pittsburgh before it became the beautiful Golden Triangle it is today. It was a very dirty city where windowsills had to be wiped off every day, and my father had to wear three different shirts every day in order to look clean. Most of this grime came from the steel mills—those roaring giants that lit up the night if you drove nearby. I never got to go into one, but I knew a man who worked in one for a while, and he said it was the hottest fire you can imagine: it blistered your face just to go near it.

Imagine how Shadrach, Meshach, and Abednego must have felt about their fire! And they didn't just stroll by…they had to go inside the furnace. There was a fourth man in there with them, however, and he kept them from harm. Only their bonds were burned away.

There are still furnaces today. And although there aren't many steel mills around, or kings to make furnaces for sacrifices, the enemy of our souls is busy night and day keeping the fires of suffering hot. We can be thankful that Christ will always be with us in the furnaces of life.

June 23: Building Blocks

Westminster Abbey has been called "A Poem to God." It sounds strange when you first hear this, but the more you ponder it, the more reasonable it becomes. It is a poem written in stone, with the meter of a thousand stanzas of winged arches and delicate fan tracery. It is a poem made of the loveliness of stone carvings, the rich colors of stained glass, and the strength of pillars and flying buttresses.

In Ephesians 2:20 we are called "God's workmanship." In this passage, the people of God are compared to a sacred temple. We are all part of this sacred building which God has designed. Some of us are stone carvings, some of us are stained glass windows, and some of us are flying buttresses.

Rome wasn't built in a day, of course, and neither was Westminster Abbey. When you come right down to it…neither are we. Stone has to be chiseled, cross beams have to be sanded, wood has to be carved, and glass has to be polished. If buildings could talk, I'm sure they would tell us it hurts to have all that construction going on; I'm afraid we don't think it's so great, either. Being made part of God's building is sometimes very painful, but, just think, one of these days it will be completed. Then, everyone will say, "What a wonderful architect!" So, I'm going to concentrate on what I am going to be, part of God's beautiful temple. I thank the Lord for His work in my life.

"So now you Gentiles are no longer strangers and foreigners. You are citizens along with all of God's holy people. You are members of God's family. We are his house, built on the foundation of the apostles and the prophets. And the cornerstone is Christ Jesus himself. We who believe are carefully joined together, becoming a holy temple for the Lord." (Ephesians 2:20-21 NLT)

June 24: Turtles

Turtles are slow, lumbering tanks without much zip or personality; yet, they are immortalized in *Aesop's Fables* for their steady, unspectacular progress. One step at a time, they lurch on toward their destination, plodding serenely over every impediment in their path, and retreating cleverly into their shells whenever danger threatens.

Frankly, I don't suppose a lot of us rate very high on the charisma scale either, and we are more likely to be remembered for plodding rather than exploding into "hare-raising" feats of glory (with the exception of course of Olympic athletes, whose energy is beyond the comprehension of most of us). Even with all that speed the "Energizer Bunny" had in that race, he put too much trust in his speed, and forgot the real goal, winning the race. I think this shows us that, in order to finish the race set before us, steadfastness and faithfulness are the qualities God looks for—not just drum rolls of exhibitionism.

For us, as Christians, as well as for turtles, there are times when it is wise to be prudent and retreat into the shell of God's protection. This will not be possible if we leave our shell at home on the dresser. Our adversary knows just where we are the weakest and most vulnerable. Our enemy is very clever, indeed, for he is aware that out weak place might be in the place where we feel the strongest and most competent…rather like Mr. Rabbit. This is why we need the whole armor of God, for Satan can turn us over like a turtle, so that with feet waving helplessly in the air, we would seem to be at his mercy. But, God can turn us right side up, for He is omnipotent as well as loving. This is a promise to remember as we plod on without seeing the finish line—or even much progress. God charts motives not miles, however, so let us keep racing, however slow we are.

Prayer: May I be a person who is known for the faithfulness that come only from You, just as Moses was: "Moses was faithful in all God's house" (Hebrews 3:2a NIV).

"My son, do not forget my teaching, but keep my commands in your heart…." (Proverbs 3:1 NIV)

June 25: The Heart of the Matter

We were renting a four-story home in Boston that was over 100 years old. It was charming, of course, but 100 years of charm wears a little thin at times. We knew we were only going to be there for a short time, however, so renting was the only solution—and this one had enough room to racket around in. The biggest drawback was the basement. It did have an outlet for the washer and dryer, but the floors were dirt, and the stairs were steep. This meant if you killed yourself falling downstairs, at least it wouldn't be hard to bury you.

I advertised for a maid without any real hope, and my hopes were realized. No one really wanted to come out there and go up and down all those stairs doing wash for seven people any more than I did. I tried praying. The only answer the Lord gave was "As a man thinketh in his heart, so is he." I not only didn't understand that, I didn't like it, so I asked Him for another verse. Nothing doing: same one. Same one each day as I stumped grouchily up and down thinking how much more valuable I could be if I were out speaking somewhere. Finally, in desperation, I asked the Lord to show me what He meant by that verse so we could get on to something else. And back came the answer: "You must learn to be valuable to me where you are. The thoughts that you are thinking in your heart are thoughts of pride and until you learn to be content working for me here, I cannot use you anywhere else."

I had to resolve to learn to do what I was doing with a cheerful heart, and remember Paul's advice, "Do your work willingly, as though you were serving the Lord himself…" (Colossians 3:23a CEV).

Prayer: Forgive me for thinking I know best how I can be used, Lord…and train me in the ways You want me to go.

June 26: Japanese Lesson

While traveling, I happened to sit next to a woman who had served in the State Department in Japan for nearly fifteen years. "How wonderful!" I enthused. "Did you get time to visit many people in their homes? Did you learn any of their language? Did you get any interesting recipes?" When I had run down, she said coldly, "I never left the American compound."

Although I struggled not to let my face betray me, I was horrified at this example of insularity. What opportunities she had missed! She had absolutely cut herself off from any contact with new ideas, and new friends (not to mention new food!). She had not enlarged her cultural horizons nor exerted herself to learn of the country in which she resided.

We may never have the chance to live in Japan, but we do serve in a land far from home. As ambassadors of the King of Kings, we have been commanded to reach out in love to all people, not just those who look and act the way we do. We dare not neglect this commission we have been given, for as loyal subjects we must do what we can to further His kingdom before we are called home.

Prayer: I know it is Your desire that all come to know You in a personal way. Help me to do what I can where You have placed me.

"Then he told me, 'The God of our ancestors has chosen you to know his will, and to see the Righteous One and hear him speak. You are to take his message everywhere, telling the whole world what you have seen and heard." (Acts 22:14-15 NLT)

June 27: On Closets

I often wonder what other people's closets look like. Mine is usually an untidy jumble of dresses, sweaters, shoes and a couple of leftover Christmas presents that I never found at the right time. I know a professional who makes her living reorganizing and prettifying closets. She can make any jungle look like Kew Gardens because that's her business.

The closet of my mind is a little trickier. It is a jumble of things I wouldn't want even my mother to see (maybe especially not my mother!). There are hangers of hatred, shelves of selfishness, racks of rancor, and floor space filled with left over bits of independence, self-pity, and greed. There is possibly even a big package of pride hidden in the back corner.

What can I do about this? The Bible says in I Corinthians 2:16b that we have "the mind of Christ" (NIV), and I think there is no question that Christ would not be thinking like this. I must go to Him and ask Him for a complete reorganization. He can make our hangers filled with the Holy Spirit, our shelves with service, our racks with the refreshment of his presence, and our floor covered with genuine gratitude, kindness and faithfulness. God can do this, giving us a wonderful makeover, because that's His business.

"You were taught, with regard to your former way of life, to put off your old self, which is being corrupted by its deceitful desires; to be made new in the attitude of your minds; and to put on the new self, created to be like God in true righteousness and holiness." (Ephesians 4:22-24 NIV)

June 28: Overlooking Facts

"Look, the little tribe of Benjamin leads the way. Then comes a great throng of rulers from Judah and all the rulers of Zebulun and Naphtali." (Psalm 68:27 NLT)

A friend of mine who lives in the Chicago area was scheduled to speak in Iowa. Since her car was not well and was in the shop for some surgery, so to speak, her husband suggested she rent one for the time she would be away. After listening through the usual explanations about the placement of the various knobs and switches, she set off.

Chicago roads have a lot of tollbooths, and when she came to the first one, she couldn't find the switch to lower the window. Frantically she searched, growing more nervous every minute, pushing and pulling at buttons, while cars piled up ominously behind her. Finally, she opened the door, got out, stuck the money in the basket, and then tried to look nonchalant as she crawled back into the car. It was at that very moment that she noticed the extra handle on the door; it was a crank, it was there to roll down the window.

Sometimes, it's the overlooked things that throw me, too. Sometimes, it's overlooked facts that turn out to be pivotal. Some people view the life, death, and resurrection of Jesus Christ as a mere blip on the computer screen of life. They seek to add to their fund of knowledge by delving deeper into science and history. But, just as the little tribe of Benjamin was the one who led the way in this psalm of praise (v. 27) so the overlooked facts of Christianity can lead us to discover the real meaning and purpose of life. When we are honest about wanting to know the God of creation and redemption, He will reveal Himself.

June 29: Yokefellows

Vacationing at Buck Hill Falls some years ago, we attended a Sunday service in the hotel where we were staying. The theologian Elton Trueblood spoke, and I was interested in what he had to say. He talked about yokefellows, which was the first time I had heard the term used. I was quite struck by it. A speaker at our church retreat echoed this same thought just recently, and I was delighted to get more of a grasp of the thoughts behind the expression.

She pointed out that when oxen were used for plowing, young, inexperienced oxen were always yoked with older ones who had been in harness for many years. The young ones always fussed and fumed or kicked against the goads because they did not want to be yoked. Gradually, however, they discovered that the less they kicked, the smoother things went, because the old ox was carrying most of the burden.

I don't know of anyone who actually just longs to be yoked: for it's a loss of freedom. If we are willing to be yoked with Jesus, however, our yoke will be light, because He carries the heavy end of the burden. We will discover that if we do not fuss and fume, but accept our part, saying in effect, "Yes, Lord, I am willing to put my head in the yoke with You," we will have discovered the secret of being content whatever the circumstances.

"If you are tired from carrying heavy burdens, come to me and I will give you rest. Take the yoke I give you. Put it on your shoulders and learn from me. I am gentle and humble, and you will find rest. This yoke is easy to bear, and this burden is light." (Matthew 11:28-30 CEV)

June 30: Family Reunion

My husband and I are among the (seemingly) statewide Floridian exodus to North Carolina in the summer, and, for several years, we rented various houses there. Since there were eighteen of us in the immediate family at the time, we had what I once saw billed in a pet shop above a hamster: "Hours of mirth and entertainment."

With this number of people, there is always someone with whom to share a story, play a game, or illustrate a skill. The best part is not the fun and laughter (lots), the helping hands (lots), the doting aunts and uncles (lots), or even the sharing of what God is doing in our lives (lots). The best part is the actual and physical fact of living together and loving each other.

The unhappy parts are the cooking (lots), late night noise (lots), trips to the grocery store (lots), or childish screams of one variety or another, but the worst part is when everyone has gone. The refrigerator that seemed too small now seems too large. The dishwasher that seemed too full is now too empty. The days that seemed too short now seem too long. There is the constant tendency to look around for someone to talk to and then realize that they are not there. Then comes the thought that, of course, someday we will be together again—and then, it will be forever.

"And I heard a loud voice from the throne saying, 'Now the dwelling of God is with men, and he will live with them. They will be his people, and God himself will be with them and be their God. He will wipe every tear from their eyes. There will be no more death or mourning or crying or pain, for the old order of things has passed away.'" (Revelation 21:3-4 NIV)

July 1: Clap Your Hands

One year, we had our family's summer reunion on the top of a mountain in North Carolina, in a beautiful home that belonged to our son-in-law Clint's family. It was brandy new, with a deck on three sides, and we could look across a valley to the mountains in the distance. We were in an aerie where it seemed we could float across that valley on a passing cloud.

Getting up to that aerie was a different story, however. The trip was up a winding gravel road that made old cars shudder and new cars shiver. So, when my brother and his wife came to visit, we all lined up on the balcony deck to wave and cheer them on as they crept slowly up the side of the mountain. Suddenly, we found ourselves clapping like mad, as if to say, "Thank you for coming all this way!" When they left, we clapped too, as if to say, "Be careful on the journey down because we love you!" Thus, an instant tradition was born, and any time anyone started off downward, the others would line up in a row and clap for them until they were out of sight.

As Bill and I left the final morning, and the few who were left clapped us on, I thought how wonderful it would be if those we love could be with us as we start on our final journey to heaven, just to say, "Thank you for being here with us, and we love you." Some of us might not have family or friends to do this, but we know our Savior will be on the other side to welcome us and say, "I love you."

"Bow down and worship the Lord our Creator! The Lord is our God, and we are his people, the sheep he takes care of in his own pasture." (Psalm 95:6-7 CEV)

July 2: Beavers

Except for the occasional reminiscence of the old TV comedy "Leave it to Beaver" or the reference to someone as "an eager beaver," I never spent much time pondering the mysteries of a beaver's life. It's too bad, really, because I have a lot to learn from these little creatures with buckteeth and flat tails, as I found out from a nature show I watched the other day.

It seems that beavers don't actually hurry (as in "eager"); they just swim and build one load at a time, one stick at a time. They build dams that benefit many other pond citizens, and they keep their homes in good shape. The father beaver takes his offspring around to show them how work is progressing and to encourage their participation.

One load of mud at a time and one stick at a time drives me crazy; I much prefer instant results. But patient faithfulness to a task at hand will not only benefit our family, it will affect others who live in the same pond. Our ministry should touch them not only by what we do in our work time but by what we do in our spare time, too. If it is a slow process, we need to see it through. Moreover, if we encourage those who come after us, we reach out through them to future generations in other ponds.

"And now the prize awaits me—the crown of righteousness that the Lord, the righteous Judge will give me on that great day of his return. And the prize is not just for me but for all who eagerly look forward to his glorious return." (II Timothy 4:8 CEV)

July 3: Rejected

I don't suppose that anyone thinks that every person they meet will become a friend, but it is always special when you do find a friend. At one time, I had two friends who were different. One was a Christian, and the other was what might be termed a confused seeker (a seeker who always thought that she was right). I witnessed to her for about fourteen years, and although we differed on nearly every point on the compass, I felt we were really friends. We moved to a different side of town, but I made every effort to stay in touch—calling her for luncheon dates, and taking her special places.

One day when I was in town (as opposed to out here in the country), I pulled into a gas station and saw her standing at the pump. I rushed over to give her a hug, but she pushed me away and said she didn't feel like a hug. Well, of course, every one has off days; so, I just let it go. But, subsequent efforts to get in touch with her always failed. I called, I wrote, I did everything I could think of, but she would either not answer the phone or hang up when she heard my voice. At last, I wrote asking forgiveness for whatever I had done that had upset her, but I never heard anything.

My experience with my other friend was similar. We had children the same age, liked a lot of the same things, and were sisters in Christ. Then, one day, she just stopped calling, would not talk to me on the phone, or see me if I went to her house. I never found out what I did to her either, although I wrote several times, asking her forgiveness, too.

I had to learn not to be bitter. It took a long time, but I have left it with the Lord.

"Who are you to judge someone else's servant? To his own master he stands or falls. And he will stand, for the Lord is able to make him stand." (Romans 14:4 NIV)

July 4: True Freedom

One of our granddaughters, Rebecca, went to India on a short-term mission trip. Her church had previously worked with some Christians in a village there, and sent the group of teenagers out to help them share the love of Christ with others. Rebecca and another girl had brought their flutes, and although they weren't quite ready for the London Philharmonic, they were certainly up to celebrating God's love through music.

The small village that was their main destination took a long time to reach. After the flight to Delhi, the group endured a 20-hour train ride (with no sleeping cars!), followed by a 2-hour jeep ride.

During the day, the team went to smaller outlying villages to share their testimonies and Bible stories in open-air meetings with the villagers. They also shared at night meetings, followed by a talk from one of the Indian Christians. In one village, where there were no known Christians, many indicated a desire to know more about Christ, and they were able to share more with them.

One of the most meaningful parts of the trip occurred during a meeting with the girls and some Indian women who were Christians. The girls shared with them how precious all people are in God's eyes, and then, the girls washed the women's feet as a symbol of Christ's love and sacrifice for them. The women, not feeling highly valued in their village, were overwhelmed.

In talking with her mother later, Rebecca said the thing that impressed her the most was the radiant way the people looked after they became Christians. "They had nothing, absolutely nothing," she said "but when they came into a relationship with the one true God, they had everything."

Freedom is not found in comfortable surroundings, expensive possessions, or lots of friends. It is only found in Jesus Christ.

"And you will know the truth and the truth will set you free." (John 8:32 CEV)

July 5: Nitpicking

"So David told Joab and the army officers, 'Go to every tribe in Israel…and count everyone who can serve in the army. I want to know how many there are.'" (II Samuel 24:2 CEV)

"Joab came and told David, 'In Israel there are eight hundred thousand who can serve in the army and in Judah there are five hundred thousand.' After David had everyone counted, he felt guilty and told the Lord, 'What I did was stupid and terribly wrong. Lord, please forgive me.'" (II Samuel 24:9-10 CEV)

Do you know anyone who likes to nit-pick? Of course, when I do it, I am not nit-picking but merely giving constructive, discerning criticism!

When I first read this story, I thought God was being a nitpicker. After all, weren't there other sins such as adultery and murder that made counting soldiers pale by comparison? To me it seemed pretty low on the sin scale. The thing that I hadn't stopped to consider was why David wanted his men counted. David made the mistake of thinking he was very special indeed, and he wanted to prove it by the number of men available to fight for him. He was focusing his attention on his own power, rather than the power of God.

How quickly this sort of pride can sneak in the side door! I often let numbers be my downfall, too: the number of times I've attended church, the number of Bible studies I've attended, the number of minutes I spend in prayer or Bible study, and so on. All this is done in the name of the Lord, of course, but somehow, I focus on the numbers instead of on what God has done and is doing. Pride was Lucifer's greatest sin—don't let it be mine!

Prayer: Father God, I confess that I would like to be among the chosen who do what seems to be important work for You. Give me the heart of a servant instead!

July 6: Armor in Place

We were staying at a state park for a week enjoying a family reunion. Even though I had not had a golf club in my little paws for nearly two years, I was determined to try at least four or five holes. My husband and I were in one cart and our son-in-law in another. He was slightly behind us and I must confess we were not really paying attention as he hit. The ball flew off at an angle and caught me square in the middle of my back. I felt a jolt and a simultaneous clang. Gary was not really trying to murder his mother-in-law (Agatha Christie and Hercule Poirot would have had a hey day with that!). He had shanked his shot and it had hit me in the middle of a large magnet I was wearing across my lower back (not spiritual armor, of course, but armor just the same). It was in the right place at the right time to give protection.

Probably, that wouldn't happen again in a million years, but I'm going to be mighty careful to be armed in every situation—and not just with magnets! God's armor can't be seen from the outside, but we need to be sure it is in place in order to take advantage of the provision God has given us.

"For our struggle is not against flesh and blood, but against the rulers, against the authorities, against the powers of this dark world and against the spiritual forces of evil in the heavenly realms." (Ephesians 6:12 NIV)

July 7: The Devil and Idle Hands

The summer between my sophomore and junior year in college, I found myself with nothing to do; and so when some friends from a neighboring college suggested that it would be fun to go to Colorado for the summer, I readily fell in with their plans. My parents did as well, since I convinced them that summer school would be a wonderful way for me to catch up on missing credits.

Colorado indeed proved to be great fun. Classes were fairly sporadic, and the majority of my time was spent playing instead of studying. One night the guys convinced me that it would be a riot for me to spend the night in their fraternity house (something forbidden to individuals lacking Y chromosomes). And so, the plans were laid with much hilarity. As the actual hour approached, I felt a few qualms, but I did my best to ignore them.

We partied until bedtime, and then I snuck into the girls' bathroom with a borrowed pillow and blanket. Trying valiantly to ignore the hard, cold floor beneath me, I settled down for the night.

Morning came all too soon, and I woke sore and stiff. To make matters worse, I began to wonder (albeit rather belatedly) if it might be a little harder to sneak out than it had been to sneak in. And indeed, my fears were well founded. Upon opening the door, I discovered a welcoming party (or should I say, an <u>un</u>welcoming party) waiting for me.

I hadn't realized it, but talk had been rampant around the house that a girl had spent the night. The fact that I had remained cloistered in the bathroom (and was rather the worse for wear) was completely ignored. Very soon afterwards, the Dean of Women called me in for a visit. During the "visit", I was informed that I was to leave the campus, leave Colorado, and as far as she was concerned, leave the world at large.

Frankly, I was terrified, because this meant I had to telephone my parents with the news. When I finally screwed up the courage to call them, I didn't explain the reason for my early departure; instead I promised further explanations upon my arrival.

And so I left the realm of fun and games and headed for the dreaded confrontation. When I got off of the plane, I could see my worried-looking parents waiting for me. As soon as I reached them, I managed to gasp out my sorry little confession, asking for forgiveness. I knew I had wasted their money and my time; and I waited for the ax to fall. It didn't. My parents took me in their arms and accepted me just as I was…and never mentioned it again.

Did you know this is what God does? When we come to him and confess our sin, he forgives us and "…does not punish us as our sins deserve" (Psalm 103:10 CEV).

July 8: What's Your Rag Content?

My husband, who reads the Encyclopedia for fun and already knows more than I ever want to, told me this morning that you can estimate how long a book will endure by discovering how high its rag content is; in other words, the higher the rag count, the more durable its pages. I must admit, the phrase "rag content" never before had passed through my mind. However, I feel I can bolster my spiritual rag content by practicing endurance. Unfortunately, endurance doesn't come overnight.

Sometimes my rag content is low, and I fold up. To be honest, many times I am a better talker than a walker, but as I look to the Father, He is helping me learn to endure unpleasant circumstances. Just as my muscles (such as they are!) need constant practice to keep me in shape, so I also need constant practice in enduring.

"We can rejoice, too, when we run into problems and trials, for we know they are good for us—they help us to learn to endure. And endurance develops strength of character in us, and character strengthens our confident expectation of salvation." (Romans 5:3-4 NLT)

July 9: Parcels and People

Have you ever lugged a new purchase home, only to discover (after you've opened the box) that you somehow missed the words "some assembly required"? To make matters worse, the instructions seem to usually be written by someone who does not have command of the English language, with words written in such microscopic letters that you must resort to using a magnifying glass. I've had much experience with these "some assembly required" purchases, and, to be blunt, I am no longer fooled by the word "some." After the instructions are deciphered, I still have pieces scattered haphazardly across the floor. Then I have to figure out how to affix sprocket "A" to black hole "B"—a difficult task since I am not a space engineer (a fact that all astronauts should applaud!).

With this in mind, it is very comforting to know that our bodies are not just bits and pieces that God put together haphazardly. Every part of us (even our little toe!) has a role to play. Thank God today for His creation; and that includes you!

"For you created my inmost being; you knit me together in my mother's womb. I praise you because I am fearfully and wonderfully made; your works are wonderful, I know that full well." (Psalm 139:13-14 NIV)

July 10: God's Wisdom from Bill

This is the story of a little boy named Bill, whose Mom and Dad did their best to share God's love with him. He came to know Christ personally when he was about five, and was able to understand many spiritual concepts.

Bill had an older friend at church who was a bit fragile physically, but when I first met her, I had no idea her cancer was so far advanced. Although not able to do much, she served God faithfully in every way she could, and everyone who knew her was touched by her courage and by her love for others. One time, for instance, she and her sister came and spent several hours patiently showing Bill and his sister, Sarah, how to make Advent calendars from old Christmas cards, just as though she had nothing else more important to do with her time and energy.

Bill and his family visited her when she was no longer able to get around, and somehow Bill understood her imminent departure from earth. As they left the house, he looked up and said quietly to his mom, "My friend is going back to dust soon, isn't she?"

We will all go back to dust one of these days. I reflect on the goodness and foresight of God: He made dust into love, and I thank Him that He made faithful servants who can share that love with others.

"God has made everything beautiful in it's own time. He has planted eternity in the human heart...." (Ecclesiastes 3:11a, b NLT)

July 11: And the Answer is...

Game shows seem to have proliferated like rabbits in the past couple of years, with people scrambling to accumulate great wads of money. Some shows involve screaming out letters or picking doors, other shows require contestants to answer a lot obscure and often frivolous questions; the winners of the latter type of show usually have a massive UI (useless information) file hidden somewhere in their brain.

But, there is one question that involves neither luck nor knowledge and is not influenced by prestige or fame. The Lord asks this question, and we need to understand that the things most people on Earth think are important are of no account to God. It's helpful to know this question in advance, and to know the only answer that God will find acceptable.

The question is, "Why should I let you into my heaven?"

The answer is not "Because of the good things I've done," "Because of all the money I've given away," "Because I went to church every Sunday," "Because I was baptized," or even "Because I never killed anyone (and believe me, I REALLY wanted to!)". No, the one-word answer God is listening for is "Jesus."

Prayer: Dear God, I look to the cross, and put my trust in Jesus, who, through his death, made it possible for me to be with you.

"Then the people came to Moses and cried out, 'We have sinned by speaking against the Lord and against you. Pray that the Lord will take away the snakes.' So Moses prayed for the people. Then the Lord told him, 'Make a replica of a poisonous snake and attach it to the top of a pole. Those who are bitten will live if they simply look at it!'" (Numbers 21:7-8 NLT)

July 12: Two Worlds

My husband and I had gone for a week's vacation to an island in the Caribbean. We stayed at a beautiful resort with all the amenities and had a wonderful time playing golf, swimming, and eating. The scenery was postcard perfect, with palm trees, white sand, and clear blue water.

When Sunday came, however, we discovered that there was no worship service at the hotel. So we decided to venture out and go to one of the churches listed in the phone book.

I got the shock of my life when we went past the gate of the resort. Outside, there was only sand and a few palmetto bushes. I had no idea we had been living in such an artificial atmosphere. I had assumed the whole island was beautifully cultivated and filled with tropical flowers. I guess that was what we were supposed to think. The resort was so complete that there was no reason to step outside (unless someone wanted to go to church!). When we left the resort, we saw things in a new light; we saw the island for what it really was: we saw its wild beauty, we saw its poverty.

Unfortunately, in my spiritual journey, I don't want to leave the resort of my own making, and so I miss out on seeing the world as it really is. It is only when I step outside myself, and focus on others, that I can begin to see people for who they really are: their true beauty and their needs.

Prayer: Lord, help me to look beyond myself; help me to focus on those around me, and help me to show them your love.

"Love must be sincere." (Romans 12:9a NIV)

July 13: God's Messenger

My mother had five sons before a baby daughter came. My parents named her Rebecca Louise (Becky Lou) after my mother and my grandmother. She was a sweet child as well as photogenic, as may be seen in a portrait they had painted from a snapshot.

Becky Lou was only a few months old when the family went to spend their usual vacation at a cottage on the property of Lake Mohonk, in upper New York State. It was a rustic little place we called "Piney Woods Cabin" and although it burned down when I was about five, I still remember parts of it (especially the tiny, sweet strawberries that grew on a hill in the back). My parents hadn't been there long that year when a sudden business call made it necessary for my father to return to Pittsburgh for a few days. He went to Becky Lou's crib to kiss her goodbye. In thanking God for this lovely gift of new life, his heart was stirred to realize that he had never really had a personal relationship with God, even though he was an elder in the church.

So, he asked Christ to enter his life and make him a new creation. He never saw Becky Lou again; she died quietly in her sleep a few days later. My mother felt that God had sent Becky Lou to earth on an errand to bring my father into the Kingdom. When that was done, He took her back, for she always belonged to Him.

"You created me and put me together. Make me wise enough to learn what you have commanded. Your worshipers will see me and they will be glad that I trust your word." (Psalm 119:73-74 CEV)

July 14: Golf Advice

There was an article in our paper that had an interview with British golfer Nick Faldo. Several years ago, when his game was not up to par, he went to Ben Hogan for some advice on what he should do to win the British Open. Hogan's advice was succinct, but not very helpful. All he said was, "Shoot the lowest score."

At a different tournament, Nick went and asked the same question of Sam Snead. That gracious golfer spent two days with him and gave him detailed instructions as well as various thoughts about dealing with the expectations of others.

I don't know anybody famous, so, I'm guessing here: I bet professionals in every sport have people hounding them for advice of one kind and another. But I would think that kindness and a genuine interest in others would go a long way toward making that pro more highly regarded.

When it comes to Christianity, I think the same thing applies. I don't know any famous theologians, but you don't have to have a doctorate in religion to help and love someone else. When we do this, people see the love of Christ illustrated. After all, isn't that why we're here?

Prayer: May I be a vessel so thoroughly filled with your love that you shine through all my cracks.

"Many waters cannot quench love; neither can rivers drown it." (Song of Songs 8:7a NLT)

July 15: Weight a Minute!

A trip to the bathroom scale is always depressing for me. The great big one at the Doctor's that never makes a mistake is worse. They seem to have taken a pledge to tell the truth, the whole truth, and nothing but the truth.

The thing is, I don't WANT to hear the truth, or see it either. In fact, if I want to see it, I can look in the mirror and see more than I need to. How did all these extra little pounds come about? In my case, it was cream puffs. In others, it is something probably different, but most of them involve nibble, nibble, and nibble.

It all started in my own little head with delicious thoughts of sugarplums and other delights. In fact, I was enticed by my own lust (as unattractive as that sounds), and I sank very gradually into the quicksand of extra sweet poundage.

Of course, overeating isn't the only thing that leads me into sin. Those things don't even have to be enumerated because the Spirit Himself is quick to spotlight where I go wrong in satisfying myself. It's not a happy occasion! When He does, I immediately start to justify my actions instead of confessing them. God wants me to be honest with myself as well as with Him; He is the one who can break my bonds of sin, if I will only ask Him to do it.

"When tempted, no one should say, 'God is tempting me.' For God cannot be tempted by evil, nor does he tempt anyone; but each one is tempted when, by his own evil desire, he is dragged away and enticed. Then, after desire has conceived, it gives birth to sin; and sin, when it is full-grown, gives birth to death." (James 1:13-15 NIV)

July 16: Out of Sequence

I have now had my first experience at being in a movie—and let me tell you it was an eye opener. Many years ago, I used to do theatre work where I learned lines, blocked out action, rehearsed, and then performed it. This in no way relates to the way movies are made.

There were four cameras, three French hens—no wait—and three roles (I got to play all three). The thing that tended to confuse me most, however (and of course it doesn't take much), was that everything was filmed out of sequence. We filmed all of the doctor's lines, then all the cleaning lady's lines, and then all the patient's lines. This is not an orderly or understandable way to do things. In fact, my daughter, Virginia, who was directing this piece, was the only one who knew what was going on.

My life is very often like this: all a jumble of people and events that don't seem to make much sense. God, my loving heavenly director, has things under control. May I remember to stay in touch with Him day by day, and trust His heart when I cannot see His hand; what is confusing to me, is not to Him.

"He prayed, 'O Lord, the God of our ancestors, you alone are the God who is in heaven. You are ruler of all the kingdoms of the earth. You are powerful and mighty; no one can stand against you.'" (II Chronicles 20:6 NLT)

July 17: Elastic Editing

There is a faint possibility that after reading the previous devotional, you may be surprised to learn that after many hours of filming, we ended up with only two minutes worth of film. The reason is editing.

When I did a short interview for the Billy Graham crusade when it was in Tampa, Virginia warned me to be sure and pray for the editing. Thankfully, the editor did a wonderful job.

I realize in retrospect that editing is the scariest thing since Mount Vesuvius erupted at Pompeii. It is the easiest thing in the world to take out one word (ONE word) and change the entire meaning of a statement. Pictures and films can be altered, entire sentences can be taken out of context.

We need to pray daily for those responsible for news and entertainment. Pray that they will do their best to always present the truth to their viewers and readers.

"The Lord hates cheating, but he delights in honesty." (Proverbs 11:1 NLT)

July 18: Help Wanted

It always makes me a little nervous when I start to go into a restaurant and see a sign that says, "Help wanted." I can't help wondering where they need that help and what is going to happen to my food before I get it. Is the cook missing? Are they short of butter (always a major concern of mine!)? Are they doing dishes by hand because the dishwasher is broken? Does the waiter have an infectious disease that will cause him to keel over as he passes my table?

These cumulative thoughts usually cause me to bypass the aforementioned restaurant and try somewhere else. When I hang my little mental sign out that says, "Too busy for God today," do you think the Lord might also want to try somewhere else?

Let me consider all the things I gain when I spend time with the Lord. Doesn't it make my other plans seem rather insignificant?

"Another man, one of his disciples, said to him, 'Lord, first let me go and bury my father.'" (Matthew 8:21 NIV)

July 19: Island Invasion

Leighton Ford wrote a book several years ago entitled *How Come It's Taking Me So Long to Get Better?* The premise of this book is that when we become Christians, we are invading an island that has been held by the enemy. It's great to get our feet on solid ground, but that is only the beginning of the invasion. We have to pick our way through a lot of bushy flora and fauna (some of it hiding land mines or quicksand). There may be not only times of discouragement, we also may find ourselves sidetracked by flopping into self indulgence, which causes us to lose ground. When this happens, we have to stop and look to the only one who can turn failure into a lesson and set us back on the right path.

Christianity is a far cry from the proverbial bowl of cherries; there are plenty of pits that can cause indigestion. I had no idea of this when I became a Christian; I thought once God was in my life, my problems were over. What a surprise it was for me to discover that some problems didn't begin until AFTER I had started my spiritual journey!

As someone has said, Christianity is a banquet, but not a picnic. The important thing to remember, however, is that God does not just drop us off on the beach and walk away. He walks with us, behind us, and in front of us—all the way, every day. So, since I haven't journeyed on this path before, the very best thing is to trust Him to lead me.

"Everyone who trusts the Lord is like Mount Zion that cannot be shaken and will stand forever." (Psalm 125:1 CEV)

July 20: Name Tags

Ever since we got married, there has been confusion over our names. My maiden name was Davison. It is now Davidson. When we go places with my brother Bill and his family, the misery is compounded, because he is William Davison and my husband is William Davidson. We have a son named Will and he has a son named Will. My brother has a son named Bill and he has a son named Will. Our daughter has a son named Bill.

We have two granddaughters, one named Rebecca and one Rebekah, and my brother Bill has a granddaughter named Rebecca. So, when we are all together, if anyone calls for a William or Rebecca, desk clerks and maitre d's just put their heads in their hands and cry quietly.

It's wonderful that God knows our name. He never gets mixed up or cranky, but instead, calls us all with a voice of love.

Prayer: We thank you, God, Maker of the heavens and earth, for knowing us all by name.

"For I say this to the eunuchs who keep my Sabbath days holy, who choose to do what pleases me and commit their lives to me: I will give them—in my house, within my walls—a memorial and a name far greater than the honor they would have received by having sons and daughters. For the name I give them is an everlasting one. It will never disappear!" (Isaiah 56:4-5 NLT)

July 21: Peacocks

Peacocks are beautiful birds, but they do have one serious drawback. If you have ever heard one scream, you know what I mean. It's enough to make your hair turn gray overnight. Their voices are the most grating, unpleasant sound imaginable; I can only presume they are so busy being proud of their tails that they don't notice the unpleasantness of each other's screeches.

I have been like this in my own life. I've tried to hide strident tones and a contentious spirit with designer clothing and a handsome face (perhaps not completely *au natural*). Even though I am a soldier of the Lord, I don't believe that I am expected to shout orders at others, for when I do this, I am likely to miss the voice of my Commander.

How wonderful it would be if I would be like Joshua: "Then Joshua fell facedown to the ground in reverence, and asked him, 'What message does my Lord have for his servant?'" (Joshua 5:14b NIV).

If I listen more than I speak, I am more likely to be in step with what God wants me to do. When I stop the sound of my own voice (whether preening, complaining, or admiring), I illustrate a willingness to give the authority of my life to the Lord.

July 22: Tidal Thoughts

Each summer when our children were small, we would load bag and baggage and head for a week or two to the beach. Although this was often repeated, we never tired of it. Each morning and afternoon we would run, scramble, or stumble (according to the age of the participants) to the water's edge to swim, play, or doze (again, according to the age of the participants). By the end of the day, the beach was always littered with accumulated shells, big and small piles of sand, and general debris, even though we did keep the area free of cans, paper, and food.

Sometime during the night, the tide would come in and cleanse the beach of everything that had been left over from the day's activities. It never failed to do this, and it was accomplished without fanfare. What a beautiful picture of what the Lord does for us! When we come to Him all hot and dirty with the sin of the day, He comes quietly close, and is "…faithful and just to forgive us and to cleanse us from every wrong" (I John 1:9 NLT). There is no fanfare here, either, for Christ's forgiveness is not accompanied by the sound of trumpets, but there is great joy and gratitude when we are clean before Him. So, if the beach of your soul is littered with accumulated and unconfessed debris, come to Jesus, and He will cleanse you more surely than the tide.

"Have mercy on me, O God, because of your unfailing love. Because of your great compassion, blot out the stain of my sins. Wash me clean from my guilt. Purify me from my sin." (Psalm 51:1-2 NLT)

July 23: Mirror, Mirror on the Wall

I find it extremely depressing to shop for bathing suits. I keep waiting for the good fairy to turn me into a size 6, but, so far, she hasn't proved too helpful. Shoes and hats are best to shop for, because I only have to examine a small portion of my anatomy. Dresses are in the middle category, because I can close my eyes while I'm putting them on. But when it comes to bathing suits, I can close my eyes till the cows come home, but there's no denying it—my stomach remains convex. It looks as if a pillow was mysteriously zipped in when I wasn't looking (some days I would like to be like King Belshazzar, who was "weighed in the balance and found wanting"!).

I sow what I reap, don't I? And for me, all those snacks have reaped a heap. Somehow, it's difficult to get my eyes off what pleases me for the moment, and discipline myself for the long haul. I'm not just talking about diets, but also about inward self-discipline that God wants to become part and parcel of my life.

If I am a "soldier of the cross," I should so thoroughly understand what pleases our Commander (showing love to others, having peace, joy, patience, gentleness, goodness and self-control) that I do not waffle when faced with difficult decisions—even those as mundane as whether or not to have a hot fudge sundae.

"Soldiers on duty don't work outside jobs. They try only to please their commanding officer." (II Timothy 2:4 CEV)

July 24: Who's in Charge Here?

From the age of eight, I loved overnight camp outs. Although I was never really adept at making a bedroll that didn't unravel, or finding a place for the tent that did not grow rocks in the middle of the night, there were other aspects that made up for it. To be in the lead canoe on a perfectly still morning with the mist rising quietly and curling around my paddle was a picture I can still see clearly in my mind. I can remember stars so low in a pine-scented sky it's a wonder they didn't get tangled up in our roasted marshmallows. I felt close to God at those times, but it was all rather nebulous and impersonal. And so, although Blue Bonnet margarine hadn't as yet put in an appearance, I attributed it all to "Mother Nature."

Robert Ingersol was a well-known atheist who came to visit Henry Ward Beecher, the famous preacher. Mr. Beecher had just purchased a beautifully detailed map of the world and showed it to his visitor. Mr. Ingersol was visibly impressed and asked, "Where did you get it?" "Oh, it just happened," replied Mr. Beecher with a twinkle in his eye. "It couldn't have!" retorted Mr. Ingersol, "it's much too intricate." "You are right, of course," answered Mr. Beecher. "Some one made it up just as God fashioned a world much larger than this map." Henry Ward Beecher knew the truth that God reveals himself first in creation, and that He continues to hold that world in His hands.

God is real. Have you ever stopped to thank Him not only for creating the world you live in, but for also creating you?

"The heavens declare the glory of God; the skies proclaim the work of his hands. Day after day they pour forth speech; night after night they display knowledge. There is no speech or language where their voice is not heard. Their voice goes out into all the earth, their words to the ends of the world. (Psalm 19:1-4 NIV)

July 25: The Greatest Gift

A king once gathered the wisest men in his kingdom and offered a reward to any man who could give him one sentence that would apply to every situation that comes into a life. The winning sentence was, "This, too, shall pass."

We can rejoice too when we run into problems and trials, for we know that they are meant for our good—they help us learn patience and endurance (see Romans 5:3). We know that our God is sovereign and that He has permitted what has occurred in our lives, even the heartaches.

Today, however, I want to apply this truth to the wonderful things that come to us, for they, too, shall pass. It is true of many things: the beauty of nature, the loveliness and strength of youth, the warmth of friends, and even the family in which you have been placed.

All of this will pass away. Only God and His word are eternal.

So, wherever you are in life, cherish the good times, the hard times, the times that you have shared and loved together. Accept one another with appreciation, forgive mistakes, respect individuality, and give all the love that you have. Some day that mother or child or sibling will no longer be there to hug. Find a special way to say, "I love you" today. It is a great gift.

"In ages past you laid the foundation of the earth, and the heavens are the work of your hands. Even they will perish, but you remain forever; they will wear out like old clothing. You will change them like a garment, and they will fade away. But you are always the same; your years never end." (Psalm 102:25-27 CEV)

July 26: Harley Davidson

When we moved to Tampa, we went to buy a cat. A good cat. A superlative cat with papers to prove it. It took a long time to find him, and even longer to get the breeder to part with the papers. She was for some reason, unwilling to part with them. I should have smelled a rat (or cat rat), but I was blithely ignorant of the whole thing.

We named the cat Harley, and hoped that he would be happy with us, but it was not to be. Harley climbed the walls, the ceiling, and everyone he came in contact with. He also bit me and I had to have a tetanus shot. He was not a happy cat. We were not happy, either, and we found out, not soon enough, that Harley had ringworm.

We had been through ringworm once before, and all seven of us had broken out with it—we looked like the American Leper Colony walking down the street. So, I took Harley back to his former home and thrust him at his former owner. "Here's your cat," I snarled (in a winning way, of course). "Well, you don't think you're gettin' yur money back, do ya?" she snarled back. "I certainly do!" I re-snarled (a little less winningly). "Well, you ain't," she screamed, and stamped in her house and shut the door.

I couldn't wait for Bill to come home, and the minute the poor thing walked in the door I let him have it (he was thrilled). "We are going to sue her for every cent she's got!" I announced (sweetly). My husband is a gentle man, and his statement was this: "Why don't you just forgive her." "Forgive her???" I asked incredulously. "This is not just a matter of turning the other cheek—this is about money!" He repeated his statement. And eventually, of course, I asked God to forgive me. I felt so much better, but I didn't feel 100% better. I also eventually realized I had to ask the cat lady to forgive me for my attitude.

"Instead [of being rude] be kind and merciful, and forgive others, just as God forgave you because of Christ." (Ephesians 4:32 CEV)

July 27: Desert Traveler

The Israelites must have been happy to go into the wilderness, since it meant the end of their bondage and slavery. My reaction when I hit desert places in my life, though, is not usually the same. I may start off thinking glibly that "into each life some rain must fall," but those little words can not equip me for the miles and miles of unrelenting wasteland that lie ahead. Usually I look for a way out (that does not include rocks), hoping for a ladder from the sky, or at the very least, a camel. I have discovered, though, that the only way <u>out</u> is <u>through</u>.

Michelangelo has been credited with saying, "Much does he gain, when he who loses, learns." When I am in a desert time, I grieve, and I cannot imagine benefiting from this journey through barren wilderness. But if I can learn from an experience, then it has not been wasted. Indeed, I should ask, "What can I get out of this?" instead of asking "How do I get out of this?"

In your sandy state, focus on God in faith. Remember, He is the only source of sufficiency; He knows where you are and what you are going through. When you are able to take courage from the Father, each day as it comes, He can make your desert a well-watered garden where others may find rest.

"The Lord will guide you always; he will satisfy your needs in a sun-scorched land...." (Isaiah 58:11a NIV)

July 28: Singing in the Rain

I was all of eighteen when I graduated from being a camper to a counselor, with one year of Counselor-in-Training in between. As far as I knew, C.I.T.s didn't do anything except stay in the cabins during rest hour, so, I wasn't really prepared for the rigors of the other twenty-three hours. Our training had been very brief. In fact, it consisted of one line: "Be firm, but pleasant." Not what you could call a complete course in working with children and adolescents.

That summer it rained for 28 days in a row: all day and all night. Every morning, we would gather dispiritedly in the gloom. We would drip and attempt to find new ways to interest our charges and keep the furniture from floating away. All this paled, however, when I became a mother and began to put away childish things. Motherhood lasts a lot longer than the two months of camp, and by the time my children were 3, 2, and 1, there were already a lot of rainy days under my belt that didn't leave me singing.

How do I handle rainy days? I don't suppose Noah thought they were too great—although he had quite a bit to do to keep him busy. But I think there must have been times when he wondered when the sun would shine again, and when that happened, I believe he must have gone directly to talk to the Lord. Who else was there? We, too, can look to the Father, rain or shine. He can lift our hearts, and give us a new song. We must resolve not to be overcome with mildew when it rains on our parade, but turn it into an opportunity to spend time with God. Pour your heart out to Him, and see if your outlook doesn't turn into an uplook (there may even be a rainbow, too!).

"As long as the earth remains, there will be springtime and harvest, cold and heat, winter and summer, day and night." (Genesis 8:22 NLT)

July 29: A Counter Encounter

We had gone directly to the store from the little nine-hole golf course, which is nice to play about 7:00 a.m., before the sun fries you into a permanently comatose position. I was looking my very best of course, in blue shorts that had a Clorox stain on the front, a shirt that was damp enough to qualify as being worn non-stop on the *Tour de France*, and hair mashed flat on top by the Panama hat I wore to keep from going blind in the sun.

At the checkout counter, I looked up to see a woman I had known in my younger and more civically active days—although, what she was doing way out where we live is still a mystery. She, unfortunately, also looked at me, and when our eyes met, I could tell I had turned out just as badly as she had known I would.

When I stand before God, however, my Advocate will have provided His white robe of righteousness for me; and God will see that I had turned out just as He had known I would. So, don't take what others think of you too seriously. God loves you and me just as we are: Clorox stains and all!

"Then I heard again what sounded like the shout of a huge crowd, or the roar of mighty ocean waves, or the crash of loud thunder: 'Hallelujah! For the Lord our God, the Almighty, reigns. Let us be glad and rejoice and honor him. For the time has come for the wedding feast of the Lamb, and his bride has prepared herself. ⸸ She is permitted to wear the finest white linen.' (Fine linen represents the good deeds done by the people of God.) And the angel said, 'Write this: Blessed are those who are invited to the wedding feast of the Lamb.' And he added, 'These are true words that come from God.' (Revelation 19:6-9 NLT)

July 30: What Goes Up…

One of my daughters-in-law was with me at the mountain Laundromat doing that little household chore that always seems to need attention, even on vacation. While waiting for the dryer to crisp our clothes, we noticed a flier describing nearby mountain trails. We decided it would be fun to take the entourage on a picnic, and settled on one that was a mile and a half round trip.

We packed lunches, stowed band-aids, checked sneakers for wearability, and started off. Privately, I was a little concerned that the children would not be able to keep up, as I had been walking over a mile every day, and felt not only fit, but also very superior about the whole thing. I needn't have worried about the children, and I should have spent more time worrying about myself. Our route was called "Look Out Trail" which I foolishly assumed meant it had a nice look out. What it really meant was LOOK OUT! TRAIL! Because it was a straight uphill climb over rocks and boulders, it necessitated not only pulling me from above, but also pushing me from behind.

I had felt supremely capable, and then found out that I was not only incapable, but that I needed all the help I could get! Wise advice comes from Proverbs 16:18, "Pride goes before destruction, a haughty spirit before a fall" (NIV).

July 31: On Fireflies

Did you know that fireflies have scientists stumped? They can't seem to figure out what makes them light up, or why it's a cool light and not a hot one. The wonderful thing is, however, not HOW they shine, but that they just do it. They don't try to dazzle anyone like a high-powered flashlight, or like a comet that sears your eyeballs; they just glow contentedly.

They don't seem to care if they are over a manicured lawn with symmetrical edges or over a knotty mangrove swamp. They don't seem to care if the one watching them is a physics professor or a kindergartner. They don't seem to care about skin color, or manner of dress, nor does it seem to matter about tattoos (or lack of them) or whether the watchers have just brushed their teeth. It is just their nature to glow, and they go right on lighting up their world.

Christ called us to be lights, too. Although we don't blink, we are called upon to shine. We don't have to be bright or colorful or exciting, we just have to shine. God will use you to shine His light to someone who is in the dark, and it will be a beacon of life and hope.

"Make your light shine, so that others will see the good that you do and will praise your Father in heaven." (Matthew 5:16 CEV)

August 1: Plan B

Unlike his wife, my husband plans ahead. Bill has not only a plan A, he has a plan B for every event, every trip, and every eventuality. I have a hard time organizing plan A. The one time I had everything planned to a gnat's eyebrow, the whole thing collapsed. For some reason, I didn't realize that wedding planning usually comes under the heading of "Group Activities," and I set out to organize our daughter Virginia's wedding with the help of just one other person. I had too much confidence for two reasons:

1) We had weathered our daughter Lissa's wedding without mishap 2) I had Plan A written out with a detailed time schedule (just to show Bill how efficient I was).

When he looked at it, his only comment was the mild observation that I might have scheduled things a little too tightly—a comment I brushed off. The day was to begin with picking up my friend at a local motel and having breakfast with my brother and his family. Then we were going to zoom to the church, decorate the sanctuary and fellowship hall (in exactly three hours), attend a ski party lunch some friends were giving for out of town guests, and leave about 2:30 p.m., getting home in time for a little nap before leisurely getting dressed for the ceremony. Ha. The only thing that stayed on schedule was breakfast. It took us until 5:00 p.m. to decorate the church, and I barely had time to make it home and throw on my dress with no bath and put my already screaming feet into a pair of not-so-sensible shoes. And then, of course, there was the wedding.

Fifteen minutes before the ceremony began, the groomsmen, who later blamed their misguided actions on my son (probably correctly), tried to hold down my poor prospective son-in-law in order to write messages to Virginia under his tuxedo (one of the groomsmen was an All-American wrestler in college, so Clint didn't stand much of a chance!). He struggled, nevertheless; the unexpected result was that he dislocated his shoulder, and he had to be rushed to the hospital.

The minister was sent in to announce events as they transpired. The organist played gamely on (later she said she had never played so long in her entire life). All of the grandchildren were to sing on this occasion, as well as our choir, so, there was a great deal of standing and sitting and shuffling about. Meanwhile, Clint was knocked out with muscle relaxants so that the shoulder could be set. Then they gave him another shot to revive him. They told him he had about thirty minutes before he would pass out again (he didn't, but I was ready to jump in and break his fall even though he is several times my size, and my feet were still killing me). We got through the ceremony in record time and he did not pass out (but he did wobble a little at the reception). Everything ended happily, if not quite according to schedule. Now, I, too, try to always have a Plan B.

God is the only one who doesn't need alternate plans, for "Your way is perfect, Lord…"(Psalm 18:30a CEV).

August 2: Western Lesson

I am a late convert to books about the old West. I have learned a lot of things about the early history of our country and the wonderfully brave and persevering men and women who settled it. I've also learned a great deal about cowboys and cattle driving and life in the saddle.

For example, on a trail drive to take cattle to market, there were two important positions: point and drag (unrelated to today's computer use!). The person riding point had to scout ahead for possible danger and look for streams or rivers to water the herd. The drag had to watch for a rear attack and "eat a lot of dust" that had been kicked up by the hundreds of animals. Not only that, all cowboys had to watch out for bunch jumpers. These were cattle that got fed up with being herded along, and tried to make a dash for greener pastures, so to speak.

Whether or not I like my particular position in the herd, I want to remember that I am put here to serve. God rides both the point and drag, and He certainly does not want me jumping to a pasture that He has not selected. May I remember not to concentrate on the danger, the dust, or the difficult circumstances but on the one who is the Way.

"We serve God whether people honor us or despise us, whether they slander us or praise us." (II Corinthians 6:8a NLT)

August 3: A Taste of Honey

I no longer flinch when someone calls me "Honey," despite the following experience. One late spring, as we were moving our household back up north after spending the winter in Florida, my parents made plans to transport forty pounds of orange blossom honey harvested from our family bee hives. They hired someone to drive one of the cars, which was loaded down with baggage; the honey was also in the back seat. During the trip, unfortunately, the driver evidently hit a slick spot in the road, and the car went over an embankment. Thankfully, he was not hurt, but you can guess what happened to the honey. If you have ever spilled a jar on the floor or counter, or worse on upholstery, you can understand that the mopping up operation was too horrible to contemplate. We ended up putting the car out of its misery (and ours) by selling it to the junkman, who, presumably, salvaged the engine and exterior parts.

Too much honey is not a good thing; neither is too much golf, computer time, television, travel, reading or skydiving. I sometimes get myself so entangled in the NOW that I forget the real purpose of life is not relaxation, or even working. My purpose is to glorify God. I must change my attitude and concentrate on showing the Father that I am willing to be used where He puts me. Hopefully, I will do it with true sweetness.

"If you find honey, eat just enough...." (Proverbs 25:16a NIV)

August 4: Bed and Breakfast

"Seven years later the workers finished building [the temple] during Bul, the eight month of the year. It was built exactly as it had been planned. Solomon's palace took thirteen years to build." (I Kings 6:38, 7:1 CEV)

We usually go to North Carolina via Interstate 75, but some years ago, as part of an anniversary present, our son, Allen, and his wife, Laura, persuaded us to go up Interstate 95 and spend a night in Savannah. They live about forty five minutes away from that beautiful city, and, following an old family tradition of always going to the church that's farthest from where we live, they go to church there. They gave us the gift of a night in a Bed & Breakfast in the historic district.

The furnishings were all period pieces; our bedroom, for example, featured a huge four-poster bed that looked as though Rhett and Scarlett had just left (hopefully, the sheets were changed first). The bath, though, was modern, and even had a Jacuzzi. The parlor (where a beautiful breakfast was served) had gorgeous glass-fronted cabinets filled with Ming vases, and one had tiny drawers holding an extensive butterfly and moth collection. We spent so much time wallowing around in all this luxury that we had to rush to get to church, and, then, hurriedly pack our bags to leave. So, it wasn't until the next day that we discovered we had been so busy with all of the grandeur and luxury, we hadn't taken time to be alone with God. The writer of I Kings records that Solomon spent 7 years building God's house, and 13 years building his own. What does that say about Solomon's priorities?

Prayer: God, help me to not get distracted by the many good things in life; help me keep You first in my life.

August 5: Not Miss America

After brushing my teeth at night, I pop in a black mouth guard to keep my teeth from grinding. Then I slather petroleum jelly on my face to keep the wrinkles at a respectful distance. If I am sleeping with someone who stays up much later than sunset, I also put on a mask that keeps out the light. The general effect is that of the Lone Ranger's greasy mother with a mouth full of licorice.

I was staying with my daughter, Virginia, and her husband, Clint, who were at the time living in a mobile home with 2 Chow dogs and 2 cats while Clint finished his Ph.D. I had finished all these preparations and was just dozing off on the living room couch when the doorbell rang. A friend had brought something for my daughter's new baby.

I pushed up my mask as I sat up to be introduced but forgot that I had my mouth guard firmly in place. Then I realized that the look on the guest's face was one of incredulity. There I was with a mask perched over eyebrows, a face glistening with petroleum jelly, and a black mouth.

There are lots of times in life when I'm not really presentable. However, even if my ugly goes all the way to the bone, it doesn't matter to God. He didn't choose me (or you) because of looks. And He didn't choose me because of my accomplishments or lack thereof. Thankfully, He is a Sovereign God and He loves us all no matter what! Start your day by reflecting on God's love for you, and share that love with someone else.

"The Lord did not choose you and lavish his love on you because you were larger or greater than other nations, for you were the smallest of all nations! It was simply because the Lord loves you, and because he was keeping the oath he had sworn to your ancestors." (Deuteronomy 7:7-8 NLT)

August 6: Rip Tide

To me, August is beach weather personified. Anyone who can walk, run, skate, bike, scooter or otherwise perambulate is there at every opportunity. We are no exception. The Gulf of Mexico has many moods, and it is fun to see them all: bathtub smooth to roaring lion. After a rough storm, the water remains rough for a day or two before returning to its previous somnolent calm; and, providing you are a good swimmer, it is fun to venture out into the thundering surf.

One such day, my mother-in-law was with us. She loved being in the water, but I had never noticed that, when she swam, she was still touching bottom with her feet and just moving her arms about in a swimming motion. One time, the waves and tide were so strong that she was suddenly swept out over her head. Our older children were all excellent swimmers (they had been paddling around out there since they were able to walk), so I was concentrating on Virginia, our three-year-old, trying to keep her upright in a Styrofoam tube.

By the time I noticed Mother Edith, she was already floundering, and I was torn between letting go of little Virginia and going to help Mother Edith. It was a perilous choice: I could see that Mother Edith was starting to sink. I also knew that if I let go of the insubstantial tube, Virginia might slip under the water in a minute.

Fortunately, and in God's providence, just at that very minute, our son, Will, popped up from under the water practically at my feet, and I yelled at him to get his grandmother. Will was thirteen and had taken some kind of rescue course. He managed to get Mother Edith back to dry land, and I managed to keep from fainting dead away with relief. We all went back to sit on the sand to recover, and then went to get a much needed nap (at least two of us needed it!). Mother Edith was with us at the beach many times after that, but afterwards, I noticed, she never went in past her ankles.

What happens when I get beyond my depth and the tides of life sweep me away? I have to be willing to put myself totally in the hands of the Savior, for He is the only one who can rescue me.

"We wait in hope for the Lord; he is our help and our shield." (Psalm 33:20 NIV)

August 7: Animal Life on the Windshield

We never found out exactly how or when the salamander crawled onto our car, but we didn't notice him until we were on the highway. He had inched his way almost up to the wipers and was staring beadily at us through the other side of the glass. It was rather disconcerting to be looking out and have something small and orange looking back at you.

My husband slowed the car and pulled off the road. "What are you doing?" I asked. "Getting that poor salamander," was the reply. When he opened the door and reached for him, however, the creature zipped down the hood and secreted himself somewhere in the inner reaches. All attempts to rescue him proved fruitless. Twice more this little incident was repeated before a triumphant grab was made. Bill then safely deposited the nervous salamander in the long grass of the roadside field. Almost immediately, after he had released the salamander, Bill worried that there might not be enough water for him to drink out there. I finally convinced him that 1) we would never be able to find him again in that field, 2) we didn't have any water with us, 3) we had no control over rain, and, 4) he was probably used to foraging for himself. We departed from The Freedom Trail.

As I think about how a man cared for an insignificant salamander, I think about how much more God cares for us. Sometimes I don't appreciate the extent of His love and mercy; so it took a tenderhearted husband and a small, orange salamander to remind me.

"Aren't two sparrows sold only for a penny? But your Father knows when any one of them falls to the ground. Even the hairs on your head are counted. So don't be afraid! You are worth much more than many sparrows." (Matthew 10:29-31 CEV)

August 8: Watch Where You're Going

Our entire family group had gone for a long hike in the mountains (at least I thought it was long). Eventually, we all did at last manage to reach civilization and I felt quite smug about the whole thing. The trail had been rather rough in spots. I had picked my way as carefully, as though I were walking through a minefield (I didn't want to spend the rest of the summer in a body cast).

A day or two later, as I watched some of the grandchildren work on a creek dam not far from our cabin, I had the inexplicable urge to exhibit my athletic ability. I was feeling comfortable after my great hiking success. I demonstrated this by leaping over the creek bed. I'm sure I was off the ground for a second or two there. Unfortunately, upon landing, I sprained my ankle.

Safety experts tell us that most accidents happen in the home. I suppose one reason for that could be that we spend more time there. It may be, however, that we also tend to be more careless in familiar territory. I thought I was in familiar territory with my athletic skills, but I overestimated my creek-leaping capacity.

It is exactly when I am complacent (contemplating my casseroles or relaxing in front of a re-run) that the Adversary slips in. When I become lax and careless (and proud of how well I am doing!), I am more likely to fall because I have not watched and prayed.

"If you think you are standing strong, be careful, for you, too, may fall into the same sin." (I Corinthians 10:12 NLT)

August 9: The Ice Cream Machine

Taking five children out to dinner was more than an adventure: it was an experience of both pride and prejudice, dipping down into apprehension and aggravation. Experienced as we were, somehow we were never prepared for the events that cropped up without warning.

We had taken our brood to a carefully chosen family-type restaurant and meals had been ordered and consumed in relative tranquility (probably tranquil only to relatives). Then, the waitress (who, evidently, had no children) announced the availability of a self-serve ice-cream machine. I bravely went to oversee this operation. Whether it is that I am just naturally inept, or the machine went on the fritz, the contraption would not stop. Events developed rapidly after that. I pushed the handle up, down and sideways, but the ice-cream just kept pouring out, making me feel as though I had been dropped into a Lucille Ball comedy skit. We filled up every bowl around with no stoppage in sight, so I hastily sent one of the children to get help from someone in higher authority. I had both hands cupped under the spout when the management appeared around the corner.

Sometimes, I feel my troubles are coming faster than ice-cream out of a berserk ice-cream machine. Then, it's time to quit relying on what I can handle and ask for help from the only one who knows the situation and its purpose in our lives. I need to resolve not to keep filling up dishes with various and sundry solutions of my own, but to go to God, whose ear is open to children who cannot manage on their own.

"You answer us with awesome deeds of righteousness, O God our Savior, the hope of all the ends of the earth and of the farthest seas...." (Psalm 65:5 NIV)

August 10: Toy Test

Our daughter Virginia was about three when she broke one of her favorite toys. With tears puddling in big brown eyes, she brought the offending article to my attention. "Look what happened!" she blurted, hanging on tightly to the toy. I could certainly see from the part that was not being hugged tightly that there was a definite break in things.

I have no mechanical ability. I do have glue, however, so I said, "Hand it to me, Honey, and I'll see if I can put it back together." She clasped the toy tighter and tears continued to slide down her cheeks. "You'll really have to give it to me, Sweetie," I insisted, "because I can't do a thing while you are holding on to it." I guess it boiled down to a question of trust: did she trust me enough to let go? Eventually, she decided to trust me, although with a great amount of apprehension (which matched the apprehension on the part of the gluer). Thankfully, it was repaired and returned, although not in what might be termed pristine condition.

Is there something broken in your life: a heart, dreams, hopes? God can mend that which is broken. But we must first give it completely to Him.

"I, the Lord your God, will make up for the losses caused by those swarms and swarms of locusts I sent to attack you. My people, you will eat until you are satisfied. Then you will praise me for the wonderful things I have done." (Joel 2:25-26a CEV)

August 11: Children 101

Before I was a parent, I thought I was an expert at childrearing. The truth is, of course, that I was pretty clueless. For example, before we had children, I felt the only important thing about raising children would be good manners. Because of their manners, everyone would know not only that I was perfect, but that my children were perfect as well. I had many of weird ideas like that. I had the notion that after they reached eighteen they would venture far away, and they would, once in a while, write to thank me for a job well done; meanwhile, I wouldn't really be deeply involved. Ha! Anyone could see I had a lot to learn.

I found out that, when my children were hurt or laughed at or rejected, it hurt me. I found out that it only takes a nanosecond for a toddler to disappear…or to become quiet, which can be even worse (they are most likely into something). I found out that I was emotionally involved at every stage of growth (way, way, way past eighteen). I was deeply involved in listening for the first word, and, then, I was deeply involved in wishing for silence. I was involved in school plays, cupcakes for 40, and in fending off questions about algebra, physics and chemistry. I was involved in finding out about the child who invited my third grader over to play. I was involved in bags of dirty laundry, with not enough underwear in there, and wondering why there wasn't. I was involved in SAT's and worried over the resulting scores. I was involved in graduation and in wondering why my college students didn't write home, and wondering how they managed to leave a hole in my heart big enough to fall into. I was involved in money and the lack thereof. I was involved in Parent Days far, far away. I was involved in careers, weddings, and grandbabies—and I found out that after all is said and done, there is no end to being involved, or to loving.

Manners are certainly nice, but they are not the main thing, by any means. I eventually discovered that the main thing was and is to love and to pray for my children. I do my best to illustrate Christ for them. I pray that they will they pass on the torch of faith to their children and those who follow after. May it be a line of love that reaches on forever.

"I could have no greater joy than to hear that my children live in the truth." (III John 4 NLT)

August 12: On the Road

In the 1950's, a friend of ours drove from Florida to Indiana with a neighbor to look at a certain machine, to see if they wanted to invest in it. I-75 was still a gleam in the contractor's eye at this stage, so, their trip took place on little, two-lane roads. In order to save time (and a motel room), they put a mattress in the back of their station wagon so that they could take turns driving. The one not at the wheel would thus be able to catch forty winks while the other drove. About 2 a.m., our friend couldn't keep his eyes open any longer, so he pulled over to a nearby driveway and poked his traveling companion awake. The man staggered out and got into the front seat while Buster fell on the mattress and immediately drifted off to sleep. After a while, Buster felt his friend shaking him, so he reluctantly yielded the mattress to his friend. Sitting in the driver's seat, he turned his head to check for any oncoming traffic. That's when Buster discovered they were still by the same driveway and the same mailbox. His friend had gone forward, but he had merely exchanged a supine sleeping position for a sitting one behind the wheel.

Sometimes, I feel I am going forward in my Christian walk when really I am just parked with the motor running. The funny thing is that I rarely recognize my stagnancy. I'm perfectly happy to not face anything new. Growth involves change, and often the scenery around me isn't what I would have chosen. So, when my roadside looks a little bleak, I just have to look on it as a mile closer to heaven.

"Everyone who competes in the games goes into strict training. They do it to get a crown that will not last; but we do it to get a crown that will last forever." (I Corinthians 9:25 NIV)

August 13: The French Fool

My ninth and tenth grades were spent in a small private school in Sarasota. My parents were under the impression that, because it was a small school and had a good teacher-student ratio, I would learn to be a good student.

They were mistaken, of course. Education cannot be just placed on a plate with the hope that the pupil will eat. I demonstrated this fact especially well in French class, where we had an old teacher who could be sidetracked and buffaloed three minutes into the class. We were supposed to be studying *Les Miserables*, but after one year of backtracking and sidetracking, I don't think we got beyond the fourth chapter. Idleness and treachery had won the day!

I found out many years later, that we were the fools, not the teacher. We had not won, we had lost: I missed out on an early opportunity to study a great masterpiece. Fortunately, God cannot be manipulated or sidetracked…ever.

"The Lord has said, 'These people praise me with their words, but they never really think about me. They worship me by repeating rules made up by humans. So once again I will do things that shock and amaze, and I will destroy the wisdom of those who claim to know and understand.'" (Isaiah 29:13-14 CEV)

August 14: Original Creations

I was at a conference when I received one of my more unusual requests. A lady came up to me and asked to take my picture so that her children would know that there really was someone in the world who was as old as she was—and just as crazy. Unfortunately, there was no time for this statement to be expanded into a conversation, so, I'm not sure of all the implications and ramifications. But I can pretty well see this: if that lady is like me, she has always been crazy. Old age erases and changes a lot of things but not our basic personality. Craziness does not suddenly come upon us with the birth of children (although, of course, that helps): inside we are pretty much the same as we always have been, even if the accoutrements on the outside have dropped or expanded about a foot.

In other words, we are the way God created us. Some of us are born to be solid plodders, others flit to every flower that waves a blossom. Some are extroverts, and others prefer to hole up without company. Some adore sushi and others wouldn't touch a raw fish with a ten-foot pole. A few see the negative side of things (good for photographers), while others are irritatingly positive. Some feel impelled to test every limit put upon them, and others are as tractable as butter on a hot day.

So, no matter if you are slow, fast, sober-sided, or crazy, you can just relax: God made us all different. We are each one an original—and God loves us just the way we are!

"Are we not all children of the same Father? Are we not all created by the same God?" (Malachi 2:10a-b NLT)

August 15: Flatlander

My brother, Bill, who lives in East Tennessee, teases all Floridians by calling them "Flatlanders" because they have never had to navigate in the mountains or learn the techniques of downshifting. The highest things most of us see around here are the overpasses on the highway, and we don't exactly have to "lift up our eyes unto the hills" to do that. All of this, naturally, tends to make a rather dull landscape (palmetto bushes and pine trees are just not that interesting!).

Our lives can be pretty dull sometimes, too, I guess, being the same old routine of work and work, or else work and sleep, or even sleep and sleep. And it doesn't seem to matter whether you are an office worker, a home worker, or a school worker, because it all seems to become one flat landscape after a while. We long for a mountain to break the monotony. As the drab days, the dreary days, and the dull days go by, we seem to plod on endlessly without any fresh mountain breezes. However, as Vance Havner points out in one of his books (I can't remember where!), "A humdrum day may be no less a holy day and a happy day. He is with us all the days…including this one!"

So, even if we can't look to the mountains, we can look to the Lord for His strength and joy for the day. And one of these days we will find that we have deer feet, feet that enable us to stand with confidence on the heights.

Prayer: Father, forgive me when I get tired, bored or discouraged with my daily life. Give me the feet of a deer, that can serve you in both low places and high, and may they be beautiful as I share Your love with those I meet.

"He makes my feet like the feet of a deer; he enables me to stand on the heights." (II Samuel 22:34 NIV)

August 16: Television

Television producers would be amazed, yea, verily, astounded (and no doubt appalled) to learn that not everyone in America watches the little black box. Having traveled in many of the nooks and crannies of our country, I have discovered that quite a lot of people are able to exist quite comfortably without indulging that particular medium (I think it was Malcolm Muggeridge who said it was called medium because it was neither rare nor well done).

Even so, I am not really panning television. Like books, movies, and radio, television can be used as a vehicle for either good or evil. But it just amazes me that people spend millions and millions of dollars producing shows that aren't even worth being turned on. It seems to me if you are going to invest a lot of time, money, and effort into something, it should be something worthwhile—something that's going to last.

May I also invest my time wisely!

"Those in frequent contact with the things of the world should make good use of them without becoming attached to them, for this world and all it contains will pass away." (I Corinthians 7: 31 NLT)

August 17: Communion Service

A small church in the Baltimore area left me with a particularly long-lasting and fragrant memory. We had been told at the morning service that there would be a communion service that evening. We were asked to come and leave in silence in order that our talking might not detract from the meaning and focus of the service.

When we entered the candlelit church that night, we saw in front of the pulpit a simple cross, made from two thick tree branches. When the service began, the pastor spoke from the back of the church, explaining that he did not want anything to come between the cross and us. Hymns were sung, a devotional message was given, and, then, communion was served, with time allowed for introspection and repentance. I know the Lord brought to my mind several sins that had to be confronted and confessed before I could partake of the elements, and I'm sure that was true of many others as well. We quietly left after we sang a hymn that concluded, "Jesus paid it all, all to him I owe; sin had left a crimson stain, he washed it white as snow." I think there were many who had done real business with God because of a pastor who had the vision of seeing that Christ was lifted up.

"You are kind, God! Please have pity on me. You are always merciful! Please wipe away my sins." (Psalm 51:1 CEV)

August 18: Viewpoint

The first thing I noticed was her hair. Actually, it was the only thing I could see because she was sitting directly in front of me on the plane, and her head stuck up over the top of the backrest. Her hair was the most unusual and beautiful I have ever seen. It was a honey blonde with little shiny depths and sparkles in the few hairs that the sun touched through the plane's window. It reminded me of those impossible hairdos you see in the movies where the heroine goes through fire and flood and ends up with only a few tousled curls—except this was real, and I noticed the man sitting next to her was extremely attentive. They laughed softly together and shared companionable secrets. I decided she must be a stunning model of some kind, and I couldn't wait to see her face when we landed. She stood as her husband gallantly gathered items from the overhead rack.

I want you to know she was one of the homeliest women I have ever seen. But her husband looked upon her with eyes of love.

This is how Christ looks at us. There is no one too inferior, too ugly, too handicapped, too ungraceful, or too sinful for Him to love. We are all transformed by that love into someone beautiful.

"You have stolen my heart, my sister, my bride; you have stolen my heart with one glance of your eyes, with one jewel of your necklace. How delightful is your love, my sister, my bride! How much more pleasing is your love than wine, and the fragrance of your perfume than any spice!" (Song of Songs 4:9-10 NIV)

August 19: Golf Games and Golf Clubs

It was very early in the morning when we teed off and the dew was still heavy. Berms on the course resembled rumpled blankets thrown over pillows and left out all night. A bullfrog harrumphed dieselly in the background as I prepared for my second shot. I looked down at my iron where the manufacturer had the brand name cut into it: "Faultless."

When I swung (actually every single time I swung), I noticed that my clubs didn't live up to their billing. There was always just a little something that threw them off: a bad lie, a bird that took off suddenly, sun shining in my eyes, or, of course, possibly the owner of the club.

"Faultless" does not describe my golf game, and faultless does not describe my life. I stagger from rough to rough, sometimes landing in water, which somehow attracts my ball like a magnet whenever I approach (if this mysterious attraction could be patented, surely someone could find a use for it!). I get behind trees, in sand traps, and every conceivable difficulty. Worst of all, I often three-putt the green (sometimes I even four-putt!) when I finally get there.

Life, like golf, is rarely ever in the fairway. Hazards leap out with alarming regularity, and always from an unexpected direction (I have noticed, however, that if I keep my head down it's easier to pray!). When I finally got to the fringes of the green years, I discovered it still "ain't over till it's over" as Yogi Berra used to say. In golf games and life, I must keep on persevering, even if I have clubs that aren't faultless…and I have to remember that God loves me even in the rough.

"And now, all glory to God, who is able to keep you from stumbling, and who will bring you into his glorious presence innocent of sin and with great joy. All glory to him, who alone is God our Savior, through Jesus Christ our Lord. Yes, glory, majesty, power, and authority belong to him, in the beginning, now and forevermore. Amen." (Jude 24-25 NLT)

August 20: Bridging the Gap

"The body of Christ has many different parts, just as any other body does. Some of us are Jews, and others are Gentiles. Some of us are slaves, and others are free. But God's Spirit baptized each one of us and made us a part of the body of Christ. Now we each drink from that same Spirit." (I Corinthians 12:12-13 CEV)

We were in a big city for a conference, and my friend and I were out for some morning exercise. We were walking fairly briskly, considering our age, and climbed onto a bridge surrounded by the fumes of passing cars. Suddenly, we were aware of two athletes coming toward us: one jogging and one riding a bike. We could tell they were athletes because they wore helmets, expensive sport shoes, and they weren't sweating. In our bulbous, mismatched outfits, we felt pretty much out of their league. We knew they knew we were out of their league. But, as they got closer, they both looked up from their labors and smiled a hello. We smiled back. We had been accepted even though they were younger, faster, thinner, and had muscles instead of a few quivering leg lumps. We were one of the group!

This is the way it should be in the Body of Christ: each one should be accepted because we are in the group. We may be tottery and slow, without any visible means of support; we may be unlearned, unlovely, and childish, or brilliant, wealthy and famous. None of this matters in God's Kingdom because the ground is still level at the foot of the cross. We are one of the group, not because of <u>who</u> we are but because of <u>whose</u> we are.

August 21: Impression at the Dentist's

My teeth are very soft. Added to this is the regrettable fact that I am an inveterate gum chewer. As a result, I have spent eons of time in many a dentist chair across the nation—not a problem for them, but not good for my wallet.

After fillings, of course, come crowns. I now have so many that when I cast my crowns before the Lord, I will no doubt out-do nearly everyone. Today, as I was going through one of the many stages of pricking, gouging, and grinding for yet another crown, the thought struck me that the temporary crown that was being inserted was just that: temporary. It's not the real thing; it's an imitation of a sort.

Jesus Christ, on the other hand, is not an imitation, He is the exact expression of God—the mirror image. He came to show us what God is like, because we could never look at God. When we look in a mirror, we see the image of ourselves. Jesus is what J.B. Phillips calls "the radiance and glory of God." How wonderful that He would stoop to become not just a man but a perfect man who was willing to be a servant and be crucified for sins He did not commit!

Prayer: I don't think I will ever fully realize Your glory, Lord; but I want You to see in me the possibility of another servant.

"The Son is the radiance of God's glory and the exact representation of his being, sustaining all things by his powerful word...." (Hebrews 1:3a NIV)

August 22: Our Creator God

It is almost impossible for us to imagine how God created the world and all who inhabit it. Even more mind-boggling is His attention to detail, both in flora and fauna.

Since I am visually handicapped, I listen to books on tape. I recently read one called *Ninety-Nine Gnats, Nits and Nibblers* by a professor of entomology at the University of Illinois. It was amazing to hear about all of these animals, with their various and sundry adaptations to the environment in which they live. One animal that particularly intrigued me was a mealworm that lives in the desert (although I didn't quite catch what kind of meal there is out there…). The interesting part is how this worm gets its water. In the early morning, it climbs up a sand dune and stands on its head. Then as the dew condenses, it rolls down its abdomen and falls into its mouth. Isn't that amazing?

It is also amazing that we too are fearfully and wonderfully made, and able to worship the great God who created us in His image and stooped to share His nature with us. God is seen in creation, but He is most clearly seen in us, for we may tell of His grace.

"So God created people in his own image; God patterned them after himself; male and female he created them." (Genesis 1:27 NLT)

August 23: Smoke Gets in Your Eyes (And Other Places)

It was a rather dark and dreary day, and my brother, Bill, was looking around for something to brighten up his life. At the ripe old age of 9, this should not have proved an insurmountable task, and indeed it wasn't. Earlier, he had purloined a few cigarettes from my father's study, so, with the knowledge that mother was upstairs, he sashayed casually into the downstairs bookroom.

He lit up and puffed gamely away, in spite of the rather greenish tint coming into his features. He finished the cigarette and threw it into the fireplace. After a few moments, he decided to prove that he was indeed a man of the world, and lit another. He heard footsteps just then, so he threw the second cigarette into the aforementioned fireplace and began to furiously fan the air with his hands. The door flew open, and my mother looked in at him through the thick cloud of smoke.

"Bill," she said, in an astonished voice, "are you smoking?"

My brother, always a quick thinker, said, "No, mother, I'm burning rubber bands."

My mother, who knew perfectly well he wasn't burning rubber bands, didn't lock Bill out of the house or kick him out of the family (although perhaps she made sure the cigarettes were under lock and key!). When we grieve God by actions that do not reflect him, He responds in the same way. He is not pleased, yet He is patient with children who insist on their own way, and He continues to love and accept them.

"Don't you realize how kind, tolerant, and patient God is with you? Or don't you care? Can't you see how kind he has been in giving you time to turn from your sin?" (Romans 2:4 NLT)

August 24: The Helper

If you have children, you will know there comes that happy stage in their lives when their pride and pleasure is to help. This rarely extends into the teenage years, unfortunately, but seems to end abruptly with the onset of muscular coordination. While it lasts, however, it can be quite pleasant. Every parent's heart is thrilled the first time a little voice asks anxiously if she may be of some assistance, usually proffered in the form of "Me help?" A chair is dragged to the sink so that the helper may reach the necessary tools, and instructions are lovingly given. Chaos soon reigns, however, and the decision is made to move to the bedroom where instructions are now given in a carefully controlled voice. It takes thirty minutes longer than usual to make the beds, thus throwing off the morning schedule. Soon the dynamic duo enters the living room where instructions are abandoned, and the older member just tries to keep vases and lamps from hitting the playing field. Soon there comes the fleeting, unbidden thought: "Really, it would be so much easier if I didn't have so much help."

I wonder if God ever thinks things like that? Am I guilty of helping God by trying to enter His field of operations? Do I think I can rush things along by putting in my clumsy little fingers? Am I really letting God control my life…or am I trying to help?

"Trust in the Lord with all your heart and lean not on your own understanding; in all your ways acknowledge him, and he will make your paths straight. Do not be wise in your own eyes…." (Proverbs 3:5-7a NIV)

August 25: Disappointments

Have you ever had cause to be disappointed in God? Ever had a prayer that wasn't answered? Ever had a burden that wasn't lifted? Ever had a promise that wasn't fulfilled? Ever had a need that wasn't met?

If I take time to be absolutely quiet before God and lay my anguish before Him, letting go of pride and control and demands, I sometimes find that I have been putting my faith in the answer I wanted rather than in God…desiring His presents rather than His presence. I can know with great certainty that the Father to whom I have prayed will work out every situation for my good (even though that situation may not be good in itself!).

"Just as parents are kind to their children, the Lord is kind to all who worship him" (Psalm 103:13 CEV)

August 26: Jiminy! It's a Cricket!

We live on three quiet acres in the outback of Tampa. When our bedroom window is open at night we can hear a cricket filling the darkness with sound. He is evidently a soloist, because there are no other chirps heard in answer, but he sounds cheery and happy out there…deterred neither by his lonely vigil nor the total blackness.

Sometimes, if there are no other Christians around, trying to be a light can be a lonesome experience…but don't be tempted to think that your witness doesn't count for much. It doesn't take much light to show in the darkness, nor much of a chirp to make a sound in the silence.

I need to remember that wherever I have been planted (either for a decade or a weekend), I may be the only light by which others see Christ.

"You are the light of the world—like a city on a mountain, glowing in the night for all to see. Don't hide your light under a basket! Instead, put it on a stand and let it shine for all." (Matthew 5:14-15 NLT)

August 27: Lettuce Pray

In my younger days, I often went to a small drive-in restaurant south of Tampa noted for its pies. Knowing that life is short (and that dessert should come first), I took the children to this restaurant when we actually moved to Tampa while we were waiting for the moving van to arrive. I felt it was necessary to set a good nutritional example, so I ordered a sandwich before I launched blissfully into my pie order. The children also ordered sandwiches. Virginia ordered a bacon, lettuce and tomato. The waitress explained that they were out of tomatoes at the moment, but since she wasn't that big on tomatoes anyway, she said that would be fine. The sandwiches arrived, and we discovered that they had forgotten the bacon, so she was left, momentarily, looking forlornly at a piece of limp lettuce stuffed between two slices of bread.

Sometimes, I feel that life has handed me a lettuce sandwich; a life that just lies there—limp and uninteresting. May I remember that there are many who have neither lettuce nor bread, and there are many who do not have God's sustaining power.

When life seems dull, I will think of others instead of myself: I'll write a letter, send an encouraging email, bake a pie—because the more I give to others the less time I'll have to grumble over my lettuce. May I turn it into a feast of love for someone else.

"Each one should use whatever gift he has received to serve others, faithfully administering God's grace in its various forms." (I Peter 4:10 NIV)

August 28: Wedding Plans

When Bill and I first started making plans for our wedding, we decided that the end of September would be a good time to get married. Accordingly, when mother and I were ordering the bridesmaid's dresses, I wondered aloud about velvet. "Perfect, Dahling," said the wedding consultant, "Velvet is exquisite for fall!" (either she was extremely fond of the word "exquisite" or her vocabulary was severely limited. She used it in every other sentence).

When May was fading, and June appeared on the horizon, Bill and I decided we couldn't wait all that time until September, so, I asked mother if we could move things up to the end of August. Mother talked to the wedding consultant who upped her exquisite count and redoubled her efforts. The order for the bridesmaid's velvet dresses was set in concrete, however, and couldn't be changed for love or money (or heat).

The day of the wedding dawned bright and sunny. And hot. And there were eight bridesmaids looking drenched and red in velvet while the temperature stood at 103? (no air conditioning, of course). Very few of them are still speaking to me. Where was my brain when I was making all those plans?

As the years have passed, I don't know that I have improved that much. I am always getting what seem to be brilliant flashes of inspiration and then jumping into the quicksand. I act first and then ask God about it, instead of the other way around. Since this seems to be my past and present *modus operandi*, I am working on my future, trying to slow down to see what God might have in mind!

"How do you know what will happen tomorrow? For your life is like the morning fog—it's here a little while, then it's gone. What you ought to say is, 'If the Lord wants us to, we will live and do this or that.'" (James 4:14-15a NLT)

August 29: Anniversary Gratitude

As some of my readers know, I collect both friends and jokes. I am happy to add to either collection. However, my husband is the resident wit. Alas, most of his quips are lost in the mists of time because I didn't think to keep track of them, but I do have two examples. We have taken to doing extra hard crosswords, hoping that a team effort will solve that which seems unsolvable. The other night Bill was laboring away at this and came upon the clue "fatty acid ester." He asked me about it (which was useless, of course) and then, said musingly, "Isn't that one of those actresses on television? (the more you say it, the more likely it sounds).

Then, another day out of a clear blue sky and apropos of nothing, he mentioned in a confidential tone, "If there were a cigarette called 'Rarely,' and you smoked it, then, when you had to fill out one of those forms at the doctors office that asked if you smoked, you could say, 'Only Rarely.'"

Of course, there is more to marriage than humor, and for a young flibberty gibbet that knew as much about marriage as a potato chip, I fell into one of God's richest blessings. I was not a Christian at the time (although I thought I was), and thus, I brought very little depth into life's most important contract. But, my gallant, always courteous Southern gentleman carried me along and changed me greatly. He has always been true "…in rich and poor, in sickness and in health," and a positive influence for integrity and kindness. He has managed to help me be a whole person, and what I would never have been without him. He has sat in doctor's offices *ad nauseum*, and once, after two ten hour days of shuttling back and forth, said, "If we ever decide to give a party, we can invite every doctor in town because we know them all personally." He re-dedicated his life to Christ the same week that Christ entered my life, and although, naturally, we have had squabbles of one kind and another (mostly due to Miss-Had-to-Have-Her-Own-Way), one of my greatest praises to the Father is that He has allowed and blessed this special relationship. On this day, in 2003, we celebrated 50 years of marriage.

"As the Scriptures say, 'A man leaves his father and mother to get married, and he becomes like one person with his wife.'" (Ephesians 5:31-32 CEV)

August 30: Hearing Loss

When I was repeating my wedding vows, I had to actually scream above what I thought was the blood roaring in my ears. I was amazed that excitement would have that effect on me. Television was in its infancy then, and there were no camcorders to immortalize this eventful occurrence, but we had rented a large tape recorder (large enough to swallow a bridesmaid), and had a record made of the ceremony.

When I heard the record, I just burst out laughing. What I had thought was blood rushing in my ears, was the roar of a train only a block away! I wasn't hard of hearing, I was hard of listening!

The same thing applies to Scripture. Hearing Scripture means it can go in your ears while all the time you are reviewing a movie, wondering about the roast in the oven, figuring out the best way to cut class Monday, or all the while drawing meaningful doodles on your bulletin. Listening to Scripture means hearing with both your ears and your heart. It not only means knowledge, it means application—application to your own life, not your spouse or the lady in front of you, who should certainly be listening because she needs it.

Through the many years of listening to sermons, I have made the terrible discovery that I am much better at hearing than I am at listening. I have also discovered that this is a habit not easily overcome. It takes motivation and a strong act of will to turn from "ho hum" to "How can I apply this to my life because of what the Lord is saying to me?" Give me ears to listen to your voice, Lord!

As Deuteronomy says, regarding the book of the law, "It is to be with him, and he is to read it all the days of his life so that he may learn to revere the Lord his God and follow carefully all the words of this law and these decrees…" (Deuteronomy 17:19 NIV).

August 31: A Change in the Weather

The end of August has always seemed to signal that summer has come to a screeching halt. It is the end of lazy days, the end of spur of the moment jaunts, the end of ocean breezes or mountain views, the end of all the things we had joyously anticipated throughout the past seasons. Even the beach, which outwardly looks pretty much the same, has a somewhat different quality of loneliness at the end of August, as if it senses change.

I have felt this feeling spiritually, too: the general loss of the sense of expectation and a general depression about the coming chill. I know, though, that my feelings are notoriously unreliable. In fact, there is fruit to be harvested in the cold of fall that could never have come in the halcyon days of summer.

Since there is not a grain of planting dirt in my body, I am not familiar with flowers or vegetables and not many fruits, but I do know that citrus is at its sweetest after there has been a frost. There are frosts that touch our lives, too. No one likes the cold dark days that seem to hang on forever. In fact, I've been known to work up a good case of resentment, wishing that the days of sunny comfort and ease were back. But the process of ripening does not happen overnight, and the end of summer may be the beginning of new sweetness.

When I feel petulant or apprehensive about what is happening, I can always turn to my heavenly Father, and let Him fill me with the fruit of the Spirit.

"All kinds of fruit trees will grow along both sides of the river. The leaves of these trees will never turn brown and fall, and there will always be fruit on their branches. There will be a new crop every month, without fail! For they are watered by the river flowing from the Temple. The fruit will be for food and the leaves for healing." (Ezekiel 47:12 NLT)

September 1: As I Stood Dyeing

I know perfectly well this subject is not what William Faulkner had in mind when he wrote his book *As I Lay Dying*, but I could not resist the urge to be silly. A while back, I needed some green dye to dye some hose for a skit I was doing. Because dye is not one of the things I have on hand, and I was not driving at the time, I had to ask Bill to go to the store for me. When he returned, I plunged the hose into a large pan and started cooking. I am a messy cook at the best of times, so naturally I managed to get green dye on my shirt. I didn't notice the problem until I had poured the water out, so I had to ask Bill to go get some more green dye so that I could dye the whole shirt green. Then I got it on my nightgown, and Bill manfully made a third trip. I now own three green articles of clothing—none of which are particularly attractive.

If you stop to think about it, sin can splatter the same way. I've heard people say, "I'm not hurting anyone but myself." This little statement is untrue in at least two ways: 1) you are not living on a planet inhabited by only one person and 2) it is impossible to keep the dye from spreading.

Not only that, but we count as individuals. In other words, if we hurt ourselves, we are hurting the Body of Christ. As John Donne has said, "No man is an island." Everything we do or say affects others in some way. It is selfishness in the extreme to think only of how things affect us and to refuse to take others into consideration. So, let's clean up our act here, and look at the big picture. When you are tempted to step into a realm that is not pleasing to God, and you know very well when that moment comes, remember that consequences have a large splatter.

"Late one afternoon, David got up from a nap and was walking around on the flat roof of his palace. A beautiful young woman was down below in her courtyard, bathing as her religion required. David happened to see her, and he sent one of his servants to find out who she was." (II Samuel 11:2-3a CEV)

September 2: Airport Vignette

We were sitting in the St. Louis airport, eating one of those non-nutritional meals you can get away with if your children aren't with you—i.e., popcorn and raspberry soda. Beside us was a moving sidewalk, on which humanity, in all its forms, came and went. My friend saw him first. He was carrying a bulging backpack, and he was lurching and stumbling badly, by appearances a victim of cerebral palsy. He was remarkably good humored about his uncoordinated progress, however, and did not seem discombobulated when he would bang into the side of the moving stairway. "He must have wonderful parents," commented my companion. "Look at his courage!" And, indeed, he was courageous, not only to be traveling alone, but to be coping with continual spasms and slow progress.

I experience spasms just in my face; I know how exhausting they are, but mine are on a small scale. My eyes filled with tears as I followed his movements, not because of his handicap, but because of his attitude. I lifted my soda in salute, and he happened to turn around and see me. A quick smile, and, then, he was gone. He was gone from sight but not from memory.

"Did I raise my children like that?" I wondered. Would they be able to go on loving and trusting God in the midst of heart breaking illness, failure, or financial loss? What kind of example am I passing on to those who come after me? Am I a teacher who can be counted on to point to a heavenly Father as the One who provides in the desert and who never leaves us?

Prayer: Oh, Lord, God, give me Your wisdom and courage day by day in order that I might be a faithful picture of You.

"Endure suffering along with me, as a good soldier of Jesus Christ." (II Timothy 2:3 NLT)

September 3: PMA

When our son, Allen, was in Junior High, the school announced its annual magazine drive. We had just moved to Tampa that summer, so we were not aware of this ghastly, local ritual that always seemed to be very costly for involved parents (and we had to go through it with two more students before we were free and clear...). Prizes were given to students selling huge numbers of magazines; and, of course, Allen wanted to win. However, since he had never sold anything in his life, he was quite apprehensive about going down a street where he knew no one, and trying to talk gun-shy neighbors into making a purchase. It has been reported that he thus compromised by walking down the middle of the road saying (none too loudly), "There isn't anyone who wants to buy a magazine, is there?" His prediction was correct. No one did!

I understand that insurance salesmen have what they call PMA: Positive Mental Attitude (I thought it was a disease of some sort when I first heard it). This must have been what my husband communicated to Allen after giving him some concrete sales techniques that were more successful than the one he had originally employed (and, yes, he did win a prize!).

My mother-in-law had one of the greatest positive mental attitudes I have ever seen. When our three oldest children were in the two to five year old range (all within thirteen months of each other) and were verging on crankiness, she would head them off at the pass by stopping what she was doing and suggesting a game. She would play with them (not just stand around and hope for the best). She never nagged; she didn't wait until the storm had turned into thunder and lightning and, then try to offer suggestions. She got down on their level and entered into the game with verve and enthusiasm. They loved her dearly—and no wonder! She had the positive mental attitude of a radiant Christian that came not from a formula, but from a life-long walk with the Lord. She used her time generously to minister to those around her.

We can't all have mothers-in-law like this, but we have the choice to minister to those around us! Let us ask the Lord to give us His attitude of love, and to love positively in all circumstances.

"Do not let any unwholesome talk come out of your mouths, but only what is helpful for building others up according to their needs, that it may benefit those who listen." (Ephesians 4:29 NIV)

September 4: Let's Play Concentration

There were three adults, three children, and two hamsters in the bedroom. I was one of the adults and my daughter, Lissa, and her husband were the others. Leading the young children in a bedtime devotion was uphill work, because the children had strategically, and with clever premeditation, placed themselves on the bed so that they were facing the hamsters. "Look!" squealed one, "He's climbing the water bottle!" All six eyes were thus firmly fixed on the hamster cage, and there was no relief in sight. When we closed our eyes in prayer, my son-in-law muttered, "This is why we don't have hamsters in church."

Children aren't the only ones distracted in their devotion time! Sometimes, when I pray, I find myself drifting off into things that were, are, or are yet to come. I don't mean to, of course, but my mind can flit faster than a confused mosquito—and, usually, just when I have settled down to have a good time of talking with God. One way I have found to anchor my mind while praying, is to whisper aloud (just as I used to when I was too frightened to pray out loud). I suppose the effort of speaking helps concentrate the mind. At least, it certainly helps me. Try writing or speaking your prayers for a while if you are having trouble. God, who loves you, is waiting to hear from you!

"But when Daniel learned that the law had been signed [forbidding prayer to anyone but the Babylonian king], he went home and knelt down as usual in his upstairs room, with its windows open toward Jerusalem. He prayed three times a day, just as he had always done, giving thanks to his God." (Daniel 6:10 NLT)

September 5: A Lesson from Captain Hornblower's Wife

My husband and I enjoy reading the stories C.S. Forester wrote about the exploits of Captain Hornblower. They take place in the late 1700's and early 1800's, and chronicle many of the sea battles between England and France. The characters are all beautifully drawn, and become as familiar as old friends after you have read a few of the books. Captain Hornblower starts as a midshipman, of course, (as did all navy personnel at that time) and rises through the ranks through many deeds of courage, and through quick, original thinking in hazardous situations.

However, it is not about the Captain that I want to write. He marries Mariah, a young serving girl, when he is not very far along in his career, mainly because he feels sorry for her (not really the best foundation for marriage). As his rank and responsibilities increase, his wife begins to increase her own sense of self-importance. She is constantly nagging at him not to demean himself by performing one task or another; and she is very careful to maintain her dignity at all costs. She becomes a ridiculous figure with an inflated view of her own importance and situation in life.

Jesus is a beautiful and striking contrast to Captain Hornblower's wife. Jesus reigned in heaven, yet did not hesitate to give up the glory He had. He was born into poverty, lived a life of hardship, and was even willing to die for our sins. What a wonderful Savior we have!

"Don't be jealous or proud, but be humble and consider others more important than yourselves. Care about them as much as you care about yourselves and think the same way that Christ Jesus thought: Christ was truly God. But he did not try to remain equal with God. Instead he gave up everything and became a slave, when he became like one of us. Christ was humble. He obeyed God and even died on a cross." (Philippians 2:3-8 CEV)

September 6: Weasels

Weasels are very sly. They not only steal to live, they seem to live to steal, slinking in and out of hen houses, chicken coops, and dove cotes with hardly the flutter of a feather in their wake. People, unfortunately (and I include myself here), have a few weasel-like qualities, although food is not what is stolen—it is time. I steal it when I have time for the morning paper and not for time for God. I steal it when I ignore people at the office or school because I am too busy. I steal it when I watch a soap opera or an irreverent talk show instead of listening to a program that would encourage or inspire me. I steal it when I rush my children from one activity to another without giving them time to dream and think. I steal it when I push ahead with a project in order to get it done instead of giving others a chance to participate or learn. I steal it when I pack the kids off to bed to get rid of them instead of implanting values of love and warmth. I steal it when I end my day in an argument or a sulk, instead of companionship and acceptance.

Prayer: Everyone has the same amount of time, Lord; I confess I have not always used it wisely. Help me to learn to use it more for You and less for me.

"And God spoke all these words.... You shall not steal." (Exodus 20:1,15 NIV)

September 7: Reflections on Reflections

I have seen and looked into many mirrors in my time…all the way from the elaborate ones at Versailles, to the cracked one in my purse. Some were so far above my eye-level, the only things visible were eyebrows looking like desiccated caterpillars under a gray fur hat. One mirror in a discount store turned me into a deliciously long quiver of color, and one I found in an old trunk was so spotted with age, it made me look as though I had a severe case of chicken pox.

In case you haven't noticed, God's mirror is not like that. It is low enough for anyone to look into, it always tells the truth without distortion, and it remains the same year after year regardless of the passing years. Both earthly mirrors and God's mirror have something in common, however. They should make me ask, "What needs to be changed?" No one looks into a mirror to see all the things that are right (except possibly Rose Red). We look into mirrors to see what is wrong, so it can be fixed.

Many times we are not thrilled with what we see, because a mirror's impartially shows us things we would rather not notice. But, we can't stop with just looking, because the purpose of the mirror is lost when no action is taken. May I not ignore what I have been shown!

"Obey God's message! Don't fool yourselves by just listening to it. If you hear the message and don't obey it, you are like people who stare at themselves in a mirror and forget what they look like as soon as they leave." (James 1:22-24 CEV)

September 8: Satisfied

When I was growing up, there were several things I wanted that I didn't have: height, curly hair, blue eyes, and dimples (naturally, I was jealous of Shirley Temple). As time passed, I could see that nothing was going to come of the first three, so I concentrated on the dimples and went to bed every night with an orange stick stuck in the side of my cheek hoping that it would make an indentation. It did not. I put this down to the fact that I must have dropped the orange stick after I fell asleep, and that if I could only concentrate more, I could produce a dimple.

I guess no one is really marvelously satisfied with the way they look, and, in fact, I have read of famous beauties that complain about their noses or skin or legs or something. I have discovered something, however, that they may not know: God made us the way we are for a purpose. My genes didn't just clump together one day and take a chance on things turning out right. They were placed by God to make someone short, with brown eyes, hair that only bends, and with no dimples. So, it is rather exciting to think that while I am not what I had in mind, I am what God had in mind. And even though I still have occasional yearnings for gracefulness instead of clumsiness, I remember that God's purpose is for me to show God's love to others, not to stand around and look gorgeous. I am satisfied.

"He is the God who made the world and everything in it. Since he is Lord of heaven and earth, he doesn't live in man-made temples, and human hands can't serve his needs—for he has no needs. He himself gives life and breath to everything, and he satisfies every need there is. From one man he created all the nations throughout the whole earth. He decided beforehand which should rise and fall, and he determined their boundaries. His purpose in all of this was that the nations should seek after God and perhaps feel their way toward him and find him—though he is not far from any one of us." (Acts 17:25-27 NLT)

September 9: Eat What's on Your Plate

When we first moved to Tampa we bought a Sheltie. After a number of years, he developed some mysterious inner problems for which the vet prescribed a cottage cheese diet—nothing else, just cottage cheese. So, for quite a while, he faithfully gobbled up all the cottage cheese we could provide, and we all grew quite accustomed to watching him eat the stuff.

This led to a remark by our youngest daughter, Margaret, who was served cottage cheese at a luncheon given for her future sister-in-law. She leaned over to me and hissed, "Why are they serving dog food???"

I also judge things by my limited experiences, thereby jumping to incorrect conclusions. I remember reading (somewhere) a remark by Spurgeon that is pertinent here: "The God who gave us understanding must also make us understand." In other words, I must look beyond what's been given, and ask God to help me understand. I may not be thrilled with what I am served in life; but, I try to remember this: "Lord, you have assigned me my portion and my cup…" (Psalm 16:5a NIV). Then, I can eat what has been put on my plate knowing that the Father always serves a balanced meal. Let me eat with good grace!

"Direct me in the path of your commands, for there I find delight." (Psalm 119:35 NIV)

September 10: A Modern Meeting in the Desert

"As for Philip, an angel of the Lord said to him, 'Go south down the desert road that runs from Jerusalem to Gaza.' So he did, and he met the treasurer of Ethiopia, a eunuch of great authority under the queen of Ethiopia. The eunuch had gone to Jerusalem to worship, and he was now returning. Seated in his carriage, he was reading aloud from the book of the prophet Isaiah. The Holy Spirit said to Philip, 'Go over and walk along beside the carriage.' Philip ran over and heard the man reading from the prophet Isaiah; so he asked, 'Do you understand what you are reading?'

"The man replied, 'How can I, when there is no one to instruct me?' And he begged Philip to come up into the carriage and sit with him. The passage of Scripture he had been reading was this: "He was led as a sheep to the slaughter. And as a lamb is silent before the shearers, he did not open his mouth. He was humiliated and received no justice. Who can speak of his descendants? For his life was taken from the earth." The eunuch asked Philip, 'Was Isaiah talking about himself or someone else?'

"So Philip began with this same Scripture and then used many others to tell him the Good News about Jesus. As they rode along, they came to some water, and the eunuch said, 'Look! There's some water! Why can't I be baptized?' He ordered the carriage to stop, and they went down into the water, and Philip baptized him. When they came up out of the water, the Spirit of the Lord caught Philip away. The eunuch never saw him again but went on his way rejoicing." (Acts 8:26-39 NLT)

We lived in Boston for the great length of nine months. Our oldest daughter was in ninth grade, and she was very (make that very, very) anxious to find a Christian friend. This of course seemed unlikely, but we prayed diligently over the situation, knowing that nothing is too hard for God.

One day, Lissa came home and announced, "I think I've found her! She's not a Christian yet, but her mother is just as mean as you are" (that sounds terrible, but Bill and I found it hilarious). A week or so later we invited this presumably suffering teenager over to spend the night—that ritual so highly prized by kids of all ages and so dreaded by parents, for whom the night is usually not spent in slumber. We had a great time, however, and at the end of her stay, Dale was presented with an opportunity to accept Christ. To Lissa's excitement, she did so. "You're the answer to my prayers," said my daughter. "I've been praying for a Christian friend." Dale looked at her very seriously and said, "You're the answer to my prayers…because I've been wondering how to find God."

We thrill at the Biblical account of how God prepared the heart of the eunuch in the desert as he met Philip and found the right person who would guide him to meet God; but God still does the same thing today. I must never miss the opportunity to share in God's plan of bringing people into His kingdom!

September 11: Remember

Americans have heard many exhortations to remember through the years: "Remember the Alamo!" "Remember the Maine!" and "Remember Pearl Harbor!" But, nothing in recent memory has struck so deeply into our hearts as the remembrance of this date in 2001 when the United States was attacked. I expect every person remembers exactly where they were when they heard the news of this devastating tragedy, and for those whose families or friends were killed or hurt, it will always be a day of mourning.

Did you know that God wants us to remember, too? He wants us to remember the times of His faithfulness and love. I Chronicles 16:11-12 says, "Search for the Lord and for his strength, and keep on searching. Think of the wonderful works he has done, the miracles, and the judgments he has handed down" (NLT). And, then, He has this promise in Jeremiah 31:33-34—and echoed in Hebrews 8:10-11—"'But this is the new covenant I will make with the people of Israel on that day,' says the Lord. 'I will put my laws in their minds, and I will write them on their hearts. I will be their God, and they will be my people. And they will not need to teach their neighbors, nor will they need to teach their family, saying, 'You should know the Lord.' For everyone, from the least to the greatest, will already know me,' says the Lord. 'And I will forgive their wickedness and will never again remember their sins'" (NLT).

God is righteous and just—this is the important thing we must remember more than anything; He is faithful, and He keeps His promises.

"…Deep in your hearts you know that every promise of the Lord your God has come true. Not a single one has failed!" (Joshua 23:14b NLT)

September 12: Incredible Edibles

There were seven of us that rocketed in the car toward Kansas City. Our conversation turned to disasters in the kitchen that we had not only known, but had eaten. Without exception, we were all victims of stupidity, carelessness, and the omission of recipe reading.

Amid shrieks of laughter at our own incompetence, we exchanged horror stories, such as the bride who cut off the heads of asparagus and made her groom eat the stalks, the one who served raw shrimp at a party because, when she had bought them, the sign said, "Ready to Go," the one who made an apple pie with only one apple and an inch-thick crust so it wouldn't fall apart on the way to the pan (my contribution!), and the young mother who, in making chicken soup, used necks to save money and, then, threw out the water in which they were cooked so her family could have fresh water and not the yellow stuff in the pot.

Since all of this gunk was actually eaten, it proves that words aren't the only thing we have to swallow when things turn out badly. If we are put in that position, however, we should make sure our words are sweet to the taste and not bitter with condemnation. The recipe for this is as follows: "Above all else, guard your heart, for it is the wellspring of life" (Proverbs 4:23 NIV). If I am working to improve my own cooking skills, I am less likely to be critical of others. Likewise, may I set my brain in motion before I turn on the sound!

"Set a guard over my mouth, O Lord; keep watch over the door of my lips." (Psalm 141:3 NIV)

September 13: Our Checkbook

Because my eyes only perform in short bursts, my husband is kind enough to read aloud to me in the evenings and in the mornings. At night, in between books he reads to me, he listens with me to the books on tape that I get from the library. This way we share adventures together. He usually falls asleep fairly quickly during the latter, and I fall asleep fairly quickly during the former. Because of my tendency to drop off before the end of a chapter, he puts a little check when he stops reading for the night to mark the place when I fall asleep, which he usually tries to erase if it's a book we want to pass on.

When he started reading me the Bible at night, he teased me saying he was going to have to do a whole lot of erasing to get rid of all those marks. He started calling it our "checkbook." Well, it really is, you know! The Bible is our checkbook to help us draw on God's resources. God says, "Every animal in the forest belongs to me, and so do the cattle on a thousand hills" (Psalm 50:10 CEV). He also says, "All silver and gold belong to me…" (Haggai 2:8 CEV).

The spiritual riches He gives are never depleted no matter how often we call upon Him. Strange as it may seem to some, it is very possible to be rich in material wealth and poor spiritually. The reverse is just as true. Many are poor in material things and overflowing with the riches of Christ. But the most wonderful thing of all is that the more of both riches we give away, the richer we are for it (explain that, all you economists!).

"Warn the rich people of this world not to be proud or to trust in wealth that is easily lost. Tell them to have faith in God, who is rich and blesses us with everything we need to enjoy life. Instruct them to do as many good deeds as they can and to help everyone. Remind the rich to be generous and share what they have. This will lay a solid foundation for the future, so that they will know what true life is like." (I Timothy 6:17-19 CEV)

September 14: Radio Daze

When I was in college, I used to do an early morning radio show with a friend at the school's big, five-watt station (really, it could only be heard downhill). It was a lot of fun, and I learned how to push and twirl all the buttons and dials.

One morning, my friend didn't show up. So, being the brave (and stupid) person that I am, I decided to do the show by myself. I adjusted my headset, pushed buttons, and pulled switches, just as I had been taught. After a wonderful show, I finished in what was surely a blaze of glory.

During my first class, I asked one of my friends how the show sounded. "It wasn't on this morning," she said. "Of COURSE it was on!" I snapped. "Nope," she answered. Mystified, I returned to the station and discovered my big mistake. I had pulled all the switches and toggles except for one: the main one that turned on the power to the transmitter.

Thankfully, we have the main power switch of the Holy Spirit living in us, helping us to communicate!

Check your sending and receiving power. Are you sure that the power is on?

Prayer: Father, I turn from sin to You. Wash me clean because of Jesus' sacrifice for me. Please send Your Holy Spirit to live in me!

"And the Holy Spirit helps us in our distress. For we don't even know what we should pray for, nor how we should pray. But the Holy Spirit prays for us with groanings that cannot be expressed in words." (Romans 8:26 NLT)

September 15: Plastic Encounter

In my early school days, I began to realize I couldn't see the blackboard very well, so I moved up to the front of the classroom (a daring move because it put me right under the nose of my teacher...). Eventually even this did not help, so mother took me to the optometrist to get glasses. To my horror, she selected little round glasses made of thin steel—just like the ones my father wore. I didn't want steel glasses; I wanted the new plastic ones. She would not be moved, however, because my father had given her strict instructions about the purchase.

I hated those glasses, and tried to leave them all over town, but, since I was the only kid in the entire world wearing this kind of glasses, they were always returned to our house. Always. Every time I had my prescription changed, I would beg mother for plastic glasses. No deal.

However, when I was fifteen, and feeling very grown up and in charge of my life, I put my foot down and absolutely insisted on plastic frames. Mother (who must have been very weary by this time) finally agreed, and we settled on a pair that were pink and turned up at the sides. I looked like a rabbit that had spent quite a bit of time with the Tartars in Outer Mongolia.

That evening, I descended the stairs for dinner wearing my new glasses. Daddy took one look at me and nearly had a stroke.

"Take those right back!" he ordered. "You look like a street walker!"

I did not know any street walkers (and wasn't exactly sure what they were anyway), but I was pretty sure they wouldn't wear pink plastic glasses.

Grudgingly, we returned the plastic frames and traded them in for steel. It was many years before I was finally allowed to get rid of those...and great day in the morning—in the 1990's, thin metal rims came back into style!

I do regret that I spent so much time and energy thinking of how glamorous I would look in my pink plastic glasses, when I should have been focusing on inner qualities, which never go out of style.

"Don't be concerned about the outward beauty that depends on fancy hairstyles, expensive jewelry, or beautiful clothes. You should be known for the beauty that comes from within, the unfading beauty of a gentle and quiet spirit, which is so precious to God." (I Peter 3:3,4 CEV)

September 16: Golden Triangle

Contrary to my accent, I was born in Pittsburgh, where they do not talk with a southern accent (even if they live on the south side of town). When I was growing up, we did not live in the city itself, but even so there was plenty of dirt and grit from the steel mills. Unless you wiped off the windowsills every day, you could write the names of your entire family in the grit.

Now they call Pittsburgh the Golden Triangle, and there has been a great change since those days. I wasn't there during its renovation, but I have seen the results, and it is truly amazing. Everything has been built up, cleaned up, and spruced up. Buildings once run-down enough to qualify as slums are all shiny and new with aluminum and glass. You could call the change in Pittsburgh a renovation. But the change in me, when I turned from the kingdom of darkness into the kingdom of light, wasn't just a renovation: it was a transformation!

When I became a Christian, our minister told me God would begin to change me; I was delighted, for I've always wanted to be tall and thin. That wasn't what happened, of course! God began to change me on the inside, and I was amazed at what He did. He changed my goals, my attitudes, my thoughts, and my actions—certainly something only God can do! A heart change does not come by self-effort; it comes as a gift from our heavenly Father. How I thank Him for it!

"And so, dear Christian friends, I plead with you to give your bodies to God. Let them be a living and holy sacrifice—the kind he will accept. When you think of what he has done for you, is this too much to ask? Don't copy the behavior and customs of this world, but let God transform you into a new person by changing the way you think. Then you will know what god wants you to do, and you will know how good and pleasing and perfect his will really is." (Romans12:1-2 NLT)

September 17: My Way

A friend of mine often plays the organ for funerals. She knows not only many hymns, but many other songs as well. In fact, whenever Stonecroft Ministries has a conference here in Florida, we call on Betty. She plays everything requested with verve and enthusiasm. Once, while attending a funeral where she was not the organist, she heard a song that seemed familiar, but she couldn't quite place it. She asked her husband if he knew what it was. "Yes," he whispered unbelievingly, "It's called 'I Did It My Way.'"

Hopefully, no Christian would ever assume he or she would get to heaven by doing it "their way," but, even so, I sometimes insist on doing other things my way. Stuart Briscoe tells of an American missionary who was late for an appointment, and was listening with irritation to two Africans discussing the best way to repair a bridge that lay in the path of the aforementioned appointment. It took a long time for them to come to an agreement, because neither brother wanted to offend the other by insisting on the method they favored. They knew it was more important to maintain a good relationship than to keep on schedule by repairing the bridge. As one man said afterward, "Americans have watches but no time. We Africans have no watches, but we have time."

Sometimes I get in so much of a hurry that I ruin relationships in the interest of efficiency. I need to practice giving those around me my full attention and consideration.

"Don't be jealous or proud, but be humble and consider others more important than yourselves. Care about them as much as you care about yourselves." (Philippians 2:3-4 CEV)

September 18: The Eyes Have It

When we lived in Tampa, we went to an ophthalmologist who had not only had extensive training in his field, but also had had further education in eye structure. He had huge posters on his office walls showing both the inside and the outside of the eye. It sounds gory, but the posters were just unbelievably gorgeous.

When God created us, His attention to the minutest detail is very evident to anyone who has studied physiology (and even to those who haven't). Philip Yancy's books on the human body are amazing and thrilling, showing how marvelously God has created us; they give us a new appreciation of the loving care God put into what was, originally, lumps of clay.

Now the question is, "What am I doing with my wonderful eyes?" Putting on lots of mascara? Taking extra care with the eyelash curler? Using mirrors along the way to admire the finished product? Or even, perhaps, looking at things that would sadden God?

A children's song goes, "Be careful, little eyes, what you see!" There is a great deal of truth in that, for I can use my eyes in the Lord's service or in mine. It just depends on my motive. When my heart is right before the Lord, I will be thinking about reflecting the love of God and the things in which He is interested. Strangely enough, that is what makes me beautiful.

"Your beauty should not come from outward adornment, such as braided hair and the wearing of gold jewelry and fine clothes. Instead, it should be that of your inner self, the unfading beauty of a gentle and quiet spirit, which is of great worth in God's sight." (I Peter 3:3-4 NIV)

September 19: Selective Memory Syndrome

Attending a Cornell College reunion with friends from before time began, I was amazed to hear some startling news about myself. It seems that several pranks that I had engineered were well remembered (and I was not even in the engineering department)—while I had forgotten them altogether. One had involved inviting Bess Truman to our annual homecoming football game. It might not have been so bad if I had issued a formal invitation, but since I evidently considered it a huge joke, I wrote it on a postcard. Naturally, the press got ahold of it, and contacted the college administration, who in turn did rather more than contact me. A good deal of time was spent trying to explain this to everyone's satisfaction. Not everyone's, actually. I was once again put on the black list of People to be Avoided at All Costs.

I have what is called a selective memory: I gloss over things I am not too proud of and rationalize that it didn't really hurt anyone, it wasn't that serious, or it must have been the other person's fault. After a while, I feel rather justified about the whole thing and consign it to oblivion. But God does not forget my sin or gloss over it, which is why I must confess it. Then, He removes it "as far away from us as the east is from the west" (Psalm 103:12 NLT), and I am cleansed and renewed (even from silly things I did in college).

"How can I know all the sins lurking in my heart? Cleanse me from these hidden faults. Keep me from deliberate sins! Don't let them control me. Then I will be free of guilt and innocent of great sin. May the words of my mouth and the thoughts of my heart be pleasing to you, O Lord, my rock and my redeemer." (Psalm 19:12-14 NLT)

September 20: On the Bench

Perhaps you were looking forward to ~~be~~ some judicial thoughts, but I'm afraid this is only about aerobics. Bench Exercises (which I particularly dislike) involve stepping up and down on a low bench to a beat, changing feet or turning as we go up so that we come down on the other side. Neither my mind nor my hips are enthused about this. When bench exercises are announced, I tend to stand numbly as if I had lost all sense of hearing. Once everyone in the front gets underway, however, I have found that I can step and turn industriously, as if I were on a bench; in reality, I am just stepping around on the floor. The other day, I was doing this so well, spinning around in time to the music, that I convinced myself I was really doing it on the bench (I'm not sure the instructor viewed it with my degree of enthusiasm!). Everywhere I looked, people were waving arms and stepping on and off, and I seemed to be moving along with the best of them (well, maybe not the best…). I had managed to fool myself into thinking I had a position I didn't really have.

I see a parallel in my life. For 31 years, I was fooled into thinking that going to church, giving money, singing, and praying was Christianity. Going through the motions did not make me a Christian. One must be on the "foundation bench" of the Lord Jesus Christ, for it is His life in me that makes me a Christian.

"Test yourselves and find out if you really are true to your faith. If you pass the test, you will discover that Christ is living in you. But if Christ isn't living in you, you have failed." (II Corinthians 13:5 CEV)

September 21: Reverse Psychology

The year I went to summer school in Colorado, I bought an old Model T Ford (an old, old one) for the sum of $200. It had little curtains on the back window, and, although it leaked in the afternoon rains, I thought it was just too cute for words. It was truly eccentric in one regard, however: it would only go up hill in reverse. Fortunately, there was only one hill that I attempted with any degree of regularity, although I remained in confusion as to which side of the road I should be on.

After forty-five years of thinking that my car had been singular in its peculiarity, I discovered that such was not the case at all. In listening to Bode Thoene's book *A Thousand Shall Fall*, I read about a young couple who had bought a Model T and drove it from Oklahoma to Arkansas. The last leg of their journey was a hill next to their old farm, and they had to go in reverse, too. The gas tank, the book explained, was under the floorboard, and if they went up the hill in first gear, the gas would flow away from the engine. I just had to laugh, thinking that all those years I had put that poor old car under a cloud of suspicion, when, in reality, it was just doing what it was made to do.

People snicker about those who march to the sound of a different drummer, but like my old Model T, Christians are to do what they're made to do. I'm sure we seem eccentric to most of the world (especially when we have to go in reverse to get where we're going). Our source of power is not a gas tank under the floorboards, but it lies in the indwelling Christ. Because of this, we have the "power of an indestructible life" (Hebrews 7:16b NIV). We can rely on the Lord no matter what kind of a hill we have to climb, and He will see us to our journey's end.

"Proclaim the power of God, whose majesty is over Israel, whose power is in the skies. You are awesome, O God, in your sanctuary; the God of Israel gives power and strength to his people." (Psalm 68:34-35a NIV)

September 22: Lost in (Cyber) Space

Along with probably 50% of the people in the world, I hate change. My favorite lipstick isn't made any more, my perfume has been discontinued, and my favorite magazines, such as *Look*, are as extinct as dodos. Not only that, but restaurants I like are closed up, area codes splinter as quickly as I memorize them, maps go out of date as soon as they're printed, friends move away, and my body keeps changing in a way which does not bring joy to my closet (or the things in it).

Added to all this, people have jumped wholesale into faxes, e-mail, and downloading. I have been dragged kicking and screaming into the world of e-mail, but I draw the line at e-cards, decorations, and other clever devices, all of which tend to make me press the wrong buttons. I feel the world has shot into space, and I have been left without a rocket. Of course, this complaint is not new. People have probably grumbled about change ever since the wheel. As Mark Twain once remarked, "The only one who likes change is a baby with a wet diaper."

God alone remains unchanged. "...I am the Lord All-Powerful, and I never change," He assures us in Malachi 3:6b (CEV). How wonderful to know that Jehovah God will never be outmoded, out-stripped, or out of place! This is as important for us to remember today as it was during the times of the Old Testament, the four hundred years of silence, and the past two thousand years. Our world changes day by day, with ever new, improved and better inventions, and greater flux and uncertainty as well. But we may rest with confidence next to our God who is the same today as He was yesterday.

"In the beginning, Lord, you laid the earth's foundation and created the heavens. They will all disappear and wear out like clothes. You change them, as you would a coat, but you last forever. You are always the same. Years cannot change you." (Psalm 102:25-27 CEV)

September 23: Glove Boxes

I simply can't imagine how the glove box got its name, because I don't know anyone past or present who keeps their gloves in it. I can't speak for anyone else, naturally, but ours is crammed with a huge assortment of unrelated and untidy accoutrements, all accumulated bit by bit. It started off, neatly enough, with its new smell and the owner's manual sitting pristinely in private splendor. But soon a map was added, and then a box of tissue, followed by sunglasses and a flashlight…and then the accumulation became an avalanche. Like Fibber McGee's legendary closet, we dare not open it because of dreadful and irretrievable consequences.

Sometimes, I live like a glove box. I have the name of someone whose inner being should be clean, but many times, I am just an accumulation of junk. I have picked up something here, and added something there until, if I were to be opened, there would be a ghastly avalanche of things I would rather not have anyone see. I need to examine my hoarded resentments, my carefully boxed envies, and my foil wrapped fancies and give them to the One to whom they would not be a surprise. He will take care of the disposal and make me what I should be—and there won't be any charge!

Prayer: Heavenly Father, deep down, I want to be what You want me to be; and I need You to be in control of every part of my life. Please take away the things that are cluttering up my walk, and make me clean and new. Amen.

"How terrible it will be for you teachers of religious law and you Pharisees. Hypocrites! You are like white-washed tombs—beautiful on the outside but filled on the inside with dead people's bones and all sorts or impurity. You try to look like upright people outwardly, but inside your hearts are filled with hypocrisy and lawlessness." (Matthew 23:27-28 NLT)

September 24: Locked In

On a recent flight to Kansas City, I was squashed in a middle seat the size of a child's swing (but not nearly as much fun). How airlines expect normal people to fit in those center seats is beyond comprehension. When you have somebody six feet four or someone who is put in the position of unhappily overflowing into the next seat…well, I'm thinking they need to redo their thinking on the passenger's idea of comfort. Of course, this has been written about *ad infinitum* (and even done in television skits, which are hilarious mainly because you aren't there).

On this particular trip, however, the designers were not concerned with my ideas at all, and I was suffering from a case of trying to dislodge the bodies surrounding me, and dodge the stewardesses handing out peanuts for lunch. Dodging and dislodging takes a lot a wiggle, and I was triumphant as I fled to the lavatory. When I tried to return to my seat, however, I was not so triumphant. I could not open the door! I have been on hundreds and maybe even thousands of airplanes and I have never come across a door handle that wasn't there. It was a new type of lock, perhaps, or the person ahead of me had torn it off in a fit of energy. At any rate, I seemed to be locked in for the duration. In desperation I rang for the stewardess. Wouldn't you know, it was a steward who opened the door, and he looked at me as though I were an unwelcome stain on his uniform. I was too glad to be released to even care, and I re-wiggled my way back into my seat.

Perhaps you are in a locked door situation right now. I have noticed that locked doors don't keep the Lord from coming in. No matter how helpless or foolish you might feel, you can remember that you are beloved, and Christ is near. May you have the peace of His presence in any and all situations.

"On the evening of that first day of the week, when the disciples were together, with the doors locked for fear of the Jews, Jesus came and stood among them and said, 'Peace be with you!'" (John 20:19 NIV)

September 25: Becoming a Child

I suppose every child ever born wants to hurry up and grow so he or she can stop being a child and be an adult. I was no exception, and I wanted to be blasé and sophisticated like Marlene Dietrich (an unlikely scenario if there ever was one). I thought she was wonderfully world-weary and sophisticated—and she had great legs. My mother was the exact opposite. She was as short and eager to meet life as a beagle going after a fresh scent; and although I don't recall ever seeing her legs, I'm afraid they were not in the glamour category. Not only that, she had no sophistication. She showed pleasure and enjoyment at meeting everyone—from the mailman to the president of a large company. I thought she was extremely childish showing all that enthusiasm for life, and I tried without success to prod her into being bored.

I was wrong, of course, but I didn't see it for many years, even after I became a Christian. The Lord Jesus loved people who were childlike and simple enough in their faith to enjoy other people, no matter who they were, and, most of all, simple enough to accept Him at face value and believe all that He said was true. I think I'm finally growing up to be a child.

"At that time the disciple came to Jesus and asked, 'Which of us is the greatest in the Kingdom of Heaven?' Jesus called a small child over to him and put the child among them. Then he said, 'I assure you, unless you turn from your sins and become as little children, you will never get into the Kingdom of Heaven.'" (Matthew 18:1-3 NLT)

September 26: The Carry All

While I was in the Chicago area on a speaking itinerary, the friend with whom I was staying suggested that we use a free afternoon to check out the outlet of a well-known store. The store handled not only clothes and linens, but also all sorts of canvas bags. We thought it would be a great idea to get a pocketbook big enough to carry everything we ever needed for emergencies. We found just what we wanted at a reasonable price, and we each picked a favorite color.

I carried it successfully on my next two trips, gloating over my cleverness in thinking this up. When one of our daughters came home for Christmas, however, she noticed what I was carrying and burst into peals of laughter. "Why are you carrying a diaper bag?" she queried. I must admit there really was no suitable answer.

Obviously, I sometimes get carried away with my carry-alls. Possessions (whether worth nickels or millions) can become overly important and end up being baggage that is hard to squeeze into anything smaller than a tent. It's okay to carry a tent, of course, since we're called to be pilgrims and not settlers; but, if it is stuffed with loot unneeded in the kingdom, and the King asks what we are planning to do with it all, it's going to be hard to find a suitable answer

"I set out some large bowls full of wine together with some cups, and then I said to the Rechabites, 'Have some wine!' But they answered: No! The ancestor of our clan, Jonadab son of Rechab, made a rule that we must obey. He said, 'Don't ever drink wine or build houses or plant crops and vineyards. Instead, you must always move from place to place. If you obey this command, you will live a long time.'" (Jeremiah 35:5-7 CEV)

September 27: Bravery

I am not a brave person, but I admire people who are, and I enjoy reading stories of daring-do on land and sea, and of strong men whose coats of arms have lions rampant (I'm afraid if I had a coat of arms it would probably be a rampant squirrel with a draggy tail).

But, it is wonderful that when one works for God, He makes a difference. We may not be strong, but in situations of peril, God is able to make the weak a strong arrow in His quiver. There was a book published many years ago called *The Tartan Pimpernel* (yes, that is correct—not the Scarlet one). This book was about an unassuming Scottish preacher who worked secretly in France during the Second World War helping young American airmen over the border into Spain. He pottered around during the day, sometimes preaching at small churches, but at night, he became a lion of the Lord, trudging valiantly over the Pyrenees to bring many to safety.

He was eventually caught and put into a terrible prison, where I am sure the Nazis thought they had finished his career. But like Paul and Barnabas, he used the opportunity he had been given to share his faith with others. Many years later he was talking to a man who told how he had come to faith after being imprisoned in the same place, but at a later date. The man said that someone had scratched the words of Isaiah 43:2 on the walls of his cell: "When thou passest through the waters, I will be with thee; and through the rivers, they will not overflow thee: when thou walkest through the fire, thou shalt not be burned, neither shall the flame kindle upon thee" (KJV). The Tartan Pimpernel had laboriously scratched those words into the stone in hopes that they might help someone who came after him.

These are wonderful words of encouragement. We are not to think only of ourselves and those we know, but of those who come after us.

September 28: The Portrait

Her words flowed as copiously as the waters of the sea, and as deftly as the dive of a dolphin…but, alas, not as deep. She skimmed the shallow water, halting on piers of personal opinion or shores of selfish interest. There was plenty of style, but not much substance, lots of materialism, but not much meat. There was much fun, but no foundation, much examination of friends, but none of self, much talk of gains, but none of God.

Would you say that what you think or do is more important than what anyone else thinks or does? Do you feel that what you do is more important than what you are? Do you try to control your life and that of your family so that it reflects well on you? Do you pout when you don't get your way? Are you careless with the feelings of others? Do you skip away from those who are a little too serious about religion and laugh over a Christian whose fall into sin makes headlines?

I understand you then, for this is a portrait of me before I met Jesus Christ. Is it also a portrait of you?

"As the Scriptures say, 'No one is good—not even one. No one has real understanding; no one is seeking God. All have turned away from God; all have gone wrong. No one does good, not even one.' 'Their talk is foul, like the stench from an open grave. Their speech is filled with lies.' 'The poison of a deadly snake drips from their lips.' 'Their mouths are full of cursing and bitterness.' 'They are quick to commit murder. Wherever they go, destruction and misery follow them. They do not know what true peace is.' 'They have no fear of God to restrain them.'" (Romans 3:10-18 NLT)

September 29: Centipedes and Millipedes

I don't think either of these animals has as many legs as their name implies, but, of course, I haven't counted them either. However, they certainly have more than anyone else. I'm sure their mamas are glad they don't have to buy Reeboks or roller-blades for all those little feet! If you have ever watched one of these fuzzy-wuzzies in the process of locomotion, they are a real wonder. Their feet never try to go in different directions, their legs never get tangled up or trip over each other, and there's never a single foot that says, "I'm tired, let's go home." These creatures move without effort because that's the way God made them.

God made me, too, and with only two legs. But see all the trouble I get into? Sometimes, I trip and fall (and it's a lot farther to the ground than it would be for a centipede!), and sometimes I try to force my feet into shoes that are a teensy bit too small so I will look endearing. Sometimes, I get leg cramps or corns (probably from those teensy shoes). Physical problems are difficult to live with (and limp with), but it's much worse when my feet carry me down the wrong path. I can hide these paths from others, but I cannot hide them from God. No matter how I rationalize it ("Just this once," "I really need this," etc.), it is a path that will surely lead to heartache, and, perhaps, disaster. If this is true of you, let's get our act together, get our feet together, and put them where they are supposed to be. In other words, if we are planning to be in step with the Father in the hereafter, we had better start getting in step in the here.

"The Lord said: My people, when you stood at the crossroads, I told you, 'Follow the road your ancestors took, and you will find peace.'" (Jeremiah 6:16a CEV)

September 30: A Grateful Heart

Parents (and other adults who have lost their minds) like to be appreciated. Our children went to a college far away in Illinois (trading warm Florida weather for cold Chicago winters); and we found that when they came home for vacation, everything was new and wonderful. This included meals, beds, weather, and even siblings. Gratitude was in the air. We noticed, however, that when a fervent request for a motorcycle was not granted, the air was not quite so thick with thanksgiving.

We do seem to have a tendency to thank God for the blessings He gives and to feel grumpy at the things He does not. But if we truly believe that God gives what is best, then we should also believe that He will withhold what would not be best. I don't mean we should jump up and down shouting, "Hallelujah! God just refused my request to be healed!" But I do know that we must learn to be content in every circumstance. Our times are in His hands.

I was forcibly reminded of this when God did not meet a need the way that I hoped. Ready to feel bereft, a wonderful verse came to mind: "I will extol the Lord at all times…." (Psalm 34:1 NIV). All times means (in case you missed it) all times. As Charles Spurgeon once said, "Happy is he whose fingers are wedded to the harp…to bless the Lord is never unreasonable."

"I will extol the Lord at all times; his praise will always be on my lips. My soul will boast in the Lord; let the afflicted hear and rejoice. Glorify the Lord with me; let us exalt his name together." (Psalm 34:1-3 NIV)

October 1: Canned Spaghetti

At one time, we had a youth pastor who owned a large Irish setter. He was very fond of this dog and took it with him wherever he went. This included summer camping trips. One year, he took a two-week trip to the mountains in North Carolina. All went well for the first couple of days, and then the dog got into a fight with a skunk. The dog lost, unfortunately, and the smell of the fray lingered powerfully on.

This young leader had read somewhere that tomato juice poured over the smell of a skunk would eliminate it (the smell, not the skunk). He didn't have any tomato juice, so he used what he figured was the next best thing: canned spaghetti.

In case you were wondering, this does not work, even when dutifully rubbed into a dog's long hair.

People tend to use various methods to get rid of sin, too. The reason they do not work is that God's only plan for removing sin is through His Son, Jesus.

"But Christ was sinless, and he offered himself as an eternal and spiritual sacrifice to God." (Hebrews 9:14 CEV)

October 2: Free Advice

I was very intrigued by the sign hanging by the gas station that advertised "Free Advice given with oil change." The mind boggles at the sort of advice that might be offered: "Find Your Happiness on Route 66," "Best Investments on Oil in the Coming Year," or possibly, "How to build your Dream House out of Old Tires." Of course, the advice might also be very mundane: "How to clean your windshield because we're not going to...." Heaven knows, people look for advice in strange places. Many people search horoscopes, call numbers advertised on TV, and consult strangers on planes who look as if they have it all together.

But God is the only one who is intimately acquainted with such diverse needs such as financial security, discipline, comfort, and encouragement. He not only knows our needs, He is able to provide what is needed. His word, His Spirit, His people, and the circumstances we encounter all have His loving hand behind them. Isaiah 30:15 reminds us, "The Sovereign Lord, the Holy One of Israel, says, 'Only in returning to me and waiting for me will you be saved. In quietness and confidence is your strength'" (NLT).

Don't wait until you are on empty. Fill up with advice from God each day. If you plan with God first, and then plan your day, you will have the comforting knowledge that He is directing your path with the absolutely best advice!

"Taste and see that the Lord is good. Oh, the joys of those who trust in him!" (Psalm 34:8 CEV)

October 3: Caught by a Prayer

I was a theater major in college. The other theater majors and I spent the majority of our time moldering around in the basement of the drama department, rehearsing whatever we thought would stun the world. We also traveled around to unsuspecting neighboring colleges, doing what are called "Morality Plays." These plays were written centuries ago, and, understandably, didn't evoke many laughs from the audience. During these trips, we slept in the beds of students who were gone for the weekend.

At one particular college, I was assigned a room from which the occupant had understandably escaped. The condition of the bed itself was not the problem—the roommate definitely was. She was a complete loser, and I knew it the second I saw her. She wore a very long black dress, out-of-style thick black shoes, black stockings, and her hair was scraped back so tightly that her face was pulled back, too. As you can imagine, I did a marvelous imitation of her in front of my cronies.

When I finally dragged up to bed for what was sure to be a night of unmitigated disaster, I hopped into bed and waited with closed eyes for her to make her appearance. In she clomped. I opened one eye and was astounded to see her kneeling by her bed to say her prayers. "Well," I thought philosophically, "how long could it take to say 'Now I lay me down to sleep'?" (the only prayer with which I was familiar). That evidently was NOT what she was praying, for although she was not praying out loud, she just kept at it. She prayed and prayed. I despised her.

After a while, I began to get the most uncomfortable feeling…and with disbelief, I thought, "She's praying for ME!" I resented her with every bone in my body—that she would have the nerve to pray for someone who was so obviously superior to her. I hated her for her presumption, and then she turned towards me. I saw in her face that she loved me. It was the first picture of Jesus Christ I ever saw, from a stranger who certainly had no call to love me. Ten years later, I myself became a follower of Jesus Christ, and I remember, with thanks, that brave "nobody" who caught me with a prayer.

"I thank my God every time I remember you." (Philippians 1:3 NIV)

October 4: Needed: A Life

Most people, when they hear the word "needy" think of someone who is down and out. Since I considered myself to be an "up and in" it never occurred to me that the word needy could ever be applied to me. My life was very full (though I did suffer through occasional days of boredom when no parties were scheduled).

God occupied an extremely limited part of my life—at most, on Sundays and during grace before meals. God simply was not relevant. I focused solely on my physical life, which, in turn, was focused primarily on walking, talking, and partying. It never occurred to me that there were two kinds of life: physical and spiritual. The extent of my spiritual knowledge was that when I died I would go straight to heaven, and, because I was a member of my church, God would say, "Come in, Dear, I know your mother." I didn't know that my sins separated me from any relationship with God.

I suppose you've heard the phrase, "Get a life!" Well, although I don't believe that's what people have in mind when they shout it, that's exactly what I did need. I needed to find a life that would give purpose and meaning to my existence, and a life that would give me a new goal and new attitudes. I needed a life that would give me understanding as to why I was here, and where I was going, a life that would be more satisfying and fulfilling than anything I had ever experienced. And I was about to receive this new life from the very God who loved me way before I loved Him.

"I came so that everyone would have life, and have it in its fullest." (John 10:10b CEV)

October 5: In Good Time

Through the new minister at our church and the ministry of Billy Graham (along with Joe Blinco, one of his team members), I heard and finally understood that the "Gospel" meant "Good News"…good news beyond my wildest imaginings. God had sent his son, Jesus, who had no sin, to die for me, someone whose life revolved around flitting from one party to another. A new spiritual life awaited me.

As one receives a gift, I received my new life and began my spiritual journey. I know that I had not been ready to hear and understand the Gospel before the Holy Spirit prepared my heart. I had heard this Good News before, but it took the Holy Spirit to help me do more than just listen. At last, I could understand and respond to it. I believe the prayers of the "uncool" roommate so many years before were an essential part of my spiritual birth process.

If you feel you should pray for someone, try to not question the timing. Instead, ask God to draw that person to hear His message of love. I think it was Joseph Parker who said, "There is a divine parabola to prayer. God inspires the prayer, and then answers it. He dictates the language and then satisfies the petition." God may be waiting for my prayer or yours to call someone to Him!

"Jesus told him, 'I am the way, the truth and the life. No one can come to the Father except through me.'" (John 14:6 NLT)

October 6: On Course

I never knew that I had to learn to apply what the Bible says to my life. In fact, I was beginning to find out I didn't know much of anything. I had always thought the Bible was a bunch of stories about people who lived a long time ago, and, therefore, the Bible had no relevance to my life. Even as a new Christian, I was beginning to make some amazing discoveries.

There were still piles and piles of stuff I didn't understand, but our minister told me when that happened to just put it to one side and see if it didn't begin to make some sense later on. So, even though the pile on the "I don't get it" side was bigger than the "Wow! I get it!" side, I started marching off down the narrow road.

One day, a woman in our church asked me if I would like to go to a prayer meeting at the home of Sanna Rossi, a missionary who later in life had married the founder of a well-known company.

Attending a prayer meeting with strangers sounded unappealing and scary, especially as I had never prayed out loud except at church meetings. Those prayers had all been carefully written out. Prayers to me were either very formal or very private, so what would a prayer meeting be like? I especially couldn't imagine a bunch of people whom I had never met welcoming a Know-Nothing with open arms. When it came to spiritual matters, I found out that, as usual, I was wrong.

"The body is a unit, though it is made up of many parts; and though all its parts are many, they form one body. So it is with Christ." (I Corinthians 12:12 NIV)

October 7: Learning About Prayer

When I finally screwed up enough courage to ask what went on in a prayer meeting, I found out it lasted from 10 a.m. until 2 p.m.. I nearly keeled over. "Sanna gives us some lunch," I was reassured, and so I reluctantly agreed to attend one meeting, after which I planned to gracefully defect.

I walked into Sanna's lovely home and met a whole passel of older women, not a one of whom I knew (and I wasn't sure I wanted to). They were sure to be very spiritual and wonderful at praying, and I was neither very spiritual nor wonderful at praying.

What an eye-opening experience! To begin with, those dear women treated me with love. They also treated me with respect, as if I knew just as much as they did, which was completely untrue! It was my first toe-dipping experience into the Body of Christ, and I was amazed that they accepted me.

Sanna read some letters from missionaries, most of whom were in Tibet. They told how God had answered their prayers of previous months. I was stunned to the eyeballs. I didn't know God answered prayers about visas and food parcels and other mundane items. I thought he spent His time stopping wars and bubonic plagues. But, no, indeed! These little ladies were thanking Him for stuff about which it would never in this world have occurred to me to pray about. Then Sanna read another bunch of letters telling what was needed: things like sewing thread and paper on which to write translations. It was quite amazing!

My view of God (and prayer) grew quite a bit bigger during the few years I stayed in that city and I went to their meetings every month. How I thank my heavenly Father for teaching me in such a lovely way that He is interested in all our needs and in every single thing we do.

"He himself gives life and breath to everything, and he satisfies every need there is." (Acts 17:25b NLT)

October 8: Let Down

We were vacationing with our three oldest children in Mexico, and we crammed all the sightseeing we could into two weeks. Traveling with our children was very different from traveling with other adults. We met every doorman, elevator man, and waiter from here to breakfast. Although we didn't learn much about them, they learned everything there was to know about us. One of the activities we launched into was water skiing. We all signed up for lessons.

The man who was teaching didn't speak much English, but the kids picked everything up in a New York minute and zoomed happily around the bay. My husband did very well, too, but the day darkened the minute I hit the water. The instructor got up on skis beside me, and as the boat shot forward, he would put his arms under me and yell, "OOP!" My legs (with one ski attached to each foot) seemed totally deaf to this instruction and would flop off to one side. I simply could not oop. The third time this happened, one of my skis took off on its own, went under water and then popped up hitting the instructor in the head. He looked at me sorrowfully and said very distinctly, "Enough for today, Señora!"

When I couldn't perform well enough, he left. But God does not do this. No matter how poorly I perform, God is always there: His love for me is not based on performance (or lack thereof). I am accepted simply because God is love, and He loves even those who repeatedly fall.

"The eternal God is our hiding place; he carries us in his arms." (Deuteronomy 33:27 CEV)

October 9: Putting it Together

When we were first married, my husband and his father had a Ford dealership. Not long after his father retired, Bill decided to get his own company, and so he bought an Edsel dealership. Fortunately, Bill is a very good salesman, and his dealership was one of the few Edsel bought back before the company went bankrupt. Bill purchased another dealership but eventually became more interested in exploring "the other side of the fence" as an automobile company executive.

I had just become a Christian, and knew we should pray about what to do and where to go, but I didn't have a clue as to how to go about it. So I prayed timidly, and then, all of a sudden, we sold our house. Many times, people get jobs and then can't sell their houses, but, of course, we had to be different. The deal was to close on April 1st. "Great," I thought, "April Fool's Day." At the end of March, I was feeling understandably stressed.

On April 1st, Bill came home and said he had been offered a nice position in Jacksonville with American Motors. I didn't realize all the implications that moving meant, especially that of leaving my friends. I was, however, absolutely bowled over that the job had come at just the moment we needed it. That's how God works—He puts everything together in the exact right time!

Then we needed to find housing in Jacksonville. Bill had said that we should rent because we didn't know how long we would be there. We had 4 children and wanted a four-bedroom house. Our friends assured us (helpfully!) that we would never find a house to rent with four bedrooms, and after nearly a week of searching through every crook and cranny of that city, I began to think they were right. Then, one morning in the paper, I read an ad that offered a four-bedroom house to rent. We jumped in the car and found the realtor's office. "I'm so sorry," he said, "I just rented that this morning." Two big tears rolled down my cheeks. "But," he said, "I have a five bedroom house you might like." We liked it!

"And my God will meet all your needs according to his glorious riches in Christ Jesus." (Philippians 4:19 NIV)

October 10: Laundry 101

Unfortunately, I was brought up in a home where there were five live-in maids and a houseman (The words you might be groping for here are "spoiled," verging extremely close to "pampered," "cosseted," and 'indulged"). I say "unfortunately" because an existence where meals were always served on snowy white linen cloths, rooms were cleaned daily, and clothes left lying on the floor were magically washed, ironed and replaced neatly in the correct drawer was about as much preparation for marriage as reading *Peter Pan* would prepare you for flight.

Marriage did come, however, and I was thrust into an unknown world. I managed to keep reality at bay for several years with a succession of maids whom I hired in desperation, and who aged quickly after they had been with us. When my husband accepted a job that required us to relocate, I was jerked away from my little cocoon of helplessness and put in a tiny one-bedroom apartment while we looked for a house. Even though the older children were at camp, I was suddenly faced with a great many things to do. Things did not seem to be done until I did them (what a concept!), and my knowledge of housekeeping was about the size of a milk dud.

In the meantime, as is its wont, the laundry continued to mount up. I did not understand how two people (one expecting her fifth child and feeling pretty grumpy about it) could heap up such piles of dirty clothes. Since there was no room in that apartment for a washer and dryer, I grudgingly took them to a nearby Laundromat. The only thing I had ever heard about laundry was that damask cloths had to be ironed and starched while damp. I therefore assumed this meant all laundry, and dragged several baskets of damp, damp laundry to our apartment. I got out the iron, the ironing board and the starch (all newly purchased) and set to work. I decided to start with the underwear, as it might not show wrinkles as much as shirts would. It was horrendous. The whole apartment filled with steam and mixed nicely with the tears streaming down my face as I started my practice by spraying starch liberally over Bill's underwear. He came home in time to stop too much of this tomfoolery; and as he took me in his arms, he explained gently that underwear did not have to be ironed or starched. I had been struggling under a self-imposed burden. Acceptance from Bill came because he loved me, even if he did crinkle when he walked. Likewise, we cannot find God's favor by trying to obey laws. Acceptance from Him comes from believing in Christ.

"No one can please God by simply obeying the Law. So we put our faith in Christ Jesus, and God accepted us because of our faith." (Galatians 2:16 CEV)

October 11: It Was the Best of Times

It was God's timing that sent us to Jacksonville, but I began to doubt if it were mine. We were expecting our fifth child (fairly depressing subject right there), we couldn't find a church, I couldn't find any friends, and I hated being lumpy, dumpy, and grumpy. I had not made the first preparation for this new baby—no clothes, no crib, no nothing (we had given everything away after our fourth—always a bad move). I was so anxious for someone to talk to I started cornering the milkman. It made him so nervous he started rolling the bottles down the hill to our door. Bill had some aunts that lived on the other side of town, but they never showed up, which, of course, made me feel like a rejected rum ball. I stopped reading my Bible, stopped praying (was God really in Jacksonville?), and just ignored the whole religion thing.

One Sunday, Bill dressed all four of the children for church (when you see him in heaven with a crown on his head, this will be one of the reasons). Bill came into the bedroom and found me still in bed. "Aren't you going to church?" he asked. "No!" I snapped, folding my fat little arms over my fat little stomach. "You can just take the children and go by yourself."

The minute he left I moaned dismally that he had gone off and left me. My lower lip was stuck out so far you could have ridden to town on it. I knew my husband loved and cared for me, but somehow even this didn't help. In my self-pity and despair, I contemplated suicide. I would have done it, except I couldn't think of a way that didn't involve energy. I had no energy. I had reached the end of my rope and let go. I just wanted to drift off someplace that didn't require any effort from me. I was in real darkness. But in that darkness there came a little light, and slowly I began to realize that even though I had let go of God, He had not let go of me. He still loved me and accepted me even though I had turned away from Him. It was a real turning point in my life: I experienced God's faithfulness and love to a sheep that had left the fold and wandered far away. It wasn't the worst of times, after all…it was the best of times!

"The sea belongs to him, for he made it. His hands formed the dry land, too. Come let us worship and bow down. Let us kneel before the Lord our maker, for he is our God. We are the people he watches over, the sheep under his care." (Psalm 95:5-7 NLT)

October 12: Speaking of Limpets…

Limpets don't really have a lot going for them: they have a drab looking shell and spend their time among the rocks near the seashore without a coffee break. Their name, however, has become a synonym for stick-to-it-tiveness because, when they are disturbed, instead of running away (difficult, of course, inside a shell…) they just dig in and adhere.

If I adhere tightly to God, even when I am not aware of His presence, then I show the same stick-to-it-tiveness. I do realize this is not very exciting or dramatic and will probably not be written up in the newspaper, but, then, limpets aren't known for their dramatic qualities either. To emulate this excellent quality of endurance, I must concentrate on what Psalm 119:68a says about God: "You are **good**, and what you do is good…" (NIV, emphasis added). Because God is good, I can trust Him when times are hard. And, of course, I know times will get hard, be it financial disaster, rejection by a loved one, or an incurable illness. These things are terrible, unexplainable and draining emotionally, physically, and spiritually. It is especially in those hard times when it is important to trust God!

I am continually reminded that although I cannot choose my circumstances, I can choose my reactions. May I cling to God even when I don't understand.

"Let us hold unswervingly to the hope we profess, for he who promised is faithful." (Hebrews 10:23 NIV)

October 13: Traffic Signals

Did you ever stop to think about the impartiality of traffic signals? All cars have to stop when they turn red, whether that car is a Rolls Royce or a battered pickup truck. The person driving may be a bank president, a steel worker, a student driver, or a convict on parole. The rules are the same for each person, and they are put there to keep us out of trouble, not just to give us something to look at. Not everyone likes traffic lights, and not everyone agrees that they are in the best places. But if they are not obeyed, one of two things almost always occurs: an accident or a ticket. There are exceptions, of course, but if we slip into the habit of expecting an exception (perhaps because we are cute, or we are best friends with the mayor, or we are someone very, very famous or we own one third of Fort Knox), then we are in for a big surprise…because we are supposed to stop on red whether we are on our way to church, to a rock concert, to the hospital, or just late for an appointment.

Traffic lights are a lot like God's commandments. They are given to everyone without partiality, and there are no exceptions. God expects each of us to obey his signals, and there is punishment given when we disobey. We cannot wheedle our way out, for He knows our thoughts and our motives, and there is actually no excuse at all, for we know what pleases the Father and what does not. If we do not listen to the warning lights that go on when we insist on going our way instead of His, there will be a day of reckoning, and it will not be just a traffic ticket. It will break our hearts and His.

"…be careful to obey that it may go well with you." (Deuteronomy 6:3a NIV)

"If you obey my commands, you will remain in my love, just as I have obeyed my Father's commands and remain in his love." (John 15:10 NIV)

October 14: Aunt Fanny's Money

I suppose everyone has heard of any number of money laundering schemes…but my Aunt Fanny was way ahead of her time. Born in 1854, she was already older than macaroni when I knew her. She was a little wisp of a woman who had led a full and interesting life teaching at the Carlisle Indian School. It was said among the family (which is why I can't guarantee it) that she taught Jim Thorpe. She may have taught him to read and write, but I doubt if she had much to offer in the way of athletics because I never saw her do anything more physical than go upstairs.

Aunt Fanny, in addition to being intelligent, was also, let's face it, eccentric. She hated dirty money. The minute she got home from a store or bank, she would suds everything out. There was no problem with coins of course. She would carefully wash the coins, wrap them in a towel, and dry them off. Paper money, however, evidently caused some trouble until she came across the idea of squeezing them out and then smoothing them carefully over the edge of the tub until they were dry.

Aunt Fanny liked clean money, but she didn't love it. She knew its value and worth, but she didn't abuse it. Although she could have had a great many things (her brother-in-law was president of Westinghouse Air Brake), she lived a simple life with her sisters, uncomplicated by a desire for wealth and power. She was eccentric, but knew better than to put her trust in riches. Her Savior was firmly in first place. She knew that nothing but His love was eternal: His love is not a prop like money, which can be lost so easily.

"Tell those who are rich in this world not to be proud and not to trust in their money, which will soon be gone. But their trust should be in the living God, who always richly gives us all we need for our enjoyment." (1 Timothy 6:17 NLT)

October 15: The Real Dirt

While on a speaking itinerary in a southern city, I spent the night at a splendiferous home that looked as though it had come straight out of *Southern Living* magazine. I had a whole wing to myself, with a private sitting room in addition to a bedroom the size of Grand Central station and a bath that had hot and cold running television.

The only thing that was a teeny bit discouraging was that there was no shower. The bathtub was long enough in which to do laps, but there was no sign of a shower, only a large ledge encircling three sides of the tub filled with large exotic plants (I have no idea how these were watered, but evidently not with the shower). I wanted to be watered by a shower, especially because I wash my hair in showers. The only solution to this dilemma was to hump over and crane my head under the faucet. In performing this not inconsiderable acrobatic feat, I managed to knock over one of the formerly beautiful plants, causing a cascade of flowers and a lot of dirt.

I don't know if you have ever been in a situation where you had to try and scrape up dirt from a tub filled with water and replace it in a planter, but believe me, it isn't easy. Luckily, the pot didn't break, but even so, my attempts at re-arrangement must have made that hostess sick for a week (not surprisingly, I was never invited back).

Fortunately, clumsiness is not something God holds against us, nor does He feel nervous about a host of other physical and mental disabilities. God is interested in the state of our heart, and searches constantly to show us any sin that stands between Him and us. It's all right to be slow or incapacitated, but we must be obedient to what He has shown us, and come to Him for washing. Do you think it might be a cleansing experience to examine your heart today and ask the Father to show you any dirt lurking on the ledges? When we are in fellowship with God, we are more likely to experience showers of blessings!

"And that is what some of you were. But you were washed, you were sanctified, you were justified in the name of the Lord Jesus Christ and by the Spirit of our God." (I Corinthians 6:11 NIV)

October 16: The Old Man and the She

Driving more than one block in a station wagon stuffed with five children and all their impedimenta calls for a weak mind and a strong body. I was going from Bradenton to Jacksonville and had the weak mind all right, but I also had a weak body to go along with it. I tried concentrating on the reunion with my husband at the end of this five-hour trip (one for each child).

We passed an old man in a truck piled high with wire crates filled with squawking chickens. I had my own squawking chickens to worry about, and I thought I had everything under control. I didn't. Five minutes after we passed him, my front tire blew out. I managed to wrestle the car over to the side of the road and sat numbly going over my choice of actions. There weren't many, but the thought did cross my mind that someone might come along and try to kidnap the children (that really WOULD take a weak mind...). I had never changed a tire in my life, and things seemed fairly hopeless in the mechanical department, as the boys were only about 9 and 10, and I doubted that their Christmas loot had included wrenches and bolts, or whatever tools it is that one uses to change a tire.

While I was pondering all these thoughts, we heard a rattling and a squawking and that old truck pulled up in back of us. "Heered ya bangin' as ya went by," he announced (which shows you the level of noise inside the car; I hadn't heard a thing!). He hopped out, extricated some tools from under the chickens and had that tire changed before I had time to ask for help. When I tried to pay him, he wouldn't take it. "Give it to your church, then," I suggested. "No Ma'am," he answered, "The Lord sez we're sposed to hep each other." Without another word, he hopped back in with the chickens and was gone.

He was a fellow traveler who took the time to "hep" a bewildered "Mother Hen." There are still Good Samaritans around after all.

"Kneeling beside him, the Samaritan soothed his wounds with medicine and bandaged them. Then he put the man on his own donkey and took him to an inn, where he took care of him." (Luke 10:24 NLT)

October 17: Heaven Scent

It's funny how certain smells bring back memories. In fact, I read recently that scientists have found that we retain all sorts of odor memories that are triggered by scent. Some are pleasant (such as a favorite flower, a pie baking, Balsam pine, or sea air), and some are fairly icky (such as old garbage or moldy towels). My dear mother always wore the same perfume, and although it is no longer made, one of my sisters-in-law gave me an old bottle that has just a trace of perfume lingering in the bottom. It reminds me so poignantly of her.

The Bible tells us that we, too, have a fragrance—good for some, and bad for others. Those who love the Lord, or who are searching for Him, find the smell attractive; those who are self-centered and indifferent to the God who loves them find it repulsive. When we spend time with Jesus, our fragrance must be particularly strong, for people sense this in a way we really do not understand.

Remember to treat those who scoff and laugh derisively about the cross with the love of Christ, and ask that His fragrance would draw them to Him.

"Our lives are a fragrance presented to Christ by God." (II Corinthians 2:15a NLT)

October 18: The Everlasting Fur Coat

On my sixteenth birthday, I was presented with a large box. As I opened it, tissue paper crackled enticingly. Glancing excitedly at my parents, I caught my first good look at the contents: a fur coat. At that time in history, I suppose, most young girls (north of the Mason Dixon line anyway) dreamed of a fur coat. At least, I did. The coat I envisioned was gray or black, preferably of chinchilla or some other fur that would swing enticingly as I walked and make me look like a shorter version of, say, Cleopatra or, at the very least, Lauren Becall. I had even practiced what I hoped was a sultry look, but which was probably only petulant.

As I opened the coat, however, I quickly realized that it did not meet any of my specifications. First of all, it was a beaver coat. My parents were far too practical to be presenting a sixteen year old with chinchilla. But worst of all, it was brown; I hate brown. And I hated that coat from the minute I put it on.

When I left for boarding school in the fall, I had to take that coat. I wore it my Junior and Senior years with slow and grudging steps, and no matter what I did to it, it would not wear out. I wore it to college with ever mounting distress; but after two years, I noticed happily that the lining was quite torn, and gaily returned it to my mother. In the fall, she gave it back. She had relined it. Fortunately, the following year, a friend of mine was moving to Colorado and had no winter coat ("There is a God in heaven after all!!" I thought). So I parted at last with my nemesis, and it went on, I presume, to see several more years' duty before being retired from active service.

Now, what should I learn from this little scenario of selfishness? Well, since becoming a Christian, I discovered that although God is a loving God, He sometimes presents me with things I would rather not have: death, illness, heartaches and disappointments. But, He does not do this haphazardly, for they are sent to be lessons in order that I might grow in the grace and knowledge of Christ.

"Therefore, among God's churches we boast about your perseverance and faith in all the persecutions and trials you are enduring. All this is evidence that God's judgment is right, and as a result you will be counted worthy of the kingdom of God, for which you are suffering." (II Thessalonians 1:4-5 NIV)

October 19: Façade

In one of our city parks, there used to be an elaborate structure that looked exactly like the front of an old antebellum plantation. It was all white, with big columns on the porch and second story windows overlooking graceful magnolia trees. It was so real you expected to see Scarlett and Rhett strolling around the corner. But if you went to the back, you would see it wasn't a house at all. There was only a front held in place by long boards and cross beams. I don't know what it was used for (maybe weddings or a postcard made up for friends who were easily impressed) but I can still hear my mother's opinion given down the long corridor of time: "Just a Queen Anne front and a Mary Anne back."

While this statement was reserved for family opinions about one thing or another, it mainly referred to people who were a little snobbish and didn't have any reason to be that way. Unfortunately, I am not exempt from this description, and I know it's one of the reasons that many unbelievers shy away from Christianity. Who can blame them? No one likes hypocrites, and people who profess one thing and do another can make the milk of human kindness curdle quite quickly.

Not only that, it must grieve God to see me acting in a way that is not pleasing to Him. So I must not waste time and energy putting up false fronts that are not really part of my framework. I pray that God will make me into a person who is genuine and sincere, front and back!

"Rather, we have renounced secret and shameful ways; we do not use deception, nor do we distort the word of God. On the contrary, by setting forth the truth plainly we commend ourselves to every man's conscience in the sight of God." (II Corinthians 4:2-3 NIV)

October 20: The Mattress Firm

The Mattress Firm is the clever name of a store that sells mattresses in our city. I think a wonderful spiritual application can be drawn from a firm mattress. Everyone knows we need a good firm mattress on which to rest the old bod because we spend at least a quarter of our lives in the sack (I spend more time than that, because I do a lot of heavy napping. I also seem to spend more time in a horizontal position than the general public due to various ailments, detailed descriptions of which I will mercifully spare you).

Just as we need a firm mattress, we also need a firm foundation for life. People seem to build their lives on an extraordinary number of things (fame, talent, wealth, power, etc.), all of which are going to prove to be sand. Sand is notoriously unstable, but many overlook this and build their houses there because of the great view. How sad this will be when the water of death and judgment comes in and washes it away! "Disaster strikes like a cyclone, whirling the wicked away; but the godly have a lasting foundation" proclaims Proverbs 10:25 (NLT).

I must think carefully about what is most important in my life: family? friends? things? attainments? All of these are wonderful, of course, but unless Jesus Christ is the true foundation of my life, I will be bitterly disappointed when my life is over.

"For no one can lay any other foundation than the one we already have—Jesus Christ." (I Corinthians 3:11 NLT)

October 21: Home Sweet Home

I was looking at my paper towels the other day (although, yes, I do have other reading material) and noticed what was imprinted on them. It said, "Home is where love surrounds you." That's not always true, is it? There are homes where love couldn't even get in a window, much less be a real part of home. There are abusive homes, lonely homes, and uncaring homes. In all of these, love is an unknown quality.

Perhaps your home is like one of these. But if you are a Christian, you not only have the mind of Christ, you have the love of Christ within you. You can start to make that love bloom by loving those within your home, manifesting His love to each one. You may not see a response, and love may never surround your home, but there can be a steady glow of acceptance because Christ Himself has accepted you. It will make an impression that will never be forgotten if you are willing to love without any strings attached, forgiving with kindness and compassion. You may be the only love they ever see.

"Be kind and compassionate to one another, forgiving each other, just as in Christ God forgave you." (Ephesians 4:32 NIV)

October 22: Dilly Crystal

When Bill and I were engaged, one of the first things that came into my brain (small as it was...) was that brides-to-be had a wonderful time picking out silver, china and crystal. Mother and I set out immediately upon this exciting errand of self-gratification. Although I didn't really need any china or silver because Mother had given me three complete sets of silver and a huge set of English china (none of which I appreciated); I did feel I was in desperate need of everyday china and exotic crystal.

Lost in the mist of time is the reason that I picked out white china with black designs—I think I thought it looked sophisticated. And my dear Mother obediently crocheted black and white edging around white linen place mats and napkins. I'm sure she wondered where in the world I had picked up such strange opinions, as she and Daddy were very conservative. So she really gets a lot of points for going along with this.

Then came crystal. Ah yes, what one uses to drink water or other beverages, and stores carefully on a secure shelf when not in use. I had my eye firmly on a set that had wide gold rims. Mother didn't seem too awfully enthused about this. She told me, "The gold will wash off, Dear." She tried steering me toward plain cut glass. I resisted. We came close to open warfare. But in the end, she gracefully gave in and allowed me to choose the ones with the gold rims.

Five days before the wedding, we were seated at the dining room table when there came a ring at the door. I rushed out, because the doorbell had hardly ever stopped ringing since the invitations went out, so I knew it was another gift.

Glowingly, I opened the huge box. Inside there were twelve cut glass water goblets. Anyone in their right mind would have been ecstatic. I was furious—because my wishes had been thwarted; and I rushed upstairs weeping copious tears of rage and frustration.

Of course, I also got my set of gold-rimmed glasses; so one would think it all ended happily. But actually, I learned a lesson the hard way...for every time those gold rimmed glasses were washed, a little of the gold came off. And when I became a Christian, I realized that, in a way, it was a symbol of all the gold and precious things that the world offers...for one day they will all be gone.

"How the gold has lost its luster, the fine gold become dull!" (Lamentations 4:1 NIV)

"Now listen you rich people, weep and wail because of the misery that is coming upon you. Your wealth has rotted, and moths have eaten your clothes. Your gold and silver is corroded…." (James 5:1-3a NIV)

October 23: The Teacher

Do you get antsy waiting for things that are late? I do! I feel this way about people, planes, and even prayers. Sometimes it seems the first two come sooner than the last.

One of my favorite hymns has this line: "Teach me the patience of unanswered prayer." Unanswered prayers often drive me to distraction—and sometimes despair, because I don't want to be patient. Yet, I think unanswered prayer clears away a lot of my dead wood. If I don't really care about what I am praying, I don't keep praying for it.

Of course, unanswered can also mean delayed, which doesn't necessarily mean no. I am often reminded of the story of Mary and Martha and how heartsick they were when Jesus delayed his coming in answer to their request for their sick brother Lazarus.

It seems to me that the most important thing to learn about unanswered prayer is that the thing prayed for is not to be our focus. We are to keep believing in the goodness and mercy of God, and believe that in His time and in His way He will answer, not so that we might be gratified (or satisfied!), but that He might be glorified. When we are trusting, He is working. Am I going to be teachable in the waiting time?

"The Lord God is waiting to show how kind he is and to have pity on you. The Lord always does right; he blesses those who trust him." (Isaiah 30:18 CEV)

October 24: Chair Person

I am not, and, probably, never will be a chair person. I am a bed person. I feel that a horizontal position is superior to one that forces you to bend, fold, staple, and be mutilated. The problem really is that chairs are not built for people like me. Ladder-backs are too stiff and hard, rockers make me feel dizzy, lounge chairs put me to sleep, and dental chairs make me stiff with apprehension. When I am at the beauty shop, my neck is too short to reach the basin, and, unless a car has a four way motorized seat, I can't see over the wheel and reach the pedal at the same time. All in all, there just aren't many chairs made for someone who is really low down.

Fortunately, this does not in any way apply to God. As one who stooped to become a man, He does not let anything touch us that is not individualized and sized to fit. Every human being is unique, and while there are physical resemblances, our fingerprints show that we are special to Him, for they point to God's power in creating separate and distinct children. Times of heartache and loss must not be viewed as happenstance or bad luck, but as something that the Father means for eventual good. I admit it is hard to believe in a good God when the things I am going through are not good; but, loyalty to Him in times of crises are what it means to trust in Him.

Am I willing to trust in God even when I do not understand? I must make every effort to be comfortable in the chair that God has provided for me.

"Then Jesus told [Thomas], 'Because you have seen me, you have believed; blessed are those who have not seen and yet have believed.'" (John 20:29 NIV)

October 25: A View from the Top

Two men who had not seen each other for some time met unexpectedly. "How are you these days?" asked the first man. "All right, I guess, under the circumstances," Was the reply. "Under the circumstances!!" smiled the first man. "What in the world are you doing under there?" That is certainly true of me: I often view life from under the circumstances instead of above them.

There are two roads in Europe that, although they are in different countries and in different climates, showed me the perspective of a view from the top. The first was up and over the Swiss Alps, which I reluctantly viewed from the window of a bus that zipped speedily around snake-like curves. The other road was in Italy, bursting enthusiastically along the east coast. It was the justly famous Amalfi drive, riotous with bougainvillea blossoms and looking down on groves of olive trees and the impossibly blue Adriatic.

Both of these roads come down to earth, so to speak, but the road that we can have above our circumstances doesn't have to. As Bruce Bickel and Stan Jantz point out in their book *Keeping God in the Small Stuff*, "Instead of trying to see God through your circumstances, take the opposite approach; Look at your circumstances through God's eyes." God has already placed us above the heavens and lifted us into glory along with Christ. So because of that unseen hand of God, we may always be above our circumstances.

"But God is so rich in mercy, and He loved us so very much, that even when we were dead because of our sins He gave us life when He raised Christ from the dead. (It is only by God's special favor that you have been saved)! For He raised us from the dead along with Christ, and we are seated with Him in the heavenly realms—all because we are one with Christ Jesus." (Ephesians 2:4-6 NLT)

October 26: Do It Yourself

A new grocery store opened in our city, and a great many people were talking about it. They said that many of the items such as flour, rice and nuts were in barrels and you just scooped up as much as you wanted. This all sounded very interesting and I made a special trip to see it for myself. It was a big warehouse, with the advertised barrels holding any number of things. I remember thinking that I hoped everyone had remembered to wash their hands thoroughly before dipping in.

A big sign over the check out counter said, "You are about to bag a whole lot of savings." In reading this, I optimistically put the emphasis on "…a whole lot of savings," but I soon found out that the emphasis was on "YOU are about to bag…." What that meant was that I had to find some bags, cram everything in there, and then lug it all out of there (which was sort of a culture shock after being molly-coddled in stores where there were people eager to bag and carry everything for me).

Sometimes, I want everything done spiritually for me, too. I would love to be a Biblical fount of knowledge, but I don't spend much time at the source. I would love to be known as a prayer warrior, but ten minutes on the bended knee makes me head for the aspirin. I would love to be as revered as Mother Teresa, but I have no intentions of getting my hands dirty or going some place where I might catch some terrible disease.

Salvation is a gift, but after we receive it, we must all feed on God's Word to grow, discipline ourselves to prayer, and "do as many good deeds as they can and to help everyone" (I Timothy 6:18a CEV). Our heavenly Father makes many provisions for His children, but He will not do what we must do for ourselves.

"And Moses told them, 'It is the bread that the Lord has given you to eat.'" (Exodus 16:15 TLB)

October 27: Restaurant Life

I heard a quip the other day about a man who walked into a restaurant and said, "There's a sign out front that says 'Under New Management,' but it looks like the same manager to me." "Oh, it is," replied the waiter, "But he got married yesterday."

When we become followers of Christ, our lives are under new management, too! As employees, we must become accustomed right away to following instructions. The reason good managers are good managers is because they see the big picture and make plans accordingly.

Now this is an analogy that breaks down here, because we can't compare God to restaurant managers, no matter how good they are. But even at the beginning of my new life in Christ, I understood that I was under new management.

I knew God had a plan for me (although I couldn't imagine what it was), but I understood (in a very beginner-like fashion) that I had been chosen before the foundation of the world. This fact continues to amaze me, although I did not comprehend how He did it or why. It's a thousand times better than being picked to be a Heisman Trophy winner, or the star of a Broadway production, or the owner of Olympic medals, because it is a personal, wonderful, special, revelation that God not only likes you, He loves you! What an honor! He did this not because I had anything to offer, but simply because it is His nature to love.

"Kings will see you and arise, princes will see and bow down, because of the Lord, who is faithful, the Holy One of Israel, who has chosen you." (Isaiah 49:7b NIV)

"Praise be to the God and Father of our Lord Jesus Christ, who has blessed us in the heavenly realms with every spiritual blessing in Christ. For he chose us in him before the creation of the world to be holy and blameless in his sight." (Ephesians 1:3-4 NIV)

October 28: A Closer (and Depressing) Look

I have always looked upon sheep as adorable creatures, especially since I had only seen them from a distance. My literary acquaintance was pretty much limited to "Mary had a little lamb." They seemed to be deliciously round and wooly, and I envisioned them cropping their placid and unhurried way up green hillsides. All in all, I was enchanted to be considered in Scripture as one of these enchantingly fuzzy animals.

On a trip to Scotland with my husband, I had good reason to change my mind. Almost the first thing I noticed was that the sheep paid no attention to where they were going. They grazed along without a thought in their heads as to what might be around the next boulder. I saw how easily one could go astray because the next bite and then the one after that were the only things on their minds. Later, when we played golf in a sheep pasture near Loch Ness, I saw these animals up close and personal (they were in no danger from golf balls as they were on the fairway and we were mostly in the rough). I was very disillusioned, for they were extremely dirty with long hair hopelessly matted, and their smell left a great deal to be desired (perhaps this was just this one particular flock. I have been assured that most sheep are not smelly). However, I was no longer so thrilled to be labeled a sheep.

Then I stop to think how I must appear to the absolute holiness and purity of my Savior. I hang my head, realizing that God sought me to be part of his flock when I was just as dirty and mindless of the Shepherd as one of those poor creatures. I am so grateful that He laid down His life for me and made me clean, giving me a heart to know His voice. If you have never had this wonderful experience, this would be the very time to admit that you are unclean with the sin of selfishness and pride, going your own way instead of following the one who loves you and laid down His life for you, taking the punishment that you and I deserve. If you are willing to admit this need and agree with God that you are a sinner, then ask His forgiveness and invite Him into your life. He will come in, and give you eternal life, for He promises to do so; and God always keeps His promises!

"I am the good shepherd, I know my sheep, and they know me. Just as the Father knows me, I know the Father, and I give up my life for the sheep." (John 10:14-15 CEV)

October 29: A Good Patient

When you think about it, some patients are not very patient (in fact, when we were driving past some beautiful flowerbeds the other day, Bill asked what they were. Because they were one of the few flowers I recognize, I said they were impatiens. Whereupon, Bill's reply was that they should be planted outside the hospital).

I can be impatient about a lot of things actually: being last in line at the grocery store with one of the people in line having a basket that holds enough for a family of twenty, trying to struggle through to the head of the line at the post office when I have packages to juggle, or even waiting my turn on the roller coaster (well, maybe that one is a bit unlikely…).

When I am a patient in the hospital, however, it is almost impossible to be a good patient. You know what I mean: the people whose sunny replies to "And, how are we today?" are the talk of the corridor. I must confess that when I am sick, I turn into a curmudgeon whose only wish is to turn my face to the wall and pull the covers up over my head so that, when I suffocate, all the nurses will be sorry they weren't more attentive.

I must, instead, learn to turn from my natural reactions to supernatural ones. Philippians 4:19 promises, "And this same God who takes care of me will supply all your needs from his glorious riches, which have been given to us in Christ Jesus" (NLT).

So when we are ill, when we are harassed, when we are fed up with our circumstances, we have God's resources to call on—not so the situation might change, but that we would be willing for God to change us. Then we can rejoice, knowing that hardships help us, "learn to endure" (Romans 5:3c NLT).

"Finishing is better than starting. Patience is better than pride." (Ecclesiastes 7:8 NLT)

October 30: An Interesting Discovery

When our three oldest children were about 6, 7, and 8, I took them on a special trip to Pittsburgh to help celebrate my mother's 75th birthday. She had been the first baby born in the little suburb of Edgewood, and after my father died, she gave our home to the Western Pennsylvania School for the Deaf. My family was always careful to underplay things like that because making a big announcement of it would have been considered *nouveau riche* and uncouth, to say nothing of showing off. The head of the school decreed a special party at the school for mother (which she graciously shared with us), to show us how little they had had to adapt the house into a boarding school for the smaller children (who lived there during the week).

One of the extra things that we did while there in Pittsburgh was to visit some of the attractions, one of which was the Museum of Natural History. We more or less galloped through it, as the children's attention span was fairly miniscule. The stuffed animal exhibit however, was found to be worth slowing down for. Our six-year-old, Allen, was especially excited at this new and wonderful world, and he ran breathlessly from one case to another. Soon he hurried back to us to come quickly and see the "Tunkahangen." I had no idea what that was, but I was pleased that he seemed to be observing all the various species.

Even after pulling up in front of a woodland scene, I was unable to locate the "Tunkahangen" that Allen had been so excited about. I saw only deer in various poses. He nudged me closer to the window and pointed to a deer lying on her side. Indeed, not only was her "tunk" hanging out, it was lolling several inches from her mouth, which did make her look quite unusual. I had seen the deer Allen was excited about, but did not see her (or her tongue) as remarkable, until he pointed her out to me.

I observe many people in my daily life; thankfully, none that I know of have spent time in a taxidermist's lab. Even so, I often take them for granted, just as I did Allen's deer in the woodland scene. May the Holy Spirit point out those whose tongue is hanging out because they are thirsting for the water of life. May I always walk carefully, and observe others with my heart as well as my eyes.

"Indeed, the water I give him will become in him a spring of water welling up to eternal life." (John 4:14b NIV)

October 31: Unmasked

On Halloween night, many people put on a mask to hide their true identity. Two party costumes that I remember vividly include one that our son, Will, wore when he tried to become a mummy and wrapped himself in yards and yards of gauze. The other was when our daughter, Margaret, ensconced herself in a large plastic garbage bag and glued on MORE than 900 balls of cotton to go as a lamb. Both of these involved many trips to the local drugstore (I'm sure they must have wondered exactly what disease we had).

The kind of mask I am thinking of, however, is not seen, nor is it put on just once a year. There are two kinds of these masks: one that we put on to impress others, and the other we put on to impress God. Neither of these is successful. People eventually see the gaps in our reality, and we might as well discard the other at once, for we are never able to fool our Creator-Redeemer. We sometimes insist on doing this, under the misguided impression that God is fooled by our actions. But God reminds us in I Samuel 16:7, "People judge others by what they look like, but I judge people by what's in their hearts" (CEV).

I don't need cotton balls or gauze to disguise myself (no more trips to the drugstore!), for because of what Christ has done for me, I will always truly be one of God's sheep.

November 1: Authorization

In 1992, my daughter, Margaret, and I went to Europe. I was going to be speaking for some Christian Women's Clubs and she had accompanied me in order to 1) help me lug my bags, 2) make sure I didn't electrocute myself, and, 3) make sure someone was around who understood my Southern accent.

We landed in London and were met by a friend of Margaret's with whom she had worked at a camp in North Carolina. What we would have done without him is anyone's guess—probably we would still be wandering around Heathrow trying to find our way toward civilization. He quickly informed us that the most economical way to get around London is to buy a pass that enables one to travel by bus or underground. In order to purchase this, however, you have to have a picture of yourself taken and paste it on the card. Margaret and I had just gotten off the plane after flying all night. So we were not really bright-eyed and bushy-tailed, to say the least. At least, I wasn't. In fact, if you had seen this photo of me, you would have been tempted to send me immediately for surgery. Nevertheless, the transportation workers in London allowed me to board all manner of public conveyance with this very scary pass photo (most issued only minor gasps of horror). I soon realized that the quality of my picture was not as important as the quality of the authorizing signatures.

My entry into the kingdom of God is not dependent on how I look either, and yours is not dependent on how you look, for that matter. It is not based on family background, past achievements or how much money your great-grandfather made in the California Gold Rush. It is not based on whether or not you can recite the Apostle's Creed or the fact that you live next door to a minister. Our entry in God's kingdom is based solely on whether or not we have the authorization of the Lord Jesus Christ. In the Gospel of John, Jesus says, "No one comes to the Father except through me" (John 14:6). To get that authorization, we need to turn from the sin that has controlled us and turn around to face God. We are saved, not because of the things we do, but because of what Jesus did for us. Now that's the correct authorization!

"Only God can give authority to anyone..." (Romans 13:1b CEV).

November 2: Haarlem Globe Trotters

We had some amazing experiences in Europe, nearly all of them fun, and a few of them hair-raising (and I never even stuck a fork into an outlet).

When we were in Holland, we took time out to see Corrie ten Boom's house in Haarlem, where she hid Jews and members of the Dutch underground from the Nazis. Corrie was an amazing woman, and a staunch Christian who lived out her faith through terrible circumstances.

I had originally thought she did most of the work in Holland by herself, but, while we were at the old clock shop that her father had owned, we were told that there were many young people who had helped her. One of the young men who helped her to rescue and hide Jewish people was very proud of the work they were doing After an especially dangerous mission, he said, "We are doing wonderful things, aren't we Tante Corrie?" "Ja" she said slowly, but when you rescue these dear people do you tell them about Jesus?" "No." he answered impatiently, "That is women work." And Corrie said, "Now we haf a leetle talk." And she "talked" a long time. Soon after this the young man was caught and imprisoned, but Corrie received a letter from him just before he was executed in which he said, "I wanted you to know I have led every man in my cell to Christ."

Corrie visited the summer camp that our two youngest daughters attended, and, even though she was 83 at the time, there was no generation gap. I doubt if there is anyone who was there at the time who does not remember her gentle smile and love for Christ. What will people remember about me?

"But we continue to preach because we have the same kind of faith the psalmist had when he said, "I believed in God, and so I speak." (II Corinthians 4:13 NLT)

November 3: Clock Talk

While we were at Corrie Ten Boom's old watch shop, I bought a small clock and gave it to my daughter as a special memory of our trip. When we got to Paris, however, we discovered that the clock had been left behind, in the Murphy bed in our Amsterdam Bed & Breakfast. Frustrating phone calls had finally resulted in our realization that the manager had probably appropriated it as a reward (in addition to the tip) for carrying bags up the three flights of stairs that wound around like a corkscrew (all of which makes me stop and think twice when someone says they need to unwind).

Although he had said he had found it and would send it COD to a London address on our itinerary, nothing was forthcoming. My reaction to this did not exhibit the fruit of the Spirit. I was furious that we had lost the clock that was our one precious souvenir. Finally, I was able to realize that the loss of a clock from Corrie's shop was an opportunity to show what Corrie's whole life had stood for: forgiveness. My daughter summed it up this way, "The materials we store in our homes must not be dearer than the materials we store in out hearts." I guess I must constantly be searching my heart to look for any grudge that needs to be brought out and given to God to dispose of.

"I the Lord search the heart and examine the mind, to reward a man according to his conduct, according to what his deeds deserve." (Jeremiah 17:10 NIV)

November 4: No Favorites

The last two devotions have been about Corrie ten Boom, who called herself "A tramp for the Lord." She was known nearly all over the world, not only for her work in rescuing Jewish people from the Nazis, but for what she later became when she was released "by mistake" from her concentration camp and began to learn what it means to forgive those who had imprisoned her.

If there ever was an example of Christian love, it shone from the countenance of Tante Corrie. One would think, after all she had done, in all the places where she had shared God's love for each person, that she would be a special favorite of her God. I envisioned her home-going to join her beloved Savior and her family as something quite spectacular. I didn't have anything in mind, of course, but I did imagine that somehow God would do something special for her as she approached death. Well, you know, He didn't. She had a stroke and was partially paralyzed and, then, had another, which left her motionless and speechless. There were no angels singing in the background, there was no visible sign of God. Corrie, no doubt, suffered as do others who have had strokes in being unable to communicate with anyone. Yet she must have continued to communicate silently with God in her heart; the woman who faithfully tended Corrie for many, many months said that everyone who entered her room felt God's presence in a subtle way. She was unable to speak or move, and, yet, to her, Christ was still the Victor.

There are thousands of Christians around the world who faithfully serve the Lord Jesus Christ; and there are many who do not give Him first place in their lives, but continue to hold the right to themselves. Yet, God loves each one the same, because He is love. He pays no attention to background (good or bad), and attainments or rewards for Christian service are not part of His plan that we be conformed to the image of Christ. We must not expect any special treatment when we die, whether it be by fire or flood. It will be enough for us to know that Christ the Victor is waiting to give us our reward in heaven.

"So do your work in honor of him…" (II Chronicles 19:7a CEV)

November 5: Scrambled

Margaret and I made our first (and only) venture into Indonesian food when we were in Holland. There was a small restaurant near our third floor Bed & Breakfast, and so we labored down the same staircase we had labored up and decided to give it a try. We had no idea what to order, but we took the recommendation of the waiter. When he staggered in with a huge tray of stuff, we couldn't believe it was just for two people.

The central item was a bowl of rice surrounded by a lot of other bowls. The one thing I thought I recognized as lentils turned out to be peanuts. We were instructed to arrange all these selections around the side of the rice, but never, never to mix them with the rice. We spooned delicately, but of course after the first ten minutes, everything was hopelessly scrambled together. The waiter had neglected to tell us what would happen if we were so careless as to mix our food, so, we ate as fast as we could cram it down, draped our napkins over the offending articles, paid our bill, and rushed out into safety.

Sometimes my life gets scrambled, too. When I am involved in too many things, it is all too easy to feel grumpy (or Sleepy and Dopey). I guess I need to take a tip from the waiter (yes, we left him one, too) and just try to keep one thing central and not mix anything up with it. That one thing should be God. When He is first, then everything else falls into place (even lentils masquerading as peanuts).

"Your heavenly Father already knows all your needs, and he will give you all you need from day to day if you live for him and make the Kingdom of God your primary concern." (Matthew 6:32b-33 NLT).

November 6: Washing Behind Your Ears

Margaret and I were waiting at a bus stop shelter in Amsterdam when I noticed that the sidewalk and the sides of the bus shelter were dripping wet. We couldn't imagine why until we saw three men wielding soap and long handled brushes all over the bus stop. They not only washed the sides and the ceiling, they washed the outside and the top. We were suitably impressed: I don't recall anyone around here washing bus shelters—much less the tops. Americans, on the whole, tend to be pretty casual about dusty stuff people can't see. Not all housewives dust only when company is coming (although I confess I fall into that category). Most of those of us who don't clean all the time think there is no use killing yourself cleaning up what others won't notice.

The artisans who worked on the great European cathedrals didn't feel that way. One man, who was laboring over a small detail that couldn't possibly be seen from the ground, was asked why he was taking such pains. He replied that God could see it, and that was reason enough for it to be perfect.

Shouldn't that be my attitude, too? As I build, clean, plant, cook, teach, bandage, or use the computer, let me strive for perfection in order that the Lord might see and be pleased because I am doing it for Him. And, may I ask Him for the incentive to do even the tops.

"Praise the Lord! Praise the name of the Lord! Praise him, you who serve the Lord." (Psalm 135:1 NLT)

November 7: Correction

On the way to the train station in Amsterdam, we drove past a closed restaurant. The window curtains were open, however, and we could see a large cat lying full length on a table right by the window. "My goodness!" I gasped, "Do you suppose the owner knows she does this?" "Sure," replied the taxi driver, "she is there to catch mouses." "Mice," corrected my daughter pleasantly, thinking he had used the wrong word by mistake and really wanted to learn to speak English correctly. "Ja," he said cheerfully, "Mouses!"

Most people don't really like being corrected (naturally, I am one of them). But, when God corrects, I need to sit up and take notice—because if I don't heed the quiet voice or the gentle nudge, He will use something stronger to get my attention! We are specifically told not to "bring sorrow to God's Holy Spirit" (Ephesians 4:30a NLT) and I can do this only if I walk in the light of obedience. I sometimes find it easy to close my ears to God's instruction, thinking He can be ignored. However, I am warned to be careful not to despise the authority of God. When He corrects, He does it for my own good, not merely because of a whim. After all, when children are left to their own devices without discipline, they will not grow up to reflect the image of the heavenly Father…and, after all, he gives individual instruction!

"As you endure this divine discipline, remember that God is treating you as his own children. Whoever heard of a child who was never disciplined?" (Hebrews 12:7 NLT)

November 8: Art Lesson

We had a free day in Brussels the day after I spoke at a lovely tea. Margaret thought it would be a good opportunity to go on a day trip to the Cathedral of St. Bavo to see the Ghent Altarpiece by Hubert and Jan Van Eyck. As she was studying one of the icons there, she noticed several groups of school children dragged along by their teachers. They didn't seem particularly excited to be there and spent a good bit of time pushing one another, giggling, and whispering. "Imagine having opportunities like that all the time!" exclaimed Margaret incredulously. "They are able to look directly at the original any time they please!" It was evidently just ho-hum for the children because it was just a small part of their everyday lives, and illustrates that well-known phrase, "Familiarity breeds contempt."

Sometimes, I am like those children. I sit, happily surrounded by all the things that I have known and loved for years, and do not really appreciate what is seen and heard. Sometimes I just groan, and sit bored by what has become ritual.

Think of how this must make God feel. I have the opportunity to draw life directly from an original. I am often indifferent to His Masterpiece, and just go through the motions, missing the joy and love that is so freely given. May I not miss the beauty of the Lord because I have allowed my walk with Him to become humdrum! May I take a closer look at the treasure that has been made available to me, and appreciate it with rejoicing!

"So they all come and listen to you, but they refuse to do what you tell them. They claim to be faithful, but they are forever trying to cheat others out of their money. They treat you as though you were merely singing love songs or playing music. They listen, but don't do anything you say." (Ezekiel 33:31-32 CEV).

November 9: Good Business Techniques

One of the intriguing things we saw on the streets of Paris was men selling crepes (definitely a marvelous invention that should be exported to the US at once). I had previously seen crepes only in restaurants, of course, so it was very exciting to see them sold in little portable stands up and down the street. These vendors had a crepe for every taste. The man swirled the batter on a little griddle, painted on a wash of flavor and rolled it up before we could decide what coins were needed to pay him. The crepes were hot and delicious, and we walked away into crowds of other happy crepe eaters.

The interesting thing about these crepe sellers is this: they stay where the crowds are. We didn't see a single one in a back alley because they stay where the people are. "How elementary!" you might say. Yes, indeed, but do I do this when I present Christianity? I need to remember to get out of the choir loft and go where those who do not know Jesus are: PTA's, YWCA's, painting classes, cooking classes, and myriads of other venues where people gather. Staying only with close Christian friends will never bring me into contact with those who are hungry to hear God's word.

"But during the night an angel of the Lord opened the doors of the jail and brought them out. 'Go, stand in the temple courts,' he said, 'and tell the people the full message of this new life.'" (Acts 5:19-20 NIV)

November 10: Adventure *En Francais*

While Margaret was at the Louvre one day, I decided that the apartment where we were staying needed a little cleaning (a thought I am usually able to escape…). I plunged in, however, and then discovered I could not find any garbage bags. The little town in which we were staying was well out of Paris. There weren't any fancy stores, but they did have a small grocery store, and so, although my French is extremely limited, I thought, perhaps, if I used a French pronunciation, we could communicate. I was mistaken. I went in and asked hesitantly "*Avez vous* any bahgs de gaarbahge?" The owner was understandably mystified, but he took me by the hand all around the store until we found what I was looking for (*sacs de plastique*).

Then, I thought I should find a bank to get some money on my charge card. No bank. "Next town," I was assured. I was put on a bus and got to the next town (giving the driver a little devotional book that I had brought). I found the bank, but they said they were closing because it was noon. I gave him a booklet, too. I went back to the apartment, and gave the bus driver a booklet. At 2:00 p.m., I started off again. I took the bus and gave the driver a booklet. When I got to the bank, the man told me they didn't take Master Charge, and said that I should go to the next town. I gave him a booklet. I found the bus and went to the next town and gave that driver a booklet. I got my money and gave the teller a booklet. I tried to find the bus going back to the apartment, but I got in one that took me out to the countryside. The driver stopped and said, "*C'est fini*" (Finished). "*Fini?*" I echoed blankly. "*Oui*," he said firmly and pushed me out the door, but not before I gave him a booklet. I did eventually get back to the second town and then back to the apartment, giving away two more booklets. I was exhausted, but the Lord had arranged an adventure to give light to those who, perhaps, needed the light of Christ.

"This is the message he has given us to announce to you: God is light and there is no darkness in him at all." (I John 1:5 NLT)

November 11: Jeep Thrills

The missionary apartment in which Margaret and I stayed while in Paris had two units: one with two bedrooms, and the other with one. The second day we were there, a young girl moved into the other apartment and I met her in the hall while I was trying to unravel the mysteries of the washer and dryer. She had just returned from her first term in Africa and, after a horrendous flight, was trying to cope with both culture shock and jet lag. We struck up a conversation (about the only thing she could strike, poor dear), and she told me a little of her work. Her only mode of transportation had been an old scooter. She was hoping that her deputation would manage to raise enough money to buy a used jeep. It seemed a huge amount to both of us when she mentioned it, and I thought of the amount we had needed for our trip.

At any rate, while I was pondering all this, the Lord immediately reminded me, "You received without paying, now give without being paid." (Matthew 10:8b CEV). This was followed by the suggestion that I give her a gift as seed money to encourage her to believe that God would provide the rest. I didn't give myself too much time to think about this, for fear I would lose my nerve. I dashed back to my room and got the money. What joy! Previously I had given out of plenty, but now I gave out of a nervously low supply. The thrill it gave me was much greater than the assurance it gave her. Nearly half a year later, I got a short note from her telling me that God had indeed supplied all her need, and I think I was just as grateful as she was!

November 12: Blackout

I am usually awake by 5:00 or 5:30 a.m. (which is why my eyeballs fall shut around 8 p.m.). In our Paris apartment, Margaret and I had a living room, which meant I could go and read my Bible without rousing the entire neighborhood. One morning, as I was sitting near the window reading my Bible, all the lights went out—all the lights everywhere. I had not heard any electrical pops or fizzles, so I thought there was a good possibility I had gone blind. In a few minutes, however, as my eyes adjusted to the dark, I began to dimly distinguish a few objects near the window, and began to see the stars; then I knew it was not MY darkness but that of the electrical company. When the lights did not come on after what I considered to be a reasonable time (probably American reasonable not French reasonable), I realized that praying is certainly one thing you can do in the dark! So I had a long and especially undistracted time praying for family and friends.

A blackout like that should remind us that there are still those living in spiritual darkness: "The god of this age has blinded the minds of unbelievers, so that they cannot see the light of the gospel of the glory of Christ, who is the image of God" (II Corinthians 4:4 NIV). For them, the darkness is permanent unless they meet the Light of the World.

Ask the Lord to give you the name of just one person to pray for that they might come into the light. We have been lit by His torch to burn so brightly that those we meet might come to see God in us, for "God is light; in him there is no darkness at all" (I John 1:5 NIV).

"You, O Lord, keep my lamp burning; my God turns my darkness into light." (Psalm 18:28 NIV)

November 13: When in Rome…

While Margaret and I were in Geneva, we went to lunch with a very special lady, an International Representative with Stonecroft Ministries, who worked with clubs in France, Switzerland, Belgium, Germany, and England. Not that there were that many clubs, really—but to try to get around to encourage and support all of them was truly a Herculean task.

We went to a charming restaurant with small tables and a cozy fireplace. The one thing we found distracting was the presence of two extremely large, hairy dogs sprawled comfortably across several square yards of floor. When I first glanced in that direction, I had assumed it was a large, furry rug, but, when the rug yawned, I realized rugs don't have pink tongues. Most restaurants in the United States have restrictions against pets, except for seeing-eye dogs, because very few people think it sanitary to have dog hairs floating about over plates and soup tureens. But this was not the U.S. and that was not the rule, and I wisely kept my opinions to myself.

Philippians 2:14 is what I call an exclusive verse, because it has one of the exclusive words such as "all," "everything," "never," "always," "nothing," or the like. These words mean there is no exception, no matter what. God says, "Do everything without grumbling or arguing" (CEV), and, although I don't believe we take this very seriously, I believe that God does. After all, it was the Israelites grumbling that got them into so much trouble! When I gripe and complain about my circumstances (even dog hair), I am really grumbling against God. I need to think twice about the things that come my way, realizing that if I complain, I am telling God, "I don't like what You are allowing to happen to me!" May I, instead, find joy in all circumstances, and live every moment to the glory of God.

November 14: Non-Sightseeing

I was excited to be going through Switzerland, because I was anxious to show my daughter how beautiful the Alps are. When we went through Neuchatel, I started looking for Mont Blanc, but I didn't see it, and decided it must still be too far away. During the whole time in Geneva, I still never found Mont Blanc. When we went across the whole country on our way to Germany, I prepared myself for a lovely day of Alpine vistas. The countryside was lovely, it is true, but it was mostly flat and the skies were gray. It started to "snain" (an unpleasant combination of snow and rain that makes you wonder how Heidi ever stuck it out on bad days). We never saw the first sign of a mountain.

My vision of God is also often obscured. He hasn't moved, of course, any more than the Alps had, but when this happens to me, I jump to the conclusion that He has left the premises. But God is not only omnipresent, He is ever-present—and He is training me to walk by faith and not by sight. This is not a thrilling prospect for me, because I like to have the feeling of His presence. The more I go on in the Christian life, the more I must expect that what my Father wants is fidelity without feeling, trust without explanation. We must decide to believe that God has not moved even when we face clouds of difficulty, distress and disappointment, remembering that we do not walk by sight, but by faith.

"I cannot find God anywhere—in front or back of me, to my left or my right. God is always at work, though I never see him. But he knows what I am doing, and when he tests me, I will be pure as gold." (Job 23:8-9 CEV)

November 15: A Rainy Day In Munich Town

Margaret and I didn't have much time to play Tillie the Tourist, but we did plan to spend part of a free weekend in Munich because it was on the way to the American Air Force base where I was going to speak. Many months in advance I had called and arranged for a small apartment, but, because the lady I spoke to did not speak English well, she gave up when it came to sending a written confirmation of our reservation. Mistake number one. When we arrived in Munich (panting from trying to make train connections) it was about 5:00 p.m. and raining. When we were deposited in front of a very large and gloomy building, we found the building was locked. We waited until someone was going in who had a key and we scurried inside. The hall was very dark, and only lit up for a moment to help people find their way to the elevator. I stayed with the bags while Margaret took the aforementioned apparatus to the fourth floor. There was no answer to her repeated knocks on the door. When Margaret reappeared the light flickered on and then, in a minute, it was gone again. We stared uncomprehendingly at each other. We didn't speak a word of German, nor know how to use the telephone (or how much it cost). Mistake number two. Margaret braved the rain and found a kind soul who called the apartment manager. "Oh sorry," she said, "I rented it to someone else when you did not re-confirm." I reminded her we had given her our credit card as a guarantee, and then she said she must have forgotten to tell us about re-confirming. Ja. Mistake number three. Then she suggested we come to her apartment for the night. She recommended a Chinese restaurant for dinner. The menu was in both Chinese and German, neither of which helped us in any way at all. Mistake number four. It was all so silly we started laughing, and finally laughed so hard the manager came and wanted to know if something were the matter.

We staggered "home," unpacked our suitcases and just put stuff on the floor—which turned out to be mistake number five. Margaret had spent a good bit of her money buying Swiss chocolate for several of her friends and she had put it in her soft-sided suitcase. Unluckily, the heating system in the apartment was in the floor, so the next morning revealed several mounds of semi-melted chocolate which never got a chance to melt in the mouth. Yet, despite all our mistakes, we felt God's provision and protection, for He was with us in every situation, and He was not taken by surprise.

"Let the beloved of the Lord rest secure in him…." (Deuteronomy 33:12a NIV)

November 16: Trouble

We were in Kaiserslauten, Germany, and while we were there we stayed at a lovely home near the American Airbase. It had taken a long time to find it, and even longer to learn to pronounce it, as neither of us spoke any German at all.

I had the privilege not only of sharing my testimony at their Christian Women's Club meeting (where the special feature was Waterford glass and gorgeous linens—and the owner said "Now I know why I came!"), but also of gathering with the committee for a covered dish supper the night before (it was fun not only because they were special people, but also, because most of them were Americans, they understood my jokes).

The family we stayed with had two dogs. The name of one of them was "Trouble" because, as our hostess explained, "He's always in it—the poor thing has no brains at all."

Sometimes, I'm not much better than that dog. I wander far afield, get into things I'm not supposed to and I create tangles that have to be untangled. Do you suppose that God sometimes thinks, "The poor thing has no brains at all"?

Proverbs 28:14 says, "Blessed are those who have a tender conscience, but the stubborn are headed for serious trouble" (NLT). May I stay out of trouble today by using my brains instead of my wants, and may I open my heart to God's guidance.

November 17: Back to London

The driver of the hired car who had been sent to pick us up in London must have thought he was invincible—or at least invisible. He parked directly under a sign that said "NO PARKING." Perhaps he thought he was only going to be there long enough to pick up a passenger and a bag (little did he know how much he would have to lug, tote, and carry before he returned).

When he did arrive at the scene of the accident, so to speak, he found his wheel had been locked—or clamped, as they say there. When your wheels are in this condition, believe me, you are not going anywhere—and he was not a happy camper (or even a happy clamper). Clamping involves a device that looks as strong and impenetrable as the Tower of London, and in order to get it off, you have to find a phone (no cell phones then) and call the lock up people to come and rescue you (although I doubt he thought of it as rescuing!). It is quite a process and costs the offender £60 (about $75.00).

I, too, was under a lockup even stronger than that clamp at one point in my life. Today's Scripture says "The Law controlled us and kept us under its power until the time came when we would have faith" (Galatians 3:23 CEV). My driver paid for his freedom (reluctantly, I must admit), but the freedom that I, that we all have, in Christ has already been paid for, "You were rescued from the useless way of life that you learned from your ancestors. But you know that you were not rescued by such things as silver or gold that don't last forever. You were rescued by the precious blood of Christ, that spotless and innocent lamb" (1 Peter 1:18-19 CEV).

November 18: The Nose Knows

We were to meet my daughter's friend at Harrods, the famous department store (he was the gallant lad who had met us at the airport when we first arrived). We had no idea how huge the store was, and so we originally thought his instructions quite hilarious: "Go to the fish department—you can't miss it!"

When we actually arrived there, I was extremely glad we had someplace specific to meet: we could have been lost in there for weeks without anyone being the wiser. But Jamie was indeed correct…we couldn't miss the fish department. It was beautiful, gleaming, and even chandeliered, as I recall, but the smell was there. It's very difficult to disguise the smell of fish, I guess. Chefs can say all they want to about fresh fish not having a smell, but I can always smell them. In fact, my husband and I were on a chartered fishing boat one time when he caught a fish (and you can't get any fresher than that), and all that smell went right up the nostrils.

There's a certain odor about Christians, too. People sense, not something fishy, but that we have been with Jesus. If my time with Him is just a nod on Sunday or a giving of thanks at the dinner table, there will not be the fragrance of His presence. This only comes with unhurried delight in His word, and the sweet communion of my heart with His. The perfume accumulates little by little: when I take time to read the word of God, breathe it, chew on it, meditate on it, and then act on it.

"When they saw the courage of Peter and John and realized that they were unschooled, ordinary men, they were astonished and they took note that these men had been with Jesus. (Acts 4:13 NIV)

November 19: Home Sweet Home (and hurry up!)

By this time I was beginning to realize we weren't in Kansas any more, Toto. When we had raced to catch trains, mole our way through subways, and battle stairs that defied progress, I began to feel the traveling life was leaving me as dizzy as Dorothy was when she was in the tornado. In fact, there were several times when I would have given a lot to have some ruby slippers, so I could try clicking them three times.

Getting home proved a lot harder than that: we waited on the tarmac in London for five hours, discovered we had missed our connection in the States and had to spend the night in a place I don't want to see again, and, then, finally had to go to Orlando instead of Tampa. All of this left me not a happy camper.

Perhaps you, too, have gone through experiences where there seems to be no end to transition and struggle. The truth is that God never expected us to settle down and get too cozy here on earth. There will always be changes of one kind and another—some pleasant and some disastrous. He wants us to learn that He is the only one who does not change. If our lives are centered on Him when all the scenery is whizzing past too fast to keep up, then we may rest in the thought that He holds all things in His hand, and that no matter where we go, we are never out of His sight and care.

"He existed before everything else began, and he holds all creation together." (Colossians 1:17 CEV)

November 20: Hope

Hope is just a small word—
Unassuming and gentle.

But
It is stronger than death:
For importance is not measured in size.

Our hope is sure—
An anchor
that does not waver
in the gales of grief;
a kite
that soars beyond pain
to the Father of lights—

The Author of hope.

November 21: Llamas

Llamas are related to camels, and like them are used as beasts of burden. You are unlikely to run into any of these along Route 66: outside of their natural habitat of Peru and a few other countries, they are mainly seen in zoos. Llamas do not have humps, but they do have other interesting characteristics: linked together as they go across the Andes, they do well until they are overloaded. Then they hiss, spit and lie down. While this is certainly a way to get your point made, it definitely puts them in the category of grumblers (they would have fit in well with the Israelites as they crossed and re-crossed the desert).

Unfortunately, this grumbling tendency is one I often emulate when I feel overloaded with work or circumstances. I may not hiss or spit, but I'm often interested in just lying down. When I do this, I am saying in effect, "God doesn't care what is happening to me, and even if He does, He evidently isn't going to help." The objective view must be taken. He does care, and He tells me this over and over again in His word.

The other lesson the llamas have for me is that they simply refuse to get up if just one of them is overloaded. I don't know how this little piece of information gets passed along the ranks, but if one has too much to carry, the whole string sinks to the ground. Then the porter has to go along the entire string of animals with their lips stuck out until he finds the one who has too much. When this problem is rectified, the train will rise and go on.

Thinking about this, I am wondering how concerned I am about the cares and burdens of others in my train of acquaintances. It won't help just to lie down (although again, there is a little temptation there), but the Lord surely means for me to reach out to help and encourage those who are faced with problems or unmanageable situations. We can all be llamas that care!

"But God has combined the members of the body and has given greater honor to the parts that lacked it, so that there should be no division in the body, but that its parts should have equal concern for each other. (I Corinthians 12:24b NIV)

November 22: Tunnel Vision

The dictionary defines tunnel vision as "a narrow outlook." For the Christian, I want to give it a more interesting slant and define it as vision in the tunnel. There are numerous tunnels in our country, but I suppose the honors for the highway with the most of them should probably go to the Pennsylvania turnpike. It has tunnels practically on top of tunnels, and some of them are so long you feel practically claustrophobic by the time you actually emerge. Ah! That is what makes a tunnel a tunnel and not a cave…the road not only goes in, it comes out. In other words, "Yes, Virginia, there really is a light at the end of the tunnel!"

Some of you may be in a "tunnel experience" right now, and perhaps you find the darkness chafing or even scary. But take heart! Psalm 139 says, "I could ask the darkness to hide me and the light around me to become night—but even in darkness I cannot hide from you. To you the night shines as bright as day.

Darkness and light are both alike to you" (Psalm 139:11-12 NLT). God will not only continue to watch over me, He will walk with me. Although I do not understand why the dark times in my life come, I will continue to love Him and look to Him. I know He has lessons for me in the darkness that I could never learn in the light.

November 23: Breezy Rider

While driving down one of the main streets of our city, I saw a motorcycle rider ahead of me. He epitomized all the gladiatorial features you've ever heard used to describe a motorcycle rider: he was huge, and he was on a huge cycle that had gleaming chrome and doodads from here to yesterday. And he was hairy. Not just a little hairy, but all-over hairy.

As I came up to a stoplight, I got close enough to see the embroidered sign on the back of his jacket. It said, "Christ is the answer." I nearly fell out of the car gawking at it. The light changed and as he started to roar off, he saw me looking at him, and he smiled a gentle smile. He was a brother in Christ! I smiled back, and we saluted each other.

I doubt if there are very many bikers who would listen to what I have to say—but I bet they listen attentively to him! I need to look at my fellow travelers a little differently. God uses all sorts of people to reach all sorts of people. Very few of us minister in the same way, so I need to learn to look at others through the eyes of the Father.

"People judge others by what they look like, but I judge people by what is in their hearts." (I Samuel 16:7b CEV)

November 24: Encouragement

I am known (presumably among other things) as a "Blepharo." This means I have a neuro-muscular dysfunction characterized by a clamping of the eyelids that grows progressively worse until there is what is known as "functional blindness." I have shots of Botulism every other month that freeze certain muscles in my face (not my mouth—Bill says they are working on that). Now, of course, it's used a great deal for cosmetic reasons, and I have had to endure teasing such as "Here all this time we thought you were getting medication and you were just getting rid of wrinkles" etc., etc.

I went to what seems hundreds of doctors (this was about 1984), and they all shook their heads and more or less agreed that I was a nut case (well, of course, they were partly right…). I did not cope well with this situation, however, and any time anyone called on the phone that sounded the least bit sympathetic, I would just burst into tears. This does not make for edifying conversations. The thing is, I was terribly discouraged, especially as I couldn't drive anywhere (it makes the person in the next lane very nervous if you are driving with your eyes closed!). I couldn't read, write, or do housework (I didn't mind not being able to do housework…). But the worst part of it was I couldn't actually do anything except just lie around and spasm.

One day our son, Allen, called, and in the course of the conversation (his) and the crying (mine) he said, "We believe in you, Mom!" Well, I didn't believe in myself at that point, but those words managed to enter my soggy brain. They sat around there in the dark, until one day, in the course of rummaging around, I happened across that little encouraging statement again. In time, I began to accept my condition and to realize that God also believed in me. I began to understand that He does not turn away from failures and from people who can't cope, and that nothing can separate us from His love. I was learning to trust God in spite of what was happening in my life. It started with a son who encouraged me.

"Who shall separate us from the love of Christ? Shall trouble or hardship or persecution or famine or nakedness or danger or sword?…No, in all these things we are more than conquerors through him who loved us. For I am convinced that neither death nor life, neither angels nor demons, neither the present nor the future, nor any powers, neither height nor depth, nor anything else in all creation, will be able to separate us from the love of God that is in Christ Jesus our Lord." (Romans 9:35,37-39 NIV)

November 25: Malice in Wonderland

It had been a "Bad Day at Black Rock" from the rising of the sun to the going down of the same. There had been a constant stream of requests for help: "When is breakfast?" "Can't we have pancakes?" "I need my underwear." "Have you got any extra shoelaces? Mine busted." "Why can't I help stuff the turkey?" "Are we going to have to get dressed up?" Can you sew this button on?" "Are you going to remember to fix some dessert?"

It was the day before Thanksgiving, and I was not giving many thanks. In fact, I took all the whys and cans and hows only so long, and at the end of the day when there was one more plaintive request for a glass of water, I burst out with a statement that summed up all my frustrations: "What is the matter with you???" I fumed, "Do you think I am your SERVANT?" And in the stunned silence that followed, I heard God's question ring in my head: "Well, aren't you?" "NO!" I raged, and God said quietly, "I thought you wanted to be like Jesus."

When I resent serving others, I am in reality rebelling against Christ. His life shows that servanthood is the highest calling of all. In fact, Dawson Trotman, the founder of a Christian organization called Navigators said it best: "How do you know if you have a servant's heart? By the way you act when you are treated like one."

We have not come to be served, but to serve. When we serve even the least and the littlest, we serve God. Sometimes, Christians who are harried mothers, overworked fathers or harassed singles forget for whom they are working. Jesus' life must have seemed at times like one long interruption after another, yet we never read of Him having a temper tantrum. I think God would be pleased if He saw more love and patience in our lives. It will not come all at once, but the Spirit in us will help us if we practice more and preach less.

"Then these righteous ones will reply, 'Lord, when did we ever see you hungry and feed you? Or thirsty and give you something to drink? Or a stranger and show you hospitality? Or naked and give you clothing? When did we ever see you sick or in prison, and visit you?' And the King will tell them, 'I assure you, when you did it to one of the least of these my brothers and sisters, you were doing it to me!'" (Matthew 25:37-40 NLT)

November 26: Counting Blessings

For as long as I can remember, I was taught to give thanks to God for all the good things He gives us. So I would thank Him for our food, our home, my parents, my brothers, and nice things to wear. Then my list always sort of petered out. This went on for years and years until I became a Christian. On that first Thanksgiving Day, I suddenly realized that I had a great debt of gratitude to God for sending His Son in order that I might enter into a relationship with Him. It seemed to be an astounding revelation, and I was thrilled as I thanked Him for my salvation and for all the many attributes I was discovering about Him. Now my list was quite long!

So, in counting my blessings I want to thank my heavenly Father for my dear husband. He is my closest friend on earth—my companion and lover who has chosen to be my Barnabas and encourage me in all I do. Not everyone has a mate like this. I thank Him for our five children…all different, all unique, all gifted in different areas. I am especially thankful that they are all alike in their love for the Father God. Not everyone has children like this. I thank Him for a lovely home, food to eat, and a comfortable bed. Not everyone has a home or food or a bed.

I thank Him for a Godly heritage, and the knowledge that after this earthly life is over, someday we shall all meet again in heaven. Not everyone has this kind of background. I thank Him for friends far and near, and for their laughter and loving support. Not everyone has friends like this. Most of all I thank Him for choosing me to be part of His family. And EVERYONE may be a member if they will only respond to His message of love! When we turn from sin and ask God to come into our lives, we become His own dear children—and that's the best family of all!

"Then they will know that I, the Lord their God, am with them…. You my sheep, the sheep of my pasture, are people, and I am your God, declares the sovereign Lord." (Ezekiel 34:30-31 NIV)

November 27: Giving Thanks

I'm sure it shows what a pagan I was, but before I became a Christian it never occurred to me to give thanks for Jesus Christ. I remember the day as clearly as if it were yesterday. We were sitting in church and our minister read "Thank God for his gift that is too wonderful for words!" (II Corinthians 9:15 CEV). I was absolutely and alternately stunned and elated (poor grammar perhaps—but you get the picture). With a grateful heart, I bowed my head to thank God, not only for my family and the food, but also I thanked him for the gift of his Son…for the very first time.

Of course, my gratitude should not be limited to just one day, as many have pointed out. But, somehow, Thanksgiving warms my heart. I don't remember exactly how I used to spend this day, but I suspect I was focusing on the food more than the thanks: in a tizzy over turkey, backpedaling over broccoli, panicky over pie, and busy giving time and effort to things that are not eternal.

November 28: Check Mate

There was a knock on our door. When I opened it, one of the neighborhood boys stood there and said brightly, "I'm collecting for the American Cancer Society. Would you like to write a check?" I asked him in and sat down to write. "How shall I make it out?" I asked brilliantly (yes, indeed, I had finished college and even attended graduate school). "Just make it out to me," he answered airily. And, I actually did so (I no longer keep the household accounts…).

When the bank statement came, I happened to notice that this particular check had been cashed at the corner drug store. At this point, dawn finally dawned, belated as it was, for I was fairly certain that the American Cancer Society did not have an account at our drugstore. I finally called his mother who told me her older son had been canvassing for the ACS, and that the younger boy had evidently appropriated his brother's fund-raising materials. She promised to discuss the matter with him, which sounded a little vague to me. I don't really know what she did, which is just as well.

A week or so later, as I was driving down the street, I saw this boy sitting glumly on a wall in the hot sun. As I swept past, God said to my heart, "Go back and see if he needs help." Well, I certainly thought he needed help all right, but I knew that wasn't what God meant. I argued about this so long I was almost to town before I was convicted enough to turn around. I pulled up beside him and asked, "Do you remember me?" He nodded. "Is there anything you need?" I plowed on. He shook his head. I thought he needed God's love; so I said, "I just want you to know I'm a Christian and I've forgiven you because Christ has forgiven me. Let me know if I can do anything for you." He shook his head again. Slowly, I drove away. I hope that tiny seed of obedience (grudgingly given as it was) helped prepare the soil for what someday would be a new heart. I still pray that he listens for God's words of hope for him.

The Psalmist says of God, "You listen to the longings of those who suffer. You offer them hope, and you pay attention to their cries for help" (Psalm 10:17 CEV).

November 29: Ship to Shore

Going to Europe by ship sounds very glamorous, but you would change your mind if you had seen the ship I took at the end of my senior year in college. We didn't have to row, exactly, but it took us twelve days to get there, and our cabin was on G level—three below water level, which was not really comforting. It slept nine on 3 triple bunks (no getting up in the middle of the night!), and the weather was quite uncooperative. The second day we ran into fog that lasted the rest of the voyage, and meant that the foghorn blasted every 60 seconds. Since it was loud enough to announce our approach, it was also loud enough to make our cheeks vibrate.

Presumably, I had heard the terms "pitch and roll" before, but although this sounded picturesque at a distance, the actual experience left a great deal to be desired. It was, in a word, sickening. When I would take a step, the deck either fell away or came up to my knees to meet me, all the while lunging forward and backward and side-to-side. I felt old and gray by the time we finally arrived, and much older than 22.

Sometimes, my spiritual ship goes through some heavy weather, too. I feel fogged in with a deck that is sliding out from under me. But, the Lord knows all about my vessel, and He will not leave me. In Madeline L'Engle's autobiography she tells of a Bishop who said, "I have been down to the bottom, and it is solid." So, underneath our decks, too, are His everlasting arms and God will bring us to a safe harbor.

"I command you—be strong and courageous! Do not be afraid or discouraged. For the LORD your God is with you wherever you go." (Joshua 1:9 NLT)

November 30: The Writing on the Wall

Life with five children can be hectic, hilarious, and hysterical. Sometimes it verges on the theological, too, although we did try to keep the first three things from leaking over too much into the last.

Our first three were all thirteen months apart, which meant that when the youngest was in preschool, the middle was in kindergarten and the oldest in first grade.

One day, we came into the living room to see printing on the plate glass doors. It said not "*mene mene tekel*" as in the book of Daniel, but "Will loves—," which meant someone was going to be punished. We were upset over this, and after lining all three of the children up, my husband demanded to know who had done it. Silence. Finally Bill said that unless the culprit confessed, they would all get a spanking, but if the one who did it confessed, no one would be spanked. At last our five year old stepped forward and said, "I did it Daddy." And, so, because he confessed, no one was spanked.

It wasn't till we got in bed that night that we realized we had been hoodwinked…our oldest child was the only one who knew how to write! But, because he didn't want everyone punished (himself included, of course!), the youngest confessed to an act he hadn't done.

This should sound familiar to us (without stretching the analogy too far). Christ was actually innocent of all sin, yet He bore our sin so that we might escape the punishment of death. If you haven't remembered to thank Him for this lately, wouldn't this be a good time to do so?

"And they sang a new song: 'You are worthy to take the scroll and to open its seals, because you were slain, and with your blood you purchased men for God from every tribe and language and people and nation. You have made them to be a kingdom and priests to serve our God, and they will reign on the earth.'" (Revelation 5:9-10 NIV)

November 31: Car Talk

At one point there were just three of us at our house, and for a while we had three cars. Then one of the cars had a stroke and died...which left three people and only two cars (one held together by prayer). This worked as long as daily arrangements were made for the transfer of drivers at the necessary and appointed time, but then the sick car got worse and had to be hospitalized in the shop. Since my husband and my daughter both needed wheels to go in opposite directions, two cars were clearly a necessity. So we rented one while the patient was on the operating table.

On Sunday, as we were driving to church, my husband remarked on how smoothly this new car was running, and then, with a little grin, added, "It's sure bad for your prayer life, though!" How true! When things are going well, I don't feel the need to pray. It's when things go wrong that my attention is focused on the need for heavenly assistance. I need to remember that my character is not constructed in a crisis, it is merely confirmed. If I am to be strong in the Lord, and not just held together, I need to seek His face daily. I need to depend on Him even when I feel competent, and proficient, and my engine is running smoothly.

"We depend on you, LORD, to help and protect us. You make our hearts glad because we trust you, the only God. Be kind and bless us! We depend on you." (Psalm 33:20-22 CEV)

December 1: The Bear Essentials

When we lived in Boston for the amazing total of 9 months, our daughter, Virginia, was in the first grade. She came home one day bursting with excitement. Her teacher had broken the news that there was going to be a play toward the end of the year, and Virginia was going to sing a solo.

Everyone in the class had to dress as a bear for the play. Unfortunately that meant I had to make a bear costume. My sewing talent is limited to buttons and an occasional hem (if it's not too wide.) "It's O.K., Mom," Virginia burbled. "You can use our brown towels and pin them together." So we dragged out the brown towels, a few snaps, and with the help of Lissa (who is actually a much better seamstress than I) began draping them around Virginia.

It really was not a success (even with 13 year-old Lissa helping) because the final product did not remotely resemble a bear…it looked like towels held together with snaps. Which, of course, it was. I tried to console myself by remembering that I hadn't been given much notice for this foray into costume design—but deep down I suspected that all the other mothers had probably gotten patterns and fabric at the store and made real bear costumes.

I was correct. All the other children came on stage looking very beary. Virginia came on stage looking like a pile of dark brown beach towels waiting to be washed. My heart sank to my toes with sympathy and I dreaded the ride home. But Virginia bounced out of the auditorium as though she had just been offered 50 straight days of pancakes.

"Did you like it, Mom?" she queried.

"Indeed I did," I assured her.

"And wasn't it wonderful?" she continued. "My costume was different from everybody else's."

Talk about a good attitude! I was thunderstruck and convicted by the happy heart under those saggy towels.

"Above all else, guard your heart, for it affects everything you do." (Proverbs 4:23 CEV)

December 2: The Anchovy Paste Saga

During World War II, when my brother Bill was in the Signal Corps in Italy, my mother sent him a food parcel that contained, among other things, a tube of anchovy paste. No one ever figured out exactly why she sent this particular item, but sometimes Mother did things that were a little off the wall (rather like her daughter, I guess). Anyway, Bill ate the cookies and all the other goodies, but he thought anchovy paste sounded pretty grim.

The more he thought of it, however, he decided it would make a great gag gift for my brother John, who was on a submarine in the south Pacific. John didn't like anchovies, either, but he got the gift idea immediately and sent it back to Africa to my brother Hugh, who was in the Air Force. Hugh also jumped on the bandwagon and sent it to my brother George, who was in the Coast Guard.

Well, this thing went round and round for years, arriving in unrecognizable packages, parcels, and tins—all unknown until unwrapped. My brothers even recruited friends to mail the disguised package from many various and sundry exotic locales, until that poor anchovy paste must have finally died from travel fatigue. Probably a good thing, too. If anyone had eaten it at that late date, they would most likely have died of some weird disease.

There are many ways to give a gift, but in order to complete the transaction the gift must be accepted. For someone who's not interested, who refuses the gift, it is not a complete transaction.

God wants to give us all the gift of salvation. It doesn't matter if you are young or old, educated or untaught, rich or poor, or anything in between. He gives this gift freely to anyone who will accept it.

"And this is what God has testified: He has given us eternal life, and this life is in his Son. So whoever has God's Son has life; whoever does not have his Son does not have life."(I John 5:11-12 NLT)

December 3: Hot Spot

I have been told from time immemorial never to wash clothes made of wool (also known as "woolens"!) in hot water. But one day I thriftily decided to put one of our wool blankets in the washer instead of sending it to the dry cleaners.

So, with economy in mind, I made sure the water was only tepid, and dumped in the offending article. When it finished the cycle and looked none the worse for wear, I put it in the dryer. Upon removal, I discovered, much to my sorrow, a very small, compressed blanket. My new motto is, "If you can't stand the heat, stay out of the dryer…."

There are circumstances that shrink my self-confidence and wrinkle my bindings. Since I can't control the heat in my life, I remind myself of Paul's letter to Philemon.

"I always thank my God as I remember you in my prayers, because I hear about your faith in the Lord Jesus and your love for all the saints. I pray that you may be active in sharing your faith, so that you will have a full understanding of every good thing we have in Christ. Your love has given me great joy and encouragement, because you, brother, have refreshed the hearts of the saints." (Philemon 4-7 NIV)

In that passage Paul says, "I pray that you may be active in sharing your faith, so that you will have a full understanding of every good thing we have in Christ." Notice he didn't say that by sharing our faith we will have "a full understanding of every situation or disaster", but instead, "a full understanding of every good thing we have in Christ." My guess is, that, when we share God's love with others, we are reminded how blessed we are because God loves us.

Instead of crying over shrunken woolens (and unpleasant heat in my life!), may I focus on sharing God's love with others (and seeing it for myself!)

December 4: Humble and Proud of It…

"During the night, Paul had a vision of someone from Macedonia who was standing there and begging him, "Come over to Macedonia and help us!" After Paul had seen the vision, we began looking for a way to go to Macedonia. We were sure that God had called us to preach the good news there." (Acts 16:9-10 CEV)

I have only recently realized that I am very opinionated, and, since I only recently discovered this, I also came to the startling conclusion (startling to me—perhaps not for you!) that my powers of self-evaluation must be rather limited. In fact, several things about which I had been quite adamant were later proven to be quite incorrect. Sometimes I think if my tongue were any quicker on the draw I would have powder burns.

I noticed while reading the above passage from Acts that, although he (Paul) had the vision, he did not make the decision to go to Macedonia by himself: the decision was reached by "we." When I am truly humble, I will be all too aware that I do not have a corner on God's wisdom or direction. Since the Holy Spirit indwells every Christian, I need to hear what others have to say! This knowledge takes away my need to be dogmatic, and when I am sensitive to the input of others, I won't get sick from eating so much humble pie.

December 5: A Winter's Tale

Several years ago many Russian Christians were imprisoned for their faith. One such young man was put in a cell with four others who were there for criminal acts. They constantly made fun of him and taunted him with cruel remarks about his beliefs. Gambling was forbidden in that prison, but these four gambled as much as possible. Their favorite game was one in which, if you lost all your money, you were given one last chance to win some back, but, if you lost that second time, you had to forfeit your life. One day, one of the young men lost all his money. He was desolate, because he wasn't sure he could win some back, and he was terrified of losing his life, poor as it was.

The Christian, who had been watching, said quietly, "I will play your hand, and I will die in your place if you lose." There was much hooting and hollering, for the others knew that he understood nothing of the game. But the man who had lost his money was grateful, and accepted the Christian's offer. The game started, and as it progressed, the three were astonished to see that the Christian was winning, and at the close of the game, he had won the other man's money back.

"Why were you willing to do that for me?" asked the young criminal. "Because it is what Jesus Christ did for me," answered the Christian. "I did not deserve His gift of salvation, but He died in my place, and rose again from the dead to live in my heart." By the end of that week, all four of the young men had put their trust in Christ. Even though snow covered the ground outside that grimy prison, there was spring in the hearts of five Christians.

"Great is his faithfulness; his mercies begin afresh each day. I say to myself, 'The Lord is my inheritance; therefore, I will hope in him!'" (Lamentations 3:23-24 NLT)

December 6: A Comforting Voice

We used to live just across the lawn from my maternal grandparents, and when I was invited to go to have dinner and spend the night, it was always a special treat for me. I must have been about four or five, but I remember it all very clearly. After dinner, I would beg my grandfather to play the napkin ring game. He and I would line up our napkin rings, and then we would roll them down the table to see whose could go all the way to the end of the table without hitting anything (I was fairly easily amused…). After dinner, we would all troop into the living room to wait by the big console radio to listen to Lowell Thomas and the news. He would report live from many different, exotic places, and always signed off in his soothing, cultivated voice with the assuring phrase, "So long, until tomorrow."

I can still hear him say it in my mind after all these years. It was a comforting thought for me to know that my little world was ordered and simple, and that the next few days would bring another visit with Lowell Thomas reporting from Nepal, New England, or Nigeria.

Now I am comforted because I know that God never signs off. He never sleeps, for as Ron Mehl says, "He works the night shift." He watches over me in a way that even my devoted parents could not. Our world is not so ordered or simple anymore, and the news is no longer relegated to 7:00 p.m., but our God is still the same. His hand is over us, no matter where we are.

"I lift my eyes to the hills—where does my help come from? My help comes from the Lord, the Maker of heaven and earth. He will not let your foot slip—he who watches over you will not slumber; indeed, he who watches over Israel will neither slumber nor sleep." (Psalm 121:1-4 NIV)

December 7: Horses

"Jesus replied, 'I assure you, unless you are born again, you can never see the Kingdom of God.'
'What do you mean?' exclaimed Nicodemus. 'How can an old man go back into his mother's womb and be born again?' Jesus replied, 'The truth is, no one can enter the Kingdom of God without being born of water and the Spirit. Humans can reproduce only human life, but the Holy Spirit gives new life from heaven. So don't be surprised at my statement that you must be born again. Just as you can hear the wind but can't tell where it comes from or where it is going, so you can't explain how people are born of the Spirit.'" (John 3:3-8 NLT)

There's an old saying that goes, "You can lead a horse to water, but you can't make him drink." A similar thought might be expressed this way: "You can lead a person to the truth, but you can't make him think."

For years I heard the truth, but I just shrugged it off or took it for granted. The sun has always risen, so why not tomorrow? Spring has never failed to come after winter; why not this year? I ignored the facts of nature, and even stared stupidly at the water of life, failing to realize that while it is true that God is seen in nature, nature is meant to lead us onward to the Creator of nature.

As a Christian, I cannot make anyone either think or drink. I cannot do it because it is the work of God to draw men and women into that special loving relationship. I can pray, though, and if I present God's truth to those I meet, He will draw them to himself. It may take a long time, but our Father does not look at time the way we do: He is in eternity.

December 8: Pats and Hugs

Having spent more time than I care to think about in hundreds of airports, and having seen perhaps thousands of hellos and good-byes, I am impressed with what seems to be a common denominator (in case you were wondering, this kind of denominator is as close as I get to mathematics). I have noticed that almost without exception, there are back pats involved on the parts of both the hugger and the huggee. Since I am not a psychologist, I don't pretend to understand the meaning behind this—except that it seems to be a reassurance of continued love and affection.

People are not the only ones who give pats and hugs…I think God gives them, too: in the unexpected sight of a long-ago friend, in the thrill of His guidance on a particular matter, in a disappointment turning into a blessing beyond what we could ask or think, in the forgiving smile of a friend or parent, in the sweetness of sleep after an especially difficult day, and, of course, in many other things too.

One that was unexpected (as most of them are) came to me when I was an outpatient in a local hospital. I was to have a lump removed, and it was to be done under a local anesthetic so we could discuss the next procedure if it should prove to be malignant (if you want to know all the stuff nurses talk about when you are in an operating room, I would be glad to share this sometime…).

They put a screen up between my eyes and the action, presumably to prevent me from fainting dead away. I noticed that the nurse taking my blood pressure kept running back to take it again and again. "What's the matter with it?" I asked timidly. She looked at me accusingly. "Well, it's normal!" I took that as a little hug from God, saying that if they had to cut off my whole right side it didn't really matter, because He was there with me (in case you are wondering, the lump was not malignant).

There are many pats which God alone can give, but there are also lots in which we can participate: a letter of encouragement, an e-mail to cheer up someone's day, a helping hand when someone is tired or discouraged, a phone call to say you are thinking of that person, or a plate of cookies to someone who is feeling lonesome and left out. All of these are reflections of a loving Father who hugs through us. Are you willing to be a hugger today?

"When I felt my feet slipping, you came with your love and kept me steady. And when I was burdened with worries, you comforted me and made me feel secure." (Psalm 94:18-19 CEV)

December 9: Jumbled Jungle Gym

It was Christmas Eve, and we had waited until we were sure the children were asleep. We tried not to fall into a bed that looked all too inviting, and we tiptoed, not through tulips, but across concrete flooring to the stashed boxes of gifts. We dragged the one that had the jungle gym outside. The directions seemed incomprehensible to me (insert sprocket A into pinhole 15, etc.), but, assuming that my husband had an innate knowledge of such sprockets, I left him alone in the yard (make that left him alone in the lurch…). I went inside to set up the things that I understood around the tree (dolls, bikes, etc.—all assembled). Two hours later, I went outside to find an exhausted husband and only a semi-completed jungle gym. He has forgiven me by now, I think, but at the time, I found it hilarious to see him sitting amidst the wreckage that still had to be assembled before sunrise.

Maybe you are also sitting amidst some wreckage, and, perhaps, you are at a loss on how to fit them together. Take heart, because in God's word there is always encouragement that is meant to sustain us through the dark times of our lives. God is waiting to help, and His directions are not complicated.

He says, "Be still, and know that I am God…" (Psalm 46:10a NIV).

Then He says, remember: "Every promise has been fulfilled; not one has failed." (Joshua 23:14b NIV)

Then He reminds us: "Cast all your anxiety on him because he cares for you." (I Peter 5:7 NIV)

So let us praise the God of our salvation, for He is always with us. Sometimes He calms the storm; sometimes He calms His child. But in every situation, we may trust Him, for He is a great God, and greatly to be praised.

December 10: Dear Mother

My grandparents were wealthy, but when they ~~raised~~ eat my mother they were very careful not to let her become spoiled or cantankerous. She did manage, however, to retain certain peculiar standards that she considered extremely important…and if these standards were not met, there was a great deal of unhappiness. My father loved to tease her just to provoke her reactions, and he was rarely disappointed.

For instance, there was a swinging door between the dining room and the pantry, and mother worried a great deal about people bumping into each other when using this door. The only one using this door was the waitress (and there was only one) so it was really highly unlikely that she would bump into anyone. But my father would acknowledge Mother's concern, and then casually mention that the next time mother was away from the house he would have a glass porthole cut in the door to eliminate all potential disasters. For some reason, this irritated mother even more, and she would instantly rise to the bait. At this, Daddy would just smile mysteriously and subside into inscrutability.

Our mother was not a joker, but she did have a few favorite humorous stories that she would drag out on occasion. She also had an unusual gift for naming things. She had a dog she named "Sanka" because he didn't keep her awake at night, and a car named "Henry the 8th" because it was a two-door (Tudor!).

Mother had a guest book that she started at her wedding in 1912, and, in 1938, when that was full, she got another one (I still have it and use it). She had a funny rule that if you ate or drank anything, you had to sign the book…and I recall with amusement the time she got a glass of water for the postman so he could ink in his signature.

With all her eccentricities, our dear mother had a heart as big as God makes—and there was nothing she would not do to help anyone in need. She had money and plenty of possessions, but she never flaunted them; and when over $40,000 of her jewelry was stolen in 1955, she never said a word against the man who took it. I was infuriated, but she said quietly, "He just didn't know any better."

Prayer: Father, teach me how to hold what you give in an open hand so that you may take it whenever it is within Your will.

"He [Job] said, 'I came naked from my mother's womb, and I will be stripped of everything when I die. The Lord gave me everything I had, and the Lord has taken it away. Praise the name of the Lord!'" (Job 1:21 NLT)

December 11: The FPW Syndrome

We seem to have an alphabet soup of initials today—anything from CEO to IRS and everything in between. But I had never seen the initials "FPW" until I read an article about it in the Wall Street Journal. FPW refers to fame, power, and wealth. In fact, it goes along with the headline I saw in a paper recently that read: "In a troubled world, the only thing saving us is the arts."

Of course, there are many things that fame, power, wealth, and the arts can do, but there are things that they cannot do. They can buy the control of people, but not what they think. They can buy cars, but they cannot keep them from crashing. They can buy pleasure, but not peace or purity. They can buy education, but they cannot buy integrity or honor. They can buy lots of things for their children, but they cannot keep them from hurt or addictions.

Fame, power, wealth and the arts may buy satisfaction and self worth for a certain amount of time, but they can never make us right with God.

"You are seeing things merely from a human point of view, and not from God's." (Matthew 16:21c NLT)

December 12: Big Britches

The following three verses refer to the story of David and the Philistine giant named Goliath. The young boy David convinces King Saul to let him go and fight the giant (a bit of a no-brainer for King Saul, since no one else dared to even go near Goliath). The verses begin with David reassuring King Saul that God would protect him: "'The Lord who delivered me from the paw of the lion and the paw of the bear will deliver me from the hand of this Philistine.' Saul said to David, 'Go, and the Lord be with you.' Then Saul dressed David in his own tunic. He put a coat of armor on him and a bronze helmet on his head. David fastened on his sword over the tunic and tried walking around, because he was not used to them. 'I cannot go in these,' he said to Saul, 'because I am not used to them.' So he took them off" (I Samuel 17:37-39 NIV).

My sister-in-law was expecting her third child, and when she told my brother it was time to go to the hospital, she was pretty cool about the whole thing. She went in to take a bath and do her nails, while Bill was nervously checking last minute details and trying to jump into his clothes at the same time. There was only one problem: every time he tried to cross the room, his pants would fall down. After several repeated attempts to repel the forces of gravity, my brother grabbed another pair of pants. Miraculously, they seemed to stay in the correct position, so he yanked Dottie out of the shower and sped her to the hospital in time for the delivery of their son, Bill. It wasn't until he got home and was gradually unwinding from emergency status that he discovered the cleaners had sent him someone else's pants.

Unlike David (who knew what fit and what didn't), and like my brother (who, I admit, was justifiably distracted), I sometimes leap into situations that don't fit me.

Some years ago, I was appointed to a position that I never felt comfortable about. I found that, although there were several aspects of the position which came easily, much of it was exhausting, uphill work. Looking back on it, I don't suppose it was a real mistake to accept, but I think God wants our work for Him to be fulfilling and challenging, not a struggle and a chore. If you're facing a similar decision, pray for guidance, and ask God to show you how to best spend your time.

December 13: Coach Shoes

I had a distant cousin, both in lineage and geography, whom I was instructed to call Aunt Susan. She was not a real aunt, as both my parents were only children, but my mother never quibbled about details…and I had "aunts" in many parts of the country. Aunt Susan was well into her eighties in the 1940's and had gotten to the point where the past was more fascinating than the present (I understand this all too well at my present age).

Since she was intimately familiar with the horse and buggy era, Aunt Susan used many phrases that were not familiar to me. One of these concerned "coach shoes"—a term evidently used to denote shoes which were saved for riding in coaches, as they were too fragile to be used for walking. I must have subconsciously adopted this statement, and to this day I have shoes that are put on only if I'm going to be quite inactive.

Sometimes, I view prayer in this manner—only to be used on special occasions or in case of emergency. Actually, it's pretty hard to establish lines of communication with someone that you only see from a distance or only once a year. So I'm revving up my Reeboks—and making tracks to pray!

"Always be joyful and never stop praying. Whatever happens, keep thanking God because of Jesus Christ. This is what God wants you to do." (I Thessalonians 5:16-18 CEV)

December 14: Mockingbirds

Mocking birds are very clever, indeed, and can sound like almost any bird they hear. Mourning doves are one of their specialties, and, since I am not even faintly ornithological, I can't tell the difference.

I can identify with these mocking birds because I was one of their group for so many years. I had no idea I wasn't the real thing, and sprinkled my vocabulary with several pious phrases. Of course, if called on to pray in a meeting, I was unable to do so unless I was warned in advance and had a chance to write out some marvelously pithy thought, which I would share without the faintest notion that it was not prayer. Even my husband thought I was a Christian, and after I actually asked Christ to come into my life and our minister suggested that I go forward during the crusade meetings at the auditorium "as a witness to what I had done" if I felt led by the Holy Spirit, Bill was shocked that I had never done this. I was still recovering from shock myself, and wondering what the Holy Spirit had to do with it. I was quite certain I had never seen any sheet with the instructions "Go forward." (My remembrance of Cornelius seeing a sheet come down from heaven was a little vague, but it was my only point of reference for seeing the Holy Spirit at work).

It all goes to show that people can hear the Gospel preached but never understand until God opens their ears. When that happens, your feathers won't change, but God will begin to change attitudes and goals as you fly with Him.

"Anyone who is willing to hear should listen and understand!" (Mark 4:23 NLT)

December 15: A Fall From a Tree

When I was about ten years old, my mother decided that I should take music lessons. I visited my longsuffering music teacher each week with my best friend, and we took turns climbing trees when we weren't inside clumping over scales.

One day, while there for a lesson, I fell out of the very top of the tree. It knocked the breath out of me so that I couldn't talk (always an unusual occasion) and broke my collarbone. I arrived back at school suitably attired in a cast, sling, and the role of the suffering survivor.

I was elated because I thought that I would be unable to perform much schoolwork, since my right arm was not functional. Alas and alack, as the saying goes, my mean teachers were not impressed with my medical impediments and announced that I would, indeed, be doing my work…with my left hand. Do you know how long that took? Hours and hours, I can tell you. I was not at all pleased with their lack of sympathy.

I have found (belatedly, of course) that I cannot escape a lesson that God has for me either. I may make excuses and expect sympathy, but I have a lesson to learn anyway. God is not mean, however. He just wants us to grow up!

"Leave your simple ways and you will live; walk in the way of understanding." (Proverbs 9:6 NIV)

December 16: A Heart That Sings

Ray Schmidt, the National Chairman of Stonecroft Ministry's Couples Clubs, says that he loves to sing, but since he can't carry a tune, he whistles. When he was the principal of a high school, he always whistled as he walked down the hall, so that people would know he was coming, and had time to straighten up and fly right, so to speak. One of Ray's favorite songs was the hymn "I will glorify the King of Kings," and one day, he got a nice note about it from a teacher: "It's just wonderful to hear you always whistling "Bridge on the River Kwai."

People may not always recognize our tunes either, but we don't have to have a trained voice to make a melody in our hearts. After all, Psalm 95:2 (CEV) says, "Come to worship him with thankful hearts and songs of praise." Fortunately, we can make a joyful noise without keeping on key!

Do you know why we should have a singing heart? It is because we have the riches of Christ, and they cannot be taken away by people or circumstances. As you walk the halls of your world today, don't be so concerned with your duties that you neglect to give praise and honor to your Creator and Redeemer.

"Let the message about Christ completely fill your lives, while you use all your wisdom to teach and instruct each other. With thankful hearts, sing psalms, hymns, and spiritual songs to God." (Colossians 3:16 CEV)

December 17: The Instructor

I've never been much in the muscle business—but when you find you are too weak to hold on to the handrail of a staircase, the time has come to start shaping up. My neighbor had joined a Fitness Spa not too far from where we live, and I asked if she would take me with her (under the heading of excess baggage). I looked into the facilities and I can tell you right now that, although the swimming pool looked familiar, all the machines looked as though they had come out of Frankenstein's lab. There were stretchers and pullers and heaven knows what else—all managing to look rather menacing. I had almost decided to back out when one of the girls suggested a private trainer.

So, I gave it a try (that sounds a little half-hearted, and I guess it probably was). But, that wonderful instructor made all the difference. She started me on baby weights and waited patiently until I was strong enough to progress a little. There was lots of encouragement ("Good job!" and, "You're getting better!"). And she never once made me feel stupid or uncoordinated (believe me, I provided her with plenty of opportunities). She gave me little hints on good posture, good eating, and good habits. Most of all, she was always there to adjust weights or suggest proper stretching afterwards.

Instructors are very important in every field of endeavor, whether it is fitness, ceramics, or basket weaving. We don't always have the good fortune to get the best. However, in Jesus Christ, we have an instructor in life who gives freely of Himself, because He is the life. He encourages. He waits patiently for us to spend time with Him, and He never, never makes us feel stupid or uncoordinated. He stretches us through life circumstances, and directs us toward good habits through the ministry of the Holy Spirit. Best of all, He is always with us!

"Commit yourself to instruction; attune your ears to hear words of knowledge." (Proverbs 23:12 NLT)

December 18: Charlotte and Wilbur

Charlotte, the spider, and Wilbur, the pig, are two very interesting animals found in the E.B. White book, *Charlotte's Web*.

Wilbur is rather endearing, as pigs go, and spends his days doing various things around the barn. His only real friend, is the spider, Charlotte, who spirals down to chat and give advice.

One day, after the farmer is overheard making plans to kill Wilbur, Charlotte racks her brain for a way to save her friend. She begins by weaving the words "Some Pig" in her web. She weaves several other messages highlighting Wilbur's good points and, in the end, the farmer spares Wilbur's life.

While most of us don't have Wilbur's initial fate hanging over our head, we do have days that are frustrating, dreary, or discouraging. How wonderful to have a Charlotte in our lives, someone who can point out that we are special to God. A friend's love and encouragement can create a new outlook on life. Are you willing to be a Charlotte for someone?

"A man of many companions may come to ruin, but there is a friend who sticks closer than a brother." (Proverbs 18:24 NIV)

December 19: Movers and Shakers

When we lived in the Boston area, we resided (for all of nine months) in a hundred year old house that had four floors, one being the attic that had a bedroom, bath, and sitting area. We decided to put the boys up in the attic to keep the noise contained, more or less, and we had a sturdy coffee table we wanted to put up there with them. There was a snag, however. The coffee table had a slate top, which weighed almost as much as a piano. In order to get it to the attic, the movers had to negotiate a narrow, winding staircase. It was so narrow, in fact, that it could only be traversed by stationing one mover at the top and one at the bottom and praying that their muscles wouldn't give out. When they came gasping down those stairs after a solid hour of grunts and moans, one of them asked me in a nervous tremolo, "Are you going to be moving back out of here soon?" When I answered in the affirmative, he was quick on the trigger with his reply: "Please lady, don't call us!"

We had another interesting incident associated with that attic. If you have ever moved to a strange town (I'm not saying Boston was strange, you understand), you will identify with me when I say that you have to start everything from scratch. You don't know where to find a good doctor, or a good dry cleaner, or a good grocery store. You don't know anything about the children at school, or who their parents are, or whether they carry knives or terrible diseases.

We moved numerous times, and it never really got any easier. I remember the Boston move particularly, because Will, our oldest son, had asked one day if he could go to some kind of a party after school. He was a little vague as to the kind of party, as well as a little vague about where it would be. Even if he had told me, I probably wouldn't have known where that street was or who owned the house. I agreed (with some trepidation), and, when suppertime came, there was no Will. We called and called and tried to retrace steps. The whole thing seemed hopeless since we didn't know anything. Margaret, our three-year-old, told us several times that Will was upstairs asleep, but, since she was only three, we dismissed this information and called the police. Out they came, and were very obliging. Suddenly, we looked up and there was Will stumbling down the winding staircase. I didn't know whether to hug him or yell at him. I think I cried, relieved that we were all once more together, even though Will had been there all the time.

God is with us too, even though we may be unaware of Him and spend our time grunting and moaning over ways we think are too steep or too hopeless!

"I know the Lord is always with me. I will not be shaken, for he is right beside me." (Psalm 16:8 NLT)

December 20: ABC

When I was a teenager I would occasionally go to the drugstore for a Coke. There was always a wad of gum in my mouth, and, in order to preserve it for later pleasure, I would remove it and place it under the table in the booth. Then when I was ready to leave, I would remove said sticky substance and place it back in my mouth. I had to be careful to get the right piece, though, otherwise it would be "ABC" gum (Already Been Chewed). I know, this sounds really dreadful (and, of course, it is) but "them's the facts, ma'am".

If you are reading what someone else has written, its "ABC," second hand stuff. If you want it straight from God to you—personalized and fresh, read the Bible! It's manna from His hand to your ears and heart.

"He fed you with manna in the wilderness, a food unknown to your ancestors. He did this to humble you and test you for your own good. He did it so you would never think that it was your own strength and energy that made you wealthy." (Deuteronomy 8:16, 17 NLT)

December 21: The Christmas Caroler

Our three oldest children were about 8, 9, and 10 when they joined the children's choir at our church. Several weeks before Christmas, the children's choir director had them rehearsing for a special Sunday evening performance. He was a little on the weird side (I'm sorry, but he really was), but he always came up with ideas to make the choir more interesting. At this particular spectacular, he announced that everyone should portray old-fashioned carolers and dress accordingly. The kids were not thrilled (we lived in Florida and cold weather was nowhere to be found) and you might say there was revolt in the ranks. There were many whispers and general agreement that no one in their right mind would get dressed up like a character out of a Dickens novel. They all agreed except our daughter, Lissa, who was either not aware of the whispers, or else decided on her own it was better to do what the adult had said.

Lissa had spent the afternoon visiting our minister's daughter when she suddenly remembered the costume thing. The minister's wife was very cooperative, and arrayed Lissa in some wool clothing left over from a previous time. When Lissa arrived at the church, she found she was the only one in mufti, but she doggedly persisted in keeping on what she was wearing. When the carolers filed in that night, there were about twenty children in everyday clothes, and one who was muffled and swagged in a long skirt and overcoat, an incomprehensible outfit to most of the congregation. There were a great many smiles on our row, and we found it hard to keep the pew from shaking with smothered laughter.

Some of all that was due to her little match girl appearance, but, really, we were proud of her for her willingness to follow instructions and go against the crowd. It's hard to be the one who stands alone, but it has its own reward in strength of character. There is also the knowledge that you're not really alone, even if you're the only one people can see.

"Therefore, my dear brothers, stand firm. Let nothing move you. Always give yourselves fully to the work of the Lord, because you know that your labor in the Lord is not in vain." (I Corinthians 15:58 NIV)

December 22: An Unexpected Gift

Have you ever had something special given to you that was not only unexpected, but also extremely touching? When I was in my late teens and early twenties, my parents and I used to patronize a particular restaurant in a nearby town on a fairly regular basis—perhaps once a month or so. The food was good and so was the service, and we gladly went the extra miles to go there. In time, the waiters got to know us and remembered our names, and we also knew theirs and enjoyed the pleasure of being welcomed by them.

When my father died, there were, of course, flower arrangements of every description, but the one that made me cry was the simple one that read "From the waiters at the Plaza." It was even more lovely because it was, in a sense, unnecessary—a gesture not from the dictates of convention, but truly from the heart of men who had only known us in a more or less casual way, but who evidently appreciated the warm patronage of people who appreciated them.

There are many people that we know—from work, church, school, and, even where we spend our leisure time—who would appreciate an unexpected gift from the heart. It doesn't have to be money, or anything bought with money—but how beautiful if it's given in the way Jesus gave: warmly and with love. Ask the Lord to give you the name of someone who needs the warmth of an unexpected gift from you. (And don't be too surprised if you're given the name of someone you don't even like!) You may find that your gift (or note or kind deed) is truly a cup of cold water to a thirsty heart.

In the gospel of Luke, Jesus said, "'If you love only someone who loves you, will God praise you for that? Even sinners love people who love them. If you are kind only to someone who is kind to you, will God be pleased with you for that? Even sinners are kind to people who are kind to them. If you lend money only to someone you think will pay you back, will God be pleased with you for that? Even sinners lend to sinners because they think they will get it all back. But love your enemies and be good to them. Lend without expecting to be paid back. Then you will get a great reward, and you will be the true children of God in heaven. He is good even to people who are unthankful and cruel. Have pity on others, just as your Father has pity on you.' Jesus [continued]: 'Don't judge others, and God won't judge you. Don't be hard on others, and God won't be hard on you. Forgive others, and God will forgive you. If you give to others, you will be given a full amount in return. It will be packed down, shaken together, and spilling over into your lap. The way you treat others is the way you will be treated." (Luke 6:32-38 CEV)

December 23: Joys-R-Us

I suppose nearly everyone is familiar with the huge toy store that has a similar name. Fortunately, our children were grown by the time it appeared: I probably would have died of shock right inside the door. When I finally found myself inside one of these stores, I was overwhelmed. I had never seen so many things clicking, clanking, and blinking. Growing up in an era where toy stores were mostly dolls, trains, and bikes, I had no idea that even the world of toys had become so mechanized.

Well, by now, I have adjusted to the fact that toys have kept pace and changed with the rest of civilization—but I am delighted to find that joys have not. As has been said many times before and by a good many people, joy is not the same as happiness. We may be in bed with a heart attack or a sore toe, and we may still have joy. We may find money has disappeared like water down a fall, but joy remains. We may discover family or friends have disappointed us, but we are never disappointed in joy. We may have a house burn down, or an achievement escape us, but joy remains.

Our joy comes as a result of our relationship to Jesus Christ. It doesn't beep, bake, or bounce, but two of its nicest characteristics are its quietness (a pleasure not often found today!), and its availability—it is available to everyone, whether king or cook. Best of all, it is a gift from our Heavenly Father (and it's a gift that never has to be returned because it is the wrong size!).

"Honor and majesty surround him; strength and beauty are in his dwelling." (1 Chronicles 16:27 NLT)

December 24: Christmas Future

For the first thirty-one years of my life, Christmas was in the future tense: I knew nothing of all that it meant. I knew all the traditions, and indeed all the facts of Christianity. Although Christ had stepped from eternity to be born as a human baby in Bethlehem, He had not been born in me. Someone has wisely said, "The only requirement for becoming a Christian is knowing you can't meet the requirements."

It was only when I realized I did not deserve heaven (what terrible conceit!) and that my good deeds were like filthy rags in the sight of a holy God that I began to doubt my ability to meet those requirements. Coming from a background of a certain amount of wealth, sprinkled liberally with good manners and morals, I never dreamed that I would not be included in heaven's plan of salvation. I know there are some who feel they are too bad to be accepted by God, but I had the opposite problem—I thought I was plenty good enough for almost anything that came along. God must lift up the first and take down the second. He had a challenge when it came to me, for I sailed along, thinking I was in control of my life and not giving God the time of day.

How I thank Him that He saw fit to open my eyes and my heart and draw me to Him! He made my Christmas and Easter a seamless garment—woven together to show the power of the Incarnation and the Resurrection. The mission of the cross is in the message of the cradle. I now have a sure and glorious hope, founded on the very character of the Trinity!

"Your attitude should be the same as that of Christ Jesus: Who, being in very nature God, did not consider equality with God something to be grasped, but made himself nothing, taking the very nature of a servant, being made in human likeness. And being found in appearance as a man, he humbled himself and became obedient to death—even death on a cross! Therefore God exalted him to the highest place and gave him the name that is above every name, that at the name of Jesus every knee should bow, in heaven and on earth and under the earth, and every tongue confess that Jesus Christ is Lord, to the glory of God the Father." (Philippians 2:5-11 NIV)

December 25: Christmas Present

On Christmas we have a birthday party for Jesus. We have a cake with a candle and sing "Happy Birthday," and then we read the Scripture from Luke about the present God gave us in the birth of His Son. We each write down on a piece of paper a present that we will give or do for someone in Jesus' name. Then we burn it so that no one will know except God.

As the logs in the fireplace burn, we sit and share what God has been doing in our lives the past year. Sometimes there are tears (usually mine) as we go around the circle. One time that stands out in my memory was the year our son, Allen, was in graduate school. He had been having a difficult time, but that evening he said, "I have come to know that you don't have to understand what God is doing in order to believe in Him." That was quite an impressive statement, I thought, because that really is the essence of trust.

Most of the time I have no idea what God is doing in my life. If we understood, there would be no need for faith. We live in the present with the Presence of Christ. That is all we need.

"I offer you my heart, Lord God, and I trust you." (Psalm 25:1-2 CEV)

December 26: Christmas Passed

Nearly everyone spends both time and energy getting ready for Christmas. There is much wrapping, writing, cooking (and if there are children involved—hilarity unbounded). Before you know it, Christmas is there (even if you aren't ready), and, then, suddenly it has passed. Are you feeling a little let down? Sometimes, when we focus very hard on a special event, we experience a real feeling of absence when it is over. This is true whether we are participating in a wedding, a play, a reunion, or a final exam (although there's probably not a pang when that's over!).

All those things are a little like Christmas, aren't they? Because while it's all too true that decorations have to be taken down, wrapping paper disposed of, thank you notes written etc.... after all, we still have what is essential to our lives because Christmas is not really over! It is with us every day of our lives because of the Divine gift of the life of the Spirit living within us.

If you have not taken the time to be quiet before the Lord during this season, this might be a good time to re-group, and make this the start of a new a deeper relationship with the Person who understands you—and loves you anyway!

"For he has gathered the exiles from many lands, from east and west, from north and south. Some wandered in the desert, lost and homeless. Hungry and thirsty, they nearly died. "Lord, help!" they cried in their trouble, and he rescued them from their distress. He led them straight to safety, to a city where they could live. Let them praise the Lord for his great love and for all his wonderful deeds to them. For he satisfies the thirsty and fills the hungry with good things." (Psalm 107:4-9 NLT)

December 27: Cache of Clay

We were watching a show on antiques the other night and heard a statement that was very startling. They were filming from New Mexico, and a couple had brought in two Indian clay pots to be evaluated. The appraiser said they were ceremonial pots and dated from about 1100 A.D. As I recall, he put a value on them of between $3,000 and $5,000. He went on to say, however, that if they had been broken and pieced back together, they would have been worth nearly $12,000 apiece. He explained that this would have shown that the pots made for ceremonial use had been made for one time only, and then cracked so that they could not be used again.

I often turn away from things that have been mended, thinking they are inferior, or of little usefulness. But I must remember that the untouched piece is not always what is most valuable.

It is natural for us to feel frustrated and perhaps even irritated that we are not whole—but take time to thank the Father instead, not for your brokenness, but for the fact that, when we are in that broken state, His light can shine more clearly through the cracks.

"But everything exposed by the light becomes visible, for it is light that makes everything visible." (Ephesians 5:13-14a NIV)

December 28: The Giver and the Gifts

Did you ever get a feeling of pleasure when you see your children using a gift you have given them and think, "How wonderful that they really like what I have selected for them!" I wonder if God ever feels that way about the gifts He has given us?

What about the gift of the Holy Spirit? Do we avail ourselves of His power to live the resurrection life day by day? Or what of the gift of His Word? Is it our daily bread or merely our emergency rations? Is it our River of Life or a canteen of promises that have gone a little stale while waiting to be acted on? These two gifts are given to every one of His children, but God gives us individual gifts, too. Are you using that gift of mercy to minister to someone in need—or have you stopped because you feel no one appreciates you? Are you using that gift of teaching, or do you feel that you have done your part? Are you using that gift of giving or do you feel that the little you can give now is not anything worthwhile?

We must remember that the mind grows by taking in, but the heart grows by giving out. We show our appreciation for the gift we have been given when we use it, not to win approbation and thanks from others, but to illustrate the life of the Lord Jesus in us.

"As God's messenger, I give each of you this warning: Be honest in your estimate of yourselves, measuring your value by how much faith God has given you. Just as our bodies have many parts and each part has a special function, so it is with Christ's body. We are all parts of his one body, and each of us has different work to do. And since we are all one body in Christ, we belong to each other, and each of us needs all the others." (Romans 12:3-5 NLT)

December 29: A Bell and a Trumpet

When I was growing up (not taller, only older), we had a very strict regimen for dinner. There was a large ship's bell hung in the downstairs hall and it was rung each weekday evening at 6:00 p.m., and Sundays at 1:00 p.m. This meant that it was time to stop work, stop play, stop reading (or in my case, stop messing around), and wash up for dinner.

At 6:15 p.m. the bell rang again, and we were supposed to be walking into the dining room with clean hands and a pure heart. No one was allowed to be late for dinner, and, in fact, no one thought of being late for dinner because we all knew it was a case of the quick or the dead.

There is another hour coming that will brook no dawdling, but it will not have a fifteen-minute warning. Moreover it will not be a mere ship's bell, but the sound of a trumpet…blown so loudly that the dead in Christ will rise. Then we who are alive will be caught up to meet the Lord in the air. We need to listen—but while we are listening, we are to be walking in the light, putting on faith and love like a breastplate, and our helmet, which is "…the confidence of our salvation" (I Thessalonians 5:8 NLT).

December 30: The Lion and the Lamb

Lions and lambs are supposed to be opposites; but I have seen several lions turned into lambs by the power of God. They have not been reformed. They have been transformed by the One who is still in the creating business.

Jesus Christ exemplifies both the lion and the lamb. Just as the lamb without defect in the book of Exodus was slaughtered and the blood placed on the sides and tops of the doorframes so that the Angel of Death would see and pass over, so Christ the sinless Lamb was slaughtered, and has taken away the sin of the world as the perfect sacrifice, so that those who believe on Him would have the sting of death taken away. This is foretold all through scripture, and especially in the book of Isaiah, where He is pictured as a lamb: "he was led like a lamb to the slaughter, and as a sheep before her shearers is silent, so he did not open his mouth" (Isaiah 53:7 NIV).

In Revelation, however, Christ is also referred to as the "the Lion of the tribe of Judah, the Root of David" (Revelation 5:5b NIV). So, someday, Christ will be a different Lamb, and many will say, "Fall on us and hide us from the face of him who sits on the throne and from the wrath of the Lamb!" (Revelation 6:16 NIV).

It is difficult for us to imagine any lamb having wrath, but that is the description of the judgment of Christ. He was the Lamb who was slain and the Lamb who judges, for he is both servant and king. It is wise to keep this dual picture of our Lord before us, for if you have never accepted Him as the Lamb who died for you, then you must be prepared to face him as the Lamb who judges.

"You are a lion's cub, O Judah; you return from the prey, my son. Like a lion he crouches and lies down, like a lioness—who dares to rouse him? The scepter will not depart from Judah, nor the ruler's staff from between his feet, until he comes to whom it belongs and the obedience of the nations is his." (Genesis 49:9-10 NIV)

"Then the angel showed me the river of the water of life, as clear as crystal, flowing from the throne of God and of the Lamb.... No longer will there be any curse. The throne of God and of the Lamb will be in the city, and his servants will serve him. They will see his face, and his name will be on their foreheads." (Revelation 22:1,3-4 NIV)

December 31: An Open Door

In *Richard III*, Shakespeare uses the phrase "the winter of our discontent" to describe a time of cold peevishness. It's true that winter does have a way of leaking chill, which can often make me feel rather desolate.

Sometimes, in the personal "winter" times of my life, I waste time thinking about the wonderful summer weather I enjoyed just a short while ago. I forget that God is always with me, even in the cold and chill.

The passage from Isaiah 43:18-19 says, "Forget what happened long ago! Don't think about the past. I am creating something new. There it is! Do you see it? I have put roads in deserts, streams in thirsty lands" (CEV).

It's interesting to me that God doesn't say, "I will deliver My people from the desert." Instead, He says that He has placed streams and roads in the midst of the desert.

My prayer is that, even in times of difficulty, sorrow, and heartache, you will drink from the refreshing streams God has provided for you, and that you will stay on the roads He has made for you.

God bless you.

"I have placed before you an open door that no one can close." (Revelation 3:8b CEV)

0-595-32002-3